THE FOUNDATIONS OF
WITTGENSTEIN'S
LATE PHILOSOPHY

The Foundations
of Wittgenstein's
Late Philosophy

ERNST KONRAD SPECHT

Translated from the German
by D E Walford

Manchester University Press

Barnes & Noble Inc., New York

Original German Edition
© 1963 Kölner Universitäts-Verlag, Köln

© 1969 English edition
(translator D E Walford)
Manchester University Press
316-324 Oxford Road, Manchester 13

SBN 7190 0312 1

USA
Barnes & Noble Inc.
105 Fifth Avenue, New York, NY 10003

Printed in Western Germany by Hang Druck KG, Köln

CONTENTS

Author's Preface

The present study seeks to clarify the linguistic-philosophical and ontological foundations of Wittgenstein's late work. Wittgenstein is seen not so much as the analyst who wished "to make philosophical problems disappear" as a thinker who constructively developed those quite specific approaches to linguistic and general philosophy that are to be found in traditional philosophy. The interpretation has, in particular, set itself the task of bringing the ontological point of view into the foreground. This procedure is open to criticism. But perhaps it is precisely the ontological attitude which incites one to re-think the problems of traditional philosophy, taking Wittgenstein as a starting point, and to meditate on their possible solution.

Bonn, Summer 1961.

Translator's Preface

In the case of the many quotations from Wittgenstein it appeared appropriate to me to quote from those translations which are now accepted as standard by English-speaking philosophers. Accordingly all quotations from the *Tractatus Logico-Philosophicus* are from the translation by D. F. Pears and B. F. McGuinness (Routledge and Kegan Paul 1961); all quotations from the *Philosophical Investigations* are from the translation by G. E. M. Anscombe (Basil Blackwell 1958). I have also quoted from Miss Anscombe's translation in the case of the *Remarks on the Foundations of Mathematics* (edited by G. H. von Wright, R. Rhees and G. E. M. Anscombe (Basil Blackwell 1956). All other quotations in the text are my own translations, unless otherwise indicated.

Abbreviations

T. Ludwig Wittgenstein: *Tractatus Logico-Philosophicus*. London, 1922. (We follow Wittgenstein's numbering in quoting).

P. I. Ludwig Wittgenstein: *Philosophical Investigations*. Oxford, 1953. (In quotations we give the number of the section concerned in the case of the first part, and the page reference in the case of the second part).

F. M. Ludwig Wittgenstein: *Remarks on the Foundations of Mathematics*. Oxford, 1956. (Page references are given in quotations).

B. B. Ludwig Wittgenstein: *The Blue and Brown Books*. Oxford, 1958. (Page references are given in quotations).

M. L. G. E. Moore: "Wittgenstein's Lectures in 1930—1933". I—III, *Mind* LXIII, 1954 and *Mind* LXIV, 1955. (In quotations we give volume and page).

I. INTRODUCTION

Wittgenstein's philosophical development from the "Tractatus" to the later philosophy

Wittgenstein's late philosophy can only be understood against the background of a continual dispute with the views maintained in his early work, known as the *Tractatus*. Let us begin, then, by briefly outlining the basic ideas of this book and its effect on contemporary philosophy.

(1) On Frege's advice Wittgenstein went to Cambridge in 1912 to study philosophy under Russell.[1] The result of his studies there and of his intimate exchange of ideas with Russell was the *Logisch-Philosophische Abhandlung*, which Wittgenstein completed in Vienna in 1918 and published in the last number of Ostwald's *Annalen der Naturphilosophie* in 1921.[2] In the following year a German-English edition appeared under the title, suggested by Moore, *Tractatus Logico-Philosophicus*.

The fundamental notion dominating this work is that our ordinary, everyday language conceals its actual logical structure, or reproduces it only incompletely (4.002). But it is possible to conceive a language which represents the logical structure of our

---

[1] The biographical details are derived from the short biography by Wright (1). After Wittgenstein's death a series of obituaries and memoires appeared, which convey a lively picture of Wittgenstein's personality and influence. Cf. for example: Russell (7), Ryle (5), Wisdom (6), Malcolm (3), Mays (1), Cranston (1), D.A.T. Gasking and A. C. Jackson (1), Kraft (1), Ficker (1), *The Times* (1).

[2] The following works are of especial importance for the interpretation of the *Tractatus* : Russell (4), Ramsay (1), Weinberg (1), Anscombe (4), Black (5), Feibleman (2), Carnap (3), Colombo (1), Urmson (1), Stenius (1).

ordinary language in pure form, in other words a kind of ideal language which obeys "logical syntax" alone (3.325). The linguistic-philosophical reflections in the *Tractatus*, then, are concerned with the presuppositions and conditions of such an ideal language, and also, consequently, with the presuppositions and conditions of our ordinary language.[3]

The fundamental function of language is the picturing function (4.01): our language pictures the world in such a way that the propositions of language stand for definite states of affairs in the world. It is true, this picturing function does not always reveal itself clearly in our ordinary language (4.011), because the words and propositions of our everyday language are usually too complex.[4]

In order to reveal this function Wittgenstein analyses our language with the help of a special procedure, logical analysis; this procedure analyses each proposition unambiguously into its elements (3.2; 3.25). This procedure is based on a particular logical theory, according to which all complex significant propositions in our language are so-called "truth-functions" of simpler propositions and can thus be constructed from these simpler propositions by logical operations (like disjunction and conjunction etc.) (5). On the basis of this theory that complex propositions are truth functions, all propositional structures are reducible by logical analysis to simpler propositions, until the ultimate propositional elements, out of which the whole of language is constructed, are arrived at. In the *Tractatus*,

---

[3]   In this account we subscribe to Anscombe's interpretation, (Anscombe (4)) according to which: 1. Wittgenstein is not occupied in the *Tractatus* simply with the conditions of an ideal language, as Russell asserts in his Introduction to the *Tractatus*, but also with the structure, hidden though it is, of our ordinary language (cf. Anscombe p. 91 ff.); 2. the elementary propositions of the *Tractatus* are not to be understood as basis- or protocol-propositions, in the Vienna Circle sense (Anscombe p. 25 f.); 3. philosophical propositions are not made nonsensical because they are not reducible to empirical observation-propositions etc. (Anscombe p. 150 ff.)

[4]   The picture theory in the *Tractatus* is on closer examination very complex, above all, namely, because the picturing propositional sign is itself a fact in Wittgenstein's sense (3.14). For an extended discussion of the problems connected with this cf. Wisdom (1). A more recent interpretation is to be found in Daitz (1) and, following this, Copi (1), also Stenius (1).

these are what are known as "elementary propositions"; they are not further analysable because they consist of "simple signs" (4.221; 3.201). The elementary proposition permits the undistorted recognition of the picturing function: it is a nexus, a "concatenation" of names that stands for definite objects; the proposition as a whole therefore refers to a structure of objects, to a state of affairs (4.22; 3.203; 2.01).

The following general picture of language and its relation to the world emerges from this approach: all meaningful and significant propositions in language are truth functions of elementary propositions and are, therefore, with respect to their truth value and sense, dependent on elementary propositions. The relation between language and world rests on the picturing function, in other words, on the fact that the simple names of elementary propositions stand for objects, and the elementary proposition as a whole for a definite state of affairs. Since all other propositions are dependent on elementary propositions, all significant propositions picture the world in some way.

The only propositions that have an exceptional position in this linguistic structure are the propositions of logic, which Wittgenstein construes as tautologies or contradictions, and the propositions of mathematics, which he interprets as equations and consequently as "pseudo-propositions" (4.46 ff; 6.2).[5] These propositions do not picture any state of affairs in the world and are therefore "senseless", i.e. without reference to real or possible states of affairs (4.461; 6.21). But they are not for that reason "nonsensical", i.e. symbolic compounds running counter to the logical syntax of language (4.4611). It is true, they do not assert anything about the world, but they do "show" the logical structure which language and the world

---

[5] The status of mathematical propositions in the *Tractatus* is disputed. Ramsey tried to construe them as tautologies (Ramsey (2)); but this interpretation cannot agree with Wittgenstein's intention. We follow Weinberg's interpretation which, briefly stated, amounts to the following: "Wittgenstein's theory of mathematics thus depends on two principal theses. First, mathematics cannot be derived from logic, and second, mathematics consists in showing the internal relatedness of meanings (though not in the tautological sense)." (Weinberg (1) p. 89.)

must have in common for propositions to be able to picture the world at all (4.12; 6.22).

So much for the basic features of the theory of language in the *Tractatus*. The consequences of this theory for philosophy[6] result from the fact that philosophical problems rest "on the misunderstanding of the logic of our language" (Preface); accordingly, they can only be removed by making the logic of language clear (4.003). Philosophy does not set up any propositions (4.112); it only clarifies the status of the propositions laid before it: it is not a body of doctrine but a linguistically critical activity (4.0031; 4.112).[7] The "only strictly correct" method of philosophy would, therefore, be the following: "to say nothing except what can be said,—i. e. propositions of natural science—i. e. something that has nothing to do with philosophy—and then, whenever someone else wanted to say something metaphysical, to demonstrate to him that he had failed to give a meaning to certain signs in his propositions." (6.53). The *Tractatus* closes, therefore, with the now famous locution: "What we cannot speak about we must consign to silence." (7).[8]

(2) There followed a series of attempts at interpreting the *Tractatus*. The most important and influential of them was certainly that of "Logical Positivism", as it developed in the Vienna Circle in the twenties, and in England in the early thirties. *The Vienna Circle* took over the theory of truth functions from the *Tractatus*, i.e. the theory that all significant propositions, with the exception of mathematical and logical propositions, are truth functions

---

[6] As already mentioned, we subscribe to Anscombe's interpretation in this point as well. According to Wittgenstein, the critique of metaphysics rests on the fact that, in metaphysical propositions, no meaning has been attributed to certain signs. It does not, however, rest on the fact that only empirically verifiable propositions have meaning, as the Vienna Circle thought (Anscombe (4) p. 150 f.)

[7] An account of the relation of the Wittgensteinian linguistic analysis to Mauthner's critique of language is to be found in Weiler (1).

[8] A detailed discussion of this famous final proposition is to be found in Delius (1).

of elementary propositions.[9] Since Wittgenstein himself does not give an example of an elementary proposition and leaves it open to what kind of objects or states of affairs the elementary propositions refer, the possibilities of interpretation were here extremely varied. Generally, in the Vienna Circle an empirical basis was assumed, and elementary propositions were so interpreted as to refer to empirical data, i. e. to data given by sense-perception. Thus, Carnap in his *Logischer Aufbau der Welt* (1928) chose, for example, "elementary experiences" as the starting point of his constitution system, in which the complete structure of reality was to be built up logically. By choosing an empirical starting point the "Logical Atomism" of the *Tractatus* was transformed into a "Logical Positivism." The experiential reference of all propositions became in this way a criterion for deciding whether a proposition was meaningful or not. This is expressed in what is known as the "Empirical Verification Principle". According to this principle the meaning of a proposition consists in the method of its empirical verification.[10] The members of the Vienna Circle thought that this principle could be found in the *Tractatus*, namely where Wittgenstein says: " . . . . . . in order to be able to say, 'p' is true (or false), I must have determined in what circumstances I call 'p' true, and in so doing I determine the sense of the proposition." (4.063). Logical Positivism interpreted this passage as if the circumstances under which a proposition is called true were empirical data, as if Wittgenstein regarded the meaning of a proposition, then, as its empirical verification.[11] Anscombe, in her interpretation of this passage, draws attention to the fact that Schlick's account is not consistent with Wittgenstein's own discussions.[12]

[9] On the history of the Vienna Circle cf. Kraft (2). For a detailed account of Wittgenstein's reception, especially in the early Vienna Circle, see Weinberg (1).
[10] The first explicit formulation of this principle is to be found in Waismann (1) p. 229: "A proposition has no meaning whatever, if it is in no way possible to state when the proposition is true; for the meaning of a proposition is the method of its verification." Cf. in this connection Passmore (2) p. 371; there is also a bibliography on the verification problem in this latter work.
[11] Cf. Schlick (2).
[12] Anscombe (4) p. 152.

Wittgenstein's critique of metaphysics is also interpreted from
the standpoint of the Verification Principle. Starting from the idea
that "most of the propositions and questions to be found in philosophical works are not false but nonsensical" (4.003) the Vienna-
Circle took the propositions of metaphysics to be of a non-empirical
nature and therefore nonsensical, in the Empirical Verification Principle sense.[13] As we have already mentioned, this is an idea that is
probably not to be found in this form in the *Tractatus*.

Thus in the opinion of the Vienna Circle also, the function of
philosophy consisted in a critical analysis of language showing,
first of all, that all significant propositions are to be reduced to
elementary propositions, immediately verifiable through experience,
and then in proving that all metaphysical propositions result from
misunderstandings about the logical syntax of language.[14]

Critical arguments with Wittgenstein occurred within the Vienna
Circle when, in the logical working-out of a philosophy completely
free of metaphysics, even Wittgenstein's *Tractatus* was subject to
investigation with regard to its metaphysical foundations. The
theory of elementary propositions constituted the departure point
of the criticism. Wittgenstein, in so far as he makes assertions
about the relation between language and fact, goes beyond the
critical limits of language which he had himself drawn; for this
relation, strictly speaking, lies outside what can be said within
language. This is Neurath's opinion in his criticism of Wittgenstein: "It is true that it is possible to speak with one part of
language about another part, but it is not possible to express
oneself about language as a whole from a 'not-yet-linguistic' point
of view, so to say, as Wittgenstein and certain individual members
of the Vienna Circle try to do . . . . . . It is also not possible to
confront language as a whole with 'experiences' or the 'world'
or a 'datum' . . . . . ".[15] In order to circumvent these difficulties
in the *Tractatus*, Neurath completely renounces any firm or pre-

---

[13] Above all cf. Carnap (2) and Schlick (1).
[14] Weinberg (1) p. 177 ff.
[15] For the following account c.f. Urmson (1), where, in particular,
"Logical Atomism" is discussed in detail. Also Pears (2).

-existent basis of any kind, for example, the "world" or "sense experience". A proposition has sense and truth only within language; even the so-called "protocol propositions", i. e. the propositions from which a theory starts, can only be confronted with other propositions, but never with a datum independent of language. It is precisely this criticism of Neurath's that is illuminating for the understanding of later developments, since Wittgenstein himself modified the idea that there was some firm basis of objects, independent of language.

The *English* interpretation of the *Tractatus* has, it is true, much in common with that of the Vienna Circle, but on the whole it is not so anti-metaphysically disposed as the latter.[16] The influence of Russell's form of Logical Atomism is also much more strongly active, so that it is not always clear in detail whether the authors are related more to Russell or to Wittgenstein. Until about 1936 a form of linguistic analysis, called "Directional Analysis", was dominant in England; among other things, it consisted in analysing complex propositions into simple propositions, in accordance with the programme of Wittgenstein and Russell; it thus sought to get rid of all those symbolic entities in complex propositions which stand for complex objects. After complete analysis only simple names should still remain; they stand for ultimate indivisible elements, for logical atoms.[17] An ontological reductionalism makes itself particularly evident in this school of thought; all complex objects (for example, "the state" or "things") were construed as "logical constructions" built up from elementary data and reducible by logical analysis to these data. The influence of Russell, who had attempted similar ontological reductions in the case of classes and numbers in *Principia Mathematica*, here makes itself felt. Once more the problem of elementary propositions and their relation to reality occasioned particularly serious difficulties in the case of these reductive analyses. The "simple names" of the elementary proposition were often interpreted as demonstrative pronouns and the "objects"

---

[16] Neurath (1) p. 396.
[17] Among the most important representatives of this school of thought were, for example, Wisdom (1), (2), (3) and Stebbing (1); cf. also Black (1).

of the state of affairs as sense data, so that according to this view an elementary proposition had roughly the form: "this-red" or "this-there" etc.[18]

There was reservation in England with respect to Wittgenstein's anti-metaphysical attitude.[19] The rejection of metaphysics really first set in with Ayer's *Language, Truth and Logic*, which appeared in 1936 and which was quite definitely influenced by the Vienna Circle.

(3) After the appearance of the *Tractatus* Wittgenstein, to begin with, published no further philosophical work. In 1929 he left Vienna for Cambridge where—with various interruptions—he was active until the end of his life. His philosophical position in about 1930 can be studied from the *lecture transcripts*, drawn up by Moore and published by him in 1954—1955. They clearly show how far Wittgenstein had distanced himself from the *Tractatus*, and it is already possible to recognise the first traces of his late work.

In contrast to the *Tractatus* he above all gives up the idea that a uniform structure must underlie any form of language, and that the propositions only have sense because they picture states of affairs. The concepts "language", "proposition", "sense", "picture", "syntax" etc. are no longer construed as sharply delimited concepts, as had been assumed in the *Tractatus* (M. L. I p. 11 f.). They are "vague" and for this reason they cannot be exactly defined. Any attempt precisely to determine such concepts is bound to lead to error, as happened in the *Tractatus*. Wittgenstein withdraws the picture theory of language, *expressis verbis* (M. L. I p. 12).

The problem of meaning, which now comes more strongly into the foreground, receives an entirely new treatment. Wittgenstein in the *Tractatus* identifies the meaning of the simple signs, out of which all propositions are ultimately constituted, with the object for which the name stands (T. 3.203). However, indications are already

---

[18] Cf. for example, Wisdom (1). Carnap, incidentally, also interprets elementary propositions in a similar fashion (Carnap (1)).

[19] Urmson (1) p. 105 f.

[20] Cf. Ryle (7).

to be found in some other passages that the meaning of a symbol must be intimately connected with its use.[20] Wittgenstein develops this idea in the Moore Lectures: he becomes critical of various analyses of meaning, among others of his own analysis in the *Tractatus*. He arrives at the conclusion that the meaning of a symbol is constituted and determined by the rules of its use within a definite language system (M. L. I, p. 6 ff.). This theory of meaning, already fully developed here, is one of the mainstays of the whole of Wittgenstein's late work. It is to be found also, practically unchanged, in the *Philosophical Investigations*. In the Moore Lectures Wittgenstein's views also changed fundamentally on the question of what a proposition is and how a proposition functions. The whole theory of elementary propositions has to a large extent disappeared (M. L. III, p. 1. ff.), and with it also the view that all significant propositions are truth functions of elementary propositions (M. L. III, p. 2).

The theory of the tautological character of logical propositions is extended to a theory of necessary propositions in general (M. L. II, p. 289 ff.). Wittgenstein now investigates not only logical and mathematical propositions but also all the judgements that had been called "necessary" or "*a priori*" in traditional philosophy; (in other words, even propositions of the type: "There is no greenish-red" or "I cannot feel your toothache"). What he asserts in the *Tractatus* of logical propositions, namely, that "they do not say anything" and that they are therefore, in a way, "without sense", is true of all these propositions. And just as in the *Tractatus* tautologies are "senseless" but not "nonsensical" because they belong "to the symbolism" (T. 4.4611), so neither are the other necessary propositions nonsensical, for they relate in a definite fashion to the "symbolism". Of course, Wittgenstein now no longer talks so much about "symbolism" (he employs this expression, for example, M. L. II, p. 298), but of "grammatical system" or simply of "grammar" (M. L. I, p. 6). Necessary propositions are for him the expression of definite "grammatical rules"; hence he also calls them "tautological or grammatical statements" (M. L. III, p. 11). The expression "grammar" or "grammatical rule" is, in this context, to be understood in a very wide and somewhat unusual sense. Thus Wittgenstein asserts e. g. " . . . that the arrangement of colours in the colour octahedron is really a part of grammar, not of psychology; that 'there is such a colour as greenish-blue' is grammar; and that Euclidean geometry is also a part of grammar." (M. L. II, p. 298). These are surprising utterances which only become intelligible in the light of Wittgenstein's later investigations. Special difficulties were created for Wittgenstein by the problem of how necessary propositions should be related on the one hand to the grammar of a definite symbolic usage, and yet on the other hand still have some connection with reality. He discusses this problem in relation to mathematical propositions. For the first time appears the idea that necessary propositions have a normative character; that they do not, therefore, tell us how reality is but rather how we ought to regard reality. A quotation may clarify what Wittgenstein has in mind here: " . . . . what Euclid's proposition 'The three angles of a triangle are equal to two right angles' asserts is 'If by measurement you get any result for the sum of the three angles other than 180°, you are going to say that you've made a mistake.'" (M. L. II, p. 303) The necessity of necessary judgements consists therefore in this: that we have not derived it from reality but rather judge reality, or our dealings with reality, in accordance with it. However, Wittgenstein does not seem to be quite clear about how this is to be conceived in detail. (cf. M. L. I, p. 22).

Wittgenstein's opinions about the position of philosophy had also changed since the *Tractatus*, although certain ideas were retained. Philosophy, as Wittgenstein now understands it, is primarily concerned with philosophical problems, with "troubles in our thought". (M. L. I, p. 5). This idea is already to be found in the Preface of the *Tractatus*. But Wittgenstein now regarded the genesis of philosophical problems from a different point of view. Here, for the first time, emerges the conception, characteristic of the late work, that philosophical problems result from misleading analogies between different forms of linguistic expression, and that, consequently, they can be disposed of by reflection on these forms of expression. Of course, Wittgenstein's discussions on this theme are still very germinal in the Moore Lectures. Basically, he speaks only of a "new method" that he has found in philosophy; but he does not say precisely in what this method consists. (Cf. M. L. III, p. 26 f.).

Finally, the problems of solipsism, realism and idealism receive detailed treatment (M. L. III, p. 10. ff.). Wittgenstein tries to solve these problems by studying in detail the use of propositions concerned with what is subjective, and revealing, by comparison, the differences between a proposition like "He is in pain" and a proposition like "I am in pain." Wittgenstein regards these problem as "extraordinarily difficult" (M. L. III, p. 10). It comes therefore as no surprise that these problems repeatedly occupied him and constitute one of the major themes of the *Philosophical Investigations*.

The Moore Lectures display Wittgenstein's gradually changing position in the years 1930—1933. His further philosophical development can be seen in what are known as the *Blue and Brown Books*. They were dictated to his students in the period 1933 to 1935 in connection with his teaching activity in Cambridge. (Cf. the Preface to the *Blue and Brown Books* p. v.). These books are important because, circulated in various transcriptions, they were, until the publication of the *Philosophical Investigations*, Wittgenstein's only assertions committed to writing and known to a wider public. They are also to be valued as a step immediately prior to the *Philosophical Investigations* and already in many respects enabling one to see the basic ideas of the latter work. Indeed, many investigations are carried out in far greater detail in the *Blue and Brown Books* than in the *Investigations*, and are therefore indispensable as commentaries (for example, the investigations into the method of language-games in the *Brown Book*). Wittgenstein's late philosophy proper begins with the *Blue and Brown Books*.

All the investigations present an entirely different view of language from that in the *Tractatus*. The conception of language in the *Tractatus* was one-sided insofar as it proceeded from the assumption that a calculus-like structure must underlie our ordinary language. This "conception" continually gave rise to the idea that our ordinary language was incomplete and, consequently, that it was necessary to draw up a perfect, artificial language. Wittgenstein now asserts categorically: "Ordinary language is all right . . ." (B. B. 28).[21]

But since our ordinary language is not a calculus, i.e. does not have a uniform and well defined structure, it is, according to Wittgenstein, absurd to look for *the* essence of language, *the* status of the proposition, *the* function of the word etc. "Language", "proposition", "word" etc. are, as Wittgenstein had already suggested in the Moore Lectures, vague concepts, embracing many differing phenomena, held together only by certain analogies and not uniformly describable. Of course, certain model-concepts are repeatedly obtruding themselves and making a clear view of the functioning of our ordinary language impossible. In order to free himself of these model-concepts Wittgenstein makes use of a procedure which he invented himself. He draws up what are known as "language-games", i. e. very simplified, linguistic forms built like a game and intended, by analogy, to throw light on the relations of ordinary language. (B. B. p. 17 and pp. 77 ff.). He uses this language-games method particularly in the *Brown Book*; indeed he uses it to a far greater extent than he does in the *Philosophical Investigations*.

Wittgenstein's opinion about the treatment of philosophical problems is closely connected with this new view of language. Philosophical problems arise, as he already suggests in the Moore lectures, because different spheres of language are brought into parallel relationship with each other and because it is supposed that what is valid for the one sphere must also be valid for the other. According to Wittgenstein, such analogies conceal the actual function of the linguistic

[21] This thesis of Wittgenstein's gave rise to the extended discussion of the problem of ordinary language. Here we can only give a selection from the literature on this problem. Malcolm (1); Ryle (6); Baier (1); Chisholm (1), with bibliography; Heath (1). On the connection between common sense and ordinary language cf. the papers in Schilpp: *The Philosophy of G. E. Moore*. It is rather difficult to decide how great Moore's influence on Wittgenstein was. Cf. Broad (1); Malcolm (3) p. 66 ff., also the Wittgenstein letter on Moore on page 80; further Wright (1) p. 8 f.

symbols and consequently also the actual nature of the object signified by the linguistic symbol. This leads to philosophical difficulties. These difficulties can be settled by reflecting on linguistic usage. For this reason the task of philosophy is characterised as analytical and critical and is thus, in a way, similar to that in the *Tractatus*: "Philosophy, as we use the word, is a fight against the fascination which forms of expression exert upon us." (B. B. p. 27).

The treatment of a series of problems arising in connection with words like "understand", "think" "believe" is entirely new in the *Blue and Brown Books*. Because of their special use as active words they sound as if they signified specific mental events. Wittgenstein, by a penetrating analysis of linguistic usage, tries, in the case of these words, to make clear whether they really function in the way they appear to. In this analysis he becomes critical of the view that each of these words is, so to say, a name for a definite event; that, in other words, there is *one* definite mental act corresponding to each word. For Wittgenstein the words mentioned have very complex functions, i. e. they are used to describe complicated states of affairs in which activities, modes of behaviour and also, under certain circumstances, mental events play a rôle. They cannot, therefore, be construed as names for individual mental acts.

The problem of solipsism is one of the chief themes of the analyses in the *Blue and Brown Books*, as had already been the case in the Moore Lectures. Here too Wittgenstein proceeds by trying to clarify the status of certain propositions which play a decisive role in solipsism, in other words, propositions about private sensations, for example. Wittgenstein does not refute solipsism but shows what linguistic presuppositions it makes and from what "linguistic misunderstandings" it results. Incidentally, it is in this context that the idea occurs, an idea frequently mentioned in the Wittgenstein literature, that philosophical problems can assume the form of a "mental cramp" that can only be resolved by a special "cure". (B. B. p. 59). This has, on occasion, been interpreted as if Wittgenstein had a kind of philosophical psycho-analysis in mind here. He expressed himself decisively against this interpretation. The expressions "mental cramp" and "cure" are to be understood metaphorically only.[22]

(4) The influence of the *Blue and Brown Books* and that of the lectures and discussions held in this period had already made itself felt very early in philosophical literature in Austria and England in the thirties. In the late twenties Schlick and Waismann, who were both members of the Vienna Circle, had taken up personal contact with Wittgenstein, so that many of the ideas to be found in the Moore lectures can also be found in the writings of the Vienna Circle.[23]

This influence becomes still clearer in the thirties when a certain split showed itself within the Vienna Circle: Schlick and Waismann, among others, followed Wittgenstein's lead and turned increasingly away from the idea that an ideal structure lay at the foundation of language and that it was necessary to describe this structure in an artificial language in order to clarify philosophical problems. Carnap, Neurath and others, on the other hand, held firmly to the view that it was possible to dispose of philosophical problems by drawing up a more perfect language, framed in accordance with the rules of logical syntax.

The strength of the influence of Wittgenstein's ideas on Schlick, for example, is best seen in his famous paper: *Meaning and Verification*. Schlick first of all discusses the empirical sense criterion, availing himself, however, of a series of concepts and fundamental ideas that he himself ascribes to Wittgenstein; concepts like "grammar", "grammatical rule", the equating of meaning and use etc. In what follows Schlick turns to certain problems connected with solipsism, and tries to clarify them in Wittgenstein's sense. He even uses a particular kind of intellectual experiment which we are repeatedly finding in Wittgenstein's late work: that of imagining certain natural facts other than as we are accustomed to seeing them,

[22] Cf. Malcolm (3) p. 56 f. "I believe another thing that angered him was the suggestion that in his conception philosophy was a form of psycho-analysis, a suggestion that I heard him explicitly attack........"
[23] For example, the theory of *a priori* proposition in Schlick (3).

and then inquiring what the consequences would be for the structure of our language.

Similar influences can be traced in the works of Waismann, for example in his paper: *The Relevance of Psychology to Logic*, where, explicitly appealing to Wittgenstein, he uses the language-game method of clarifying certain relations of our ordinary language. Also in Waismann's 1936 *Einführung in das mathematische Denken*, hints of Wittgenstein's are worked up, for example his theory of meaning, his theory of the vagueness and indefinability of certain concepts, applied here to the concept of number etc. The influence of Wittgensteinian ideas can also be seen in other studies by Waismann, although the development of these ideas is entirely original.[24]

One of the first applications of Wittgenstein's ideas to the problems of empirical linguistics is to be found in the far too little appreciated book of Schächter: *Prolegomena zu einer kritischen Grammatik*. Schächter is the first to illuminate the problems of traditional grammar from the standpoint of grammar in Wittgenstein's sense, i.e. from the point of view of a grammar concerned with the analysis of meaning.

Still stronger than his influence on the Vienna Circle was the late Wittgenstein's influence on English philosophy, basically through the *Blue and Brown Books* and his teaching activity in Cambridge. His influence becomes more and more noticeable from about 1935 onwards. One of the most important documents for this development is the series of papers published by Wisdom in the period 1936 to 1944.[25]

Already in the first paper, characteristically entitled *Philosophical Perplexity*, Wisdom frequently refers to Wittgenstein. Like Wittgenstein, he starts from the view that philosophical problems are connected with language and are, therefore, to be clarified by linguistic reflections. His attitude to metaphysics, which seeks to solve philosophical problems with the help of a metaphysical theory,

[24] Cf. Waismann (5), (6), and (7).
[25] A detailed characterisation of Wisdom's philosophy, with particular reference to Wittgenstein, is given in Pole (1) p. 103 ff.

is, it is true, positive. For Wisdom metaphysical propositions are not only an expression of linguistic confusion, they are also illuminating insofar as they draw attention to similarities and differences that are hidden in our ordinary language. Wisdom distances himself from Wittgenstein in the following way; "Wittgenstein allows importance to these theories (metaphysical theories). They are for him expressions of deep-seated puzzlement...... But this is not enough..... he too much represents them as merely symptoms of linguistic confusion. I wish to represent them as also symptoms of linguistic penetration".[26] He characterises the task of philosophy positively: "The philosopher's purpose is to gain a grasp of the relations between different categories of being, between expressions used in *different ways*".[27] Here, then, is the traditional conception of philosophy as ontology, set in immediate parallel with Wittgenstein's conception. It is true, problems for philosophy arise from the fact that the different linguistic forms, in which different categorial spheres are spoken about, have very complicated relations to each other. This fact, however, ought not to hinder philosophy in its investigations. As a countermove to the concluding proposition of the *Tractatus* Wisdom explains: "Philosophers should continually be trying to say what cannot be said."[28]

In another of Wisdom's papers, *Metaphysics and Verification* these ideas are further deepened and discussed with reference to the Verification Principle of Logical Positivism. Wisdom clearly expresses himself opposed to any form of linguistic analysis that (following the *Tractatus* and Russell's Logical Atomism) attempts to reduce entities of any kind to simpler entities. All things are precisely what they are. Theories asserting propositions about numbers and universals, propositions about objects that are objectively real but not perceptible etc. are, in a way, perfectly correct (say, insofar as numbers are not ink-marks on paper, do not last only so long as a particular subject thinks them etc.). Wisdom thus grants to Realism, which works with other entities as well as individual things, a

[26] Wisdom (8) p. 41.
[27] Wisdom (8) p. 42.
[28] Wisdom (8) p. 50.

certain validity over against Reductionalism. For him the aim of philosophy is to accept all data for what they are and only to dispose of those difficulties that result from misunderstanding certain modes of speech about the data.

Wisdom's method is, in this, not so much linguistic-analytical, as "dialectical" or "therapeutical". In the progression of argument and counter-argument he seeks to test a definite philosophical formulation with regard to its sense-content and to clarify, with his discussion partner, how certain problems are arrived at and how they are to be settled. Wittgenstein's idea that philosophical problems are a kind of "mental cramp" that can only be disposed of by a particular "cure", assumes in Wisdom the form of a "therapeutic dialogue". One of the most important documents, in this respect, is his series of articles, *Other Minds*, which were written once more in close dependence on Wittgenstein.[29] In this way, Wisdom represents an interpretation and continuation of the late Wittgenstein. This development was called "Therapeutic Positivism" and it gained a foothold particularly in Cambridge among Wittgenstein's pupils.[30]

However, Therapeutic Positivism only represents one school of Wittgenstein interpretation. Another and, on the whole, much more autonomous developement of Wittgenstein's ideas is to be found in the strongly linguistically orientated *Oxford Philosophy*, represented by philosophers like Ryle, Austin, Strawson etc.[31]

Back in 1932 Ryle published a paper, *Systematically Misleading Expressions*, in many respects a kind of manifesto of this school of

[29] On "Therapeutic Method" cf. *Other Minds* p. 1 note.
[30] Along with Wisdom, G. A. Paul, M. Lazerowitz and N. Malcolm belong to this school of thought; cf. also the report on "Therapeutic Analysis" in Charlesworth (1) p. 150 ff.; Black (3) and Farrell (1).
[31] We are taking over the term "Oxford Philosophy" from M.Weitz, who has described this line of thought in contemporary English philosophy. (Weitz (2)). Oxford philosophy is by no means limited to Oxford, as is shown by the collections of papers where the most important contributions of this school of thought are collected. Cf. Flew (1), (2), (3). In the last of these is a longish chapter by A. Flew (4), who sketches the historical and systematic background.

thought. The fundamental idea of this paper is roughly as follows: there are many expressions in our everyday, non-philosophical language which, although they are understood with perfect clarity in our ordinary usage, have a grammatical form unsuited to the form of the state of affairs represented. These expressions mislead one into supposing that they describe a state of affairs quite different from that which they actually describe. Thus arise certain philosophical problems which can, however, be settled by so reformulating these expressions that, in their grammatical form, they are suited to the form of the state of affairs. Although this paper originated largely independently of Wittgenstein, the parallels with respect to the linguistic origins of philosophical problems are still clearly to be seen. Ryle (like Wittgenstein) turns increasingly away in what follows, from the idea that there are facts of some kind, quite independent of language, whose form could serve as a corrective for linguistic forms of expression. Although, in Ryle's opinion, philosophical problems still arise from linguistic "confusions", their disposal no longer consists in the search for a mode of expression suited to the form of the state of affairs, but rather in the clarification of the "logical geography" of our concepts; he understands by a concept the use of a definite expression.[32]

Ryle shares yet another interest with the late Wittgenstein: the investigation of mental words. In spite of many agreements there exist, however, considerable differences between Ryle and Wittgenstein in this respect. This is clearly shown by a comparison of Ryle's strongly behaviouristically orientated *Concept of Mind* with Wittgenstein's *Philosophical Investigations* which cannot by any means be called behaviouristic in respect of its philosophy of mind.

The orientation towards the study of ordinary language is a feature that all "Oxford philosophers" have in common with Wittgenstein. But while the study of language in Wittgenstein serves exclusively for the clarification of philosophical problems, these Oxford philosophers display a certain tendency to investigate lan-

---

[32] For this account cf. White (1) p. 216ff. and Warnock (3) p. 94ff.

guage systematically and far more for its own sake. This tendency is clearest in the case of Austin, who published a series of analyses which could be described as "philosophical linguistics".[33]

The development of philosophy in the Vienna Circle and in the Anglo-Saxon countries enables one to see how many, quite different philosophers were influenced by Wittgenstein through his *Tractatus* and his teaching activity in Cambridge. It is therefore not surprising that the *Philosophical Investigations*, which appeared in 1953, should appeal to a public already familiar with the most important of the book's basic ideas. Strawson was thus able to write in his famous review of the *Philosophical Investigations* : "It will consolidate the philosophical revolution for which more than anyone else, its author was responsible."[34] This "philosophical revolution" completed itself in the Anglo-Saxon countries during the last decades under the decisive influence of Wittgenstein.[35] From a historical point of view it would seem that its basic ideas are by no means so new as may at first appear, but that in England particularly they are built upon a long philosophical tradition.

Aristotle constitutes the starting point of this tradition; he had already investigated logical and philosophical fallacies resulting from grammatical errors, the *figura dictionis* as they were called. Similar reflections are to be found in the Middle Ages, for example in Ockham who repeatedly draws attention to the fact that certain hypostatisations have their origin in linguistic modes of expression.[36] In England it was above all Locke and Berkeley who emphasised the close connection between philosophical problems and linguistic misunderstandings and who consequently resorted to linguistic-analytical investigations to clarify philosophical questions. The following passage, frequently quoted in modern English

[33] Cf. in this connection Austin's illuminating paper *A Plea for Excuses*.
[34] Strawson (3) p. 99.
[35] Cf. in this connection the collection of papers edited by A. J. Ayer: *The Revolution in Philosophy*, particularly the contribution by Paul on Wittgenstein. A. J. Ayer (3) and G. A. Paul (1).
[36] Martin in particular has emphasised this side of Ockham's examination of language. Cf. Martin (1) p. 207 ff.

philosophy, is to be found in Locke: "The consideration, then, of ideas and words as the great instruments of knowledge, makes no despicable part of their contemplation, who would take a view of human knowledge in the whole extent of it. And perhaps if they were distinctly weighed, and duly considered, they would afford us another sort of logic and critic, than what we have hitherto been acquainted with."[37] Berkeley expresses himself still more clearly and sharply when he writes in the *Philosophical Commentaries*: "The chief thing I do or pretend to do is only to remove the mist or veil of Words. This has occasion'd ignorance and confusion. This has ruin'd the Scholeman and Mathematicians, Lawyers and Divines."[38]

This tradition was continued in the 19th Century by the English logicians, in particular by Mill and then by Moore and Russell in about 1900.[39] Russell's conception of the linguistic-critical function of philosophy eventually won influence on Wittgenstein's linguistic philosophy.[40]

(5) Wittgenstein died in Cambridge in 1951. Soon afterwards appeard the *Philosophical Investigations* (1953) which were written in the period 1936—1949 and which, with the *Remarks on the Foundations of Mathematics* (appeared 1959), represent that part of Wittgenstein's late work that had at that time been published.

In many respects the *Investigations* immediately follow on from where the *Blue and Brown Books* left off; but there are also investigations that advance in entirely new directions. The work as a whole is very heterogeneous and is by no means complete. In this connection Wittgenstein himself remarks: "After several unsuccessful attempts to weld my results together into such a whole, I realised that I should never succeed. The best that I could write would never be more than philosophical remarks...And this was,

---

[37] Locke (1) Vol. III, Chap. 21, 4.
[38] Berkeley (1) Vol. I, 641; p. 78. Cf. also in this connection Warnock (1).
[39] Broad has described the historical background against which the Cambridge philosophy of the last fifty years (in other words Moore, Russell, Wittgenstein) unfolded. Cf. Broad (1).
[40] The best information on Russell's linguistic critical papers is Black (4).

of course, connected with the very nature of the investigation. For this compels us to travel over a wide field of thought criss-cross in every direction.—The philosophical remarks in this book are, as it were, a number of sketches of landscapes which were made in the course of these long and involved journeyings." (P. I. Preface.)

In the *Investigations*, as already in the *Blue and Brown Books*, Wittgenstein discusses in detail the views about language represented in the *Tractatus*. He first of all criticises a particular picture of the function of language according to which each word as an isolated symbolic structure has a definite meaning, and the meaning is the object for which the word stands. Wittgenstein comes to the view that, although this picture has a certain limited application, it misleads if it is employed in the interpretation of the whole of language.

Wittgenstein then critically investigates, in greater detail than in the *Blue and Brown Books*, the view that language has an ideal structure that it is important to find and describe. Having overcome this idea of the "crystal purity" of language (P. I. 97) a series of presuppositions disappear. In Wittgenstein's opinion these presuppositions have decisively hindered the philosophy of language, and their rejection makes possible an undistorted view of the real function of our ordinary language.

Wittgenstein's views about the origins of philosophical problems and his characterisation of the task of philosophy have not advanced very much on the *Blue and Brown Books*; philosophical problems arise "through a misinterpretation of our forms of language" (P. I. III), through the fact that *we do not command a clear view* of the use of our words." (P. I. 122). The task of philosophy is essentially *analytic*, it should clarify the linguistic misunderstandings underlying philosophical problems and thus solve the problems.

The analysis of mental words moves to the centre of attention. Wittgenstein, to begin with, turns against an analysis of subjectivity according to which there are two fundamentally different strata of language: a public language common to all people, by means of which they agree about the objects of the external world, and a private language for the objects of an inner world, accessible only to each individual alone.[41] Wittgenstein seeks to prove that there cannot be a private language, but that all talk about mental states is from the beginning bound to the inter-subjective language. Wittgenstein's rejection of private language is, it is true, indissolubly bound up with our external modes of behaviour, but it does not consist exclusively in the description of these modes of behaviour. From this position Wittgenstein throws light on the problem of solipsism: the question about the reality of other people. Other people are revealed to us simultaneously with our inter-subjective language. Their reality is a fact rooted in our language and in our forms of life, neither requiring nor admitting a justification.[42]

Another theme is closely connected with these problems, the question about the status of words for mental processes (e.g. "understand", "mean", etc.). The starting-point of Wittgenstein's analyses is here similar to that in the *Blue and Brown Books*. The special grammatical application of these words as temporal words mislead one into interpreting them as names for actual mental processes. But closer investigation shows that the functioning of these words is much more involved and that they cannot be construed simply as names for specific processes. The advance on the *Blue and Brown Books* consists above all in a far more detailed discussion of individual words and their totally different and often very complex use.

It is no simple matter to formulate in a few theses the fundamental ideas of the *Investigations* because of the profusion of problems treated there. Strawson (3) has attempted to reduce the most

---

[41] For Wittgenstein a private language is a language that can, *in principle*, only be understood by *one* person. Malcolm, in particular, in his long review of the P. I. has drawn attention to this point. (Malcolm (2).) A rather different interpretation of the Wittgensteinian private language is to be found in Strawson (3). Hardin (1) asserts that Wittgenstein had not yet proved with his *Investigations* the logical impossibility of a phenomenalistic language.

[42] According to Wittgenstein it is not a matter of belief or opinion that the other person is real, but a question of "attitude", an attitude expressed both in our language and also in our forms of life. It is, therefore, neither to be doubted nor to be justified. For this original theory of Wittgenstein's cf. Pole (1) p. 55 and 63 ff. There is also here a longish critique of the Wittgensteinian approach.

important linguistic-philosophical ideas to the following three theses compiled from quotations:

(1). "To imagine a language means to imagine a form of life". (P. I. 19) and "What has to be accepted, the given, is—so one could say—forms of life." (P. I. p. 226). Wittgenstein, in these propositions, expresses the close connection between language and form of life. The ultimate, irreducible basis of our language is our form of life, which has to be accepted as given.

(2). "What happens now has meaning—in this context. The context gives it its importance." (P. I. 538). Here Wittgenstein is drawing attention to the fact that all our words and expressions have sense and meaning only in a wider context, in an "environment", but that they can never function as isolated symbolic entities or acts.

(3). "An 'inner process' stands in need of outward criteria." (P. I. 580). This thesis formulates Wittgenstein's view of the impossibility of a private language; the use of mental words is for him indissolubly connected with external criteria.

(6) Efforts at interpreting the *Philosophical Investigations* consist essentially of a comprehensive review literature and of commentary on specific individual questions. To the first class belong, for example, the lengthy reviews of Strawson (3), Malcolm (2), Findlay (3), Feyerabend (2), (3) and the descriptive account in Pole (1). With respect to commentary on individual questions there is a series of papers on the most varied problems from the *Investigations*, for example, on the concepts—so characteristic of Wittgenstein's linguistic philosophy—of the language-game and of the criterion, about the problem of the so-called family of meaning, about the analysis of mean, understand, believe etc. and above all, about the difficult problem of private language. In the course of the following investigations we shall come to speak about the literature in detail.

Our interpretation seeks to penetrate to the ontological and linguistic-philosophical background and to the presuppositions of the *Investigations*. It starts from the fact that at the root of all analyses lies a quite definite conception of the nature and function of language. However, this conception contains not only a theory of language, but also a philosophical theory with far reaching ontological theses. Wittgenstein, it is true, never stated this general philosophical position *in extenso*, so that we are obliged to work it out from scattered, individual investigations and remarks. Our interpretation will omit both the "therapeutic" aspect, accentuated by the "therapeutic analysis", and also the "linguistic-analytical" aspect, emphasised by the Oxford philosophy, although we are conscious that both these aspects represent essential moments of the late work of Wittgenstein.

Stegmüller, in his discussion of Wittgenstein's linguistic philosophy, has drawn attention to the fact that in the *Investigations* two different model conceptions are set up opposite each other: a "Mosaic Theory", in which language is constructed, like a mosaic, out of isolated symbolic structures with independent signification functions, and a "Chess Theory" of language, orientated on the model of a game of chess and attempting to clarify the function of language on the analogy of a game. Stegmüller discusses both theories primarily with regard to semantic questions, without going more closely into the ontological foundations.[43]

We wish to include these ontological foundations in our interpretational essay so that the following general picture results: Wittgenstein, in his linguistic philosophical investigations, is opposed to a quite definite model of language that could perhaps be thus characterised: the objects of the world exist quite independently of language; subsequently we give the objects specific names while reading off from the objects the linguistic rules for the usage of these names. In this way we set up a subsequent connection between each object and a name and are able, with the help of the names, to refer to objects. The construction of language ensues on this model, mosaic-wise, as one might say with Stegmüller. Since this model found its most extreme formulation in the linguistic theories of Logical Atomism (among other works, in the *Tractatus* also) it shall for short be called the "atomic model".

[43] Stegmüller (1) p. 282ff.

As a counter-move to this model, Wittgenstein outlines in the *Philosophical Investigations* another model of language. In constructing his theory, he starts from linguistic entities in which linguistic signs and objects are incorporated into the totality of the performance of a human action. Wittgenstein calls these totalities "language-games" (where the expression "game" is intended to bring out certain analogies between human linguistic activity and games).

A language-game is thus a homogeneous structure in which word and signified object do not occur as isolated structures, as is the case in the atomic model.

The contrast between the two linguistic models can be briefly characterised thus: the atomic model presupposes a world of given objects, in the Realist sense, to which a multiplicity of linguistic symbols is unambiguously allied. In this way the atomic model thus implies a certain Correspondence or Picture Theory of language.

By way of contrast, the language-game model at first leaves open the question about reality existing in itself and is limited to the investigation of the objects appearing in the language-games. The central question which then poses itself to us is the question how, taking the language-game model as a foundation, the connection of language and the world of objects is to be conceived. Our interpretation amounts to the view that in Wittgenstein we have to do with a linguistic "Constitution Theory", in which language is not derived from the world of objects but is somehow involved in the construction of objects.

In the following investigations the semantic and ontological presuppositions of the atomic model of language will first of all be illustrated from the example of the *Tractatus* and the Aristotelian theory of language (II). Then we shall discuss the complex and many-levelled concept of the language-game, which in Wittgenstein is the real counter-concept to the atomistic model (III). Afterwards, having first given an account of the signification function, we shall clarify Wittgenstein's theory of language, built on the concept of the language-game, along with its various ontological implications (IV). Following this, we shall take up the problem of meaning in order to show how Wittgenstein develops a theory of meaning with the help of the language-game model, a theory which tries to manage without a sphere of meanings additional to words and things (V). The really central problem of Wittgenstein's theory of language is to be treated at the end, namely in the question how, in the individual language-games, an "object-constitution" is completed simultaneously with the outline of linguistic rules (VI).

II. THE ATOMIC MODEL OF LANGUAGE

1. *The theory of language in the "Tractatus" and in Aristotle*

(1) The atomic model of language mentioned in the Introduction received its most extreme formulation in the lingustic theory of Logical Atomism and particularly in the *Tractatus*.[1]

As we have already pointed out, the fundamental conception that our ordinary, everyday language conceals its real semantic and logical structure dominates in the *Tractatus*. A special logical analysis is necessary to arrive at this structure. If this is carried out one arrives at symbolic entities lying, so to say, behind the words and sentences of our ordinary language; they are divisible into two fundamentally different classes:

(a) Signs belonging to the symbolism of language and having no relation to the world (4.4611). Among these are to be found logical symbols, the tautologies and equations of mathematics. In contrast to the view of Frege and Russell these signs do not signify anything: "My fundamental idea is that the 'logical constants' are not representatives." and "At this point it becomes manifest that there are no 'logical objects' or 'logical constants' (in Frege's and Russell's sense)." (4.0312 and 5.4). Similarly for tautologies: "In a tautology the conditions of agreement with the world—the representational relations—cancel one another, so that it does not stand in any representational relation to reality." (4.462).

---

[1] We are here taking as a basis a realistic interpretation of the *Tractatus*. Stenius (1) has shown that the *Tractatus* can also be understood transcendentally, in Kant's sense.

(b) Signs immediately refering to the world. To these belong names and the elementary propositions constructed from them. It is true, names cannot occur outside elementary propositions; within elementary propositions, however, they refer directly to objects that are their meaning: "The simple signs employed in propositions are called names. A name means an object. The object is its meaning... In a proposition a name is the reprensentative of an object." (3.202, 3.203, 3.22). Elementary propositions are immediate combinations of names and thus stand for a combination of objects, the state of affairs (2.01): "The simplest kind of proposition, an elementary proposition, asserts the existence of a state of affairs...An elementary proposition consists of names. It is a nexus, a concatenation of names." (4.21, 4.22). All other symbolic entities can be built up from these two classes in accordance with the rules of "logical syntax" (3.325), so that in the end the whole of language stands in an unambiguous, correlative relation to the world. The propositions of logic and mathematics alone are exceptions: they do not refer to the world although they do perhaps show the logical structure of language: "The propositions of logic demonstrate the logical properties of propositions by combining them so as to form propositions that say nothing." (6.121). In this way language is the "great mirror" of the world (5.511).

In the *Tractatus*, therefore, we find a very refined Picture Theory of language; but the basic characteristics of the atomic model are easily recognisable: there is a given world of objects or states of affairs to which a corresponding multiplicity of names or elementary propositions is subsequently allied so that there is an unambiguous correspondence between language and the world.[2]

---

[2] It might be thought that the Realism presupposed in the atomic model of language contradicted the linguistic Solipsism maintained in the *Tractatus*. On this point it is to be remarked that the language of which Wittgenstein speaks in his treatment of the problem of Solipsism (5.6, 5.62) is *my* private language. In addition to it there are many other languages that are not my language and which remain, therefore, unintelligible to me. It is true to say of all languages what is said of language in general, that they are, namely, pictures of the world, even if they are not always my picture of the world. For the interpretation of the very difficult Solipsism passages in the *Tractatus* cf. Anscombe (4) p. 165 and Hintikka (1).

(2) The theory of language in the *Tractatus* represents, as was said, an extreme formulation of the atomic model. A much simpler and clearer form of this model is to be found much earlier in the history of the philosophy of language, namely in Aristotle's theory of language, the basic characteristics of which we wish to sketch here. Aristotle starts from the view that the objects of the world exist in complete independence of language, and that definite words are only subsequently allied to these objects. This alliance lends to words an independent signification-function which they retain in all the wider contexts of language.

He first of all divides the entities of our language into two large groups: significant and non-significant phonetic structures; to the first group belong, for example, words and propositions; to the latter group, letters.[3]

The significant phonetic structures are particularly important for our investigation. They are divisible into two classes: *words* (*onomata* in the wider sense) and *propositions (logoi)*.[4]

In the case of *words* one has to do with signs that signify something in isolation and independently, but whose individual parts have no independent signification-function. The word "mortal", for example, thus signifies a definite property independently of all the other compounds in which the word occurs; on the other hand, its syllables "mor" and "tal" have no signification-function whatever, either in the word or in separation from verbal wholes.

Aristotle divides *words* into two kinds: *onomata* (in the narrow sense) and *rhemata*. They differ in that *onomata* have no temporal

---

[3] For the semantics of Aristotle developed in the following pages cf. the detailed description in Bochénski (1) p. 55 ff. and (2) p. 27 ff.

[4] In what follows we give only Aristotle's most important determinations in the Greek text:

Ὄνομα μὲν οὖν ἐστὶ φωνὴ σημαντικὴ κατὰ συνθήκην ἄνευ χρόνου, ἧς μηδὲν μέρος ἐστὶ σημαντικὸν κεχωρισμένον· 16 a 19—21

Ῥῆμα δέ ἐστι τὸ προσσημαῖνον χρόνον, οὗ μέρος οὐδὲν σημαίνει χωρίς, καὶ ἔστιν ἀεὶ τῶν καθ' ἑτέρου λεγομένων σημεῖον. λέγω δ' ὅτι προσσημαίνει χρόνον, οἷον ὑγίεια μὲν ὄνομα, τὸ δὲ ὑγιαίνει ῥῆμα· προσσημαίνει γὰρ τὸ νῦν ὑπάρχειν. 16 b 6—9

Λόγος δέ ἐστι φωνὴ σημαντική, ἧς τῶν μερῶν τι σημαντικόν ἐστι κεχωρισμένον, ὡς φάσις, ἀλλ' οὐχ ὡς κατάφασις ἢ ἀπόφασις. 16 b 26—28

reference, whereas *rhemata* always signify a specific time. The word "health" is thus an *onoma*, since it contains no temporal specifications whatever, whereas the word "recovers" is a *rhema*, since it signifies a specific moment of time; it does not merely signify the process of recovery but also the temporal point at which the process of recovery is completed. The *rhema* corresponds naturally to our "verb"; the *onoma*, however, includes much more than our "substantive", since adjectives, like "white", for example, also belong to *onomata*.

Under *propositions* Aristotle understands all phonetic entities of which the individual parts have a definite signification-function within and independently of the sentence-whole. Propositions can be ordered into several classes; thus, say, into the class of true or false propositions, and into the class of propositions that are neither true nor false (e.g. a request).

The problem now arises how the linguistic signs mentioned refer to things, i.e. how the words and propositions of our language really function. Aristotle, in investigating this question, starts with the following consideration: it is obviously true that the phonetic structures differ from race to race but all people refer to the same things with their respective languages; how is it possible to signify the same things with different phonetic structures?

Aristotle explains this phenomenon with the help of the *pathemata* in the mind, in other words, with the help of the ideas we have of things.[5] The phonetic structures are primarily signs for ideas in the mind; but since the ideas of things are the same for all people (everybody has the same idea of the colour red) all people are able to refer to the same things *via* ideas, in spite of the difference in phonetic structures.

There are accordingly then, three inter-related spheres: phonetic structures that are different in different languages, ideas in the mind that are the same for all people and, finally, things which are

[5] Ἔστι μὲν οὖν τὰ ἐν τῇ φωνῇ τῶν ἐν τῇ ψυχῇ παθημάτων σύμβολα, καὶ τὰ γραφόμενα τῶν ἐν τῇ φωνῇ. καὶ ὥσπερ οὐδὲ γράμματα πᾶσι τὰ αὐτά, οὐδὲ φωναὶ αἱ αὐταί· ὧν μέντοι ταῦτα σημεῖα πρώτως, ταὐτὰ πᾶσι παθήματα τῆς ψυχῆς, καὶ ὧν ταῦτα ὁμοιώματα, πράγματα ἤδη ταὐτά. 16 a 3—8

naturally the same for all people, according to Aristotle's realist mode of thought. Phonetic structures are primarily signs for ideas, ideas are images of things; phonetic structures thus refer to things by means of ideas.[6]

Word and proposition also differ from each other here. Words, namely, signify individual ideas or thoughts *(noemata)* and thus refer to individual things; propositions, on the other hand, signify combinations of *noemata* (the so-called *logos* in the mind); in doing so propositions also signify corresponding combinations in or of things.

But this account does not yet by any means exhaust the semantic function of individual linguistic symbols. In particular a more precise characterisation of individual kinds of words is lacking.

To begin with, Aristotle's theory of language could be construed as if each phonetic structure signified one thing. But that would be a misunderstanding. When it is said that Aristotle interprets language from the point of view of the representational function of names, this is not to be understood to mean that words like "indeed", "but", "in order to", "and" stand for definite things. These so-called "conjunctions" and links (σύνδεσμος and ἄρδρον as Aristotle calls them) are not included by Aristotle among meaningful phonetic structures; he classifies them as "non-significant sounds" (φωνὴ ἄσημος) and in their case the question as to what they really signify cannot occur at all.[7]

Nor is Aristotle to be understood to mean that every *significant* phonetic structure in language signified one thing (a view discussed from time to time in Scholastic Philosophy: *tot notiones, tot res*). There are limits that have to be drawn here. Aristotle by no means held to the rigid name-thing schema, not even in the case of significant phonetic structures. A well known example in this connexion is the word "being" when used as a copula in a proposition: "is" does not of itself signify a thing. However, insofar as it indicates the

---

[6] We are following the traditional interpretation with this account, found, say, in Ammonius. Cf. Ammonius (1) p. 18 and (2) p. 9.

[7] 1456b 21 and 1456b 38.

connection between subject and predicate, it has a definite semantic function within the sentence-whole.

The same is true of the words "being" and "entity" when used as transcendental determinations. "ὄν" and "ἕν" do not designate special entities, whether individual substances or attributes of individual substances. If, for example, they are attached to an *onoma* that indicates a substance, no newly appearing determination, no peculiar "factuality" additional to the signified thing is asserted as a result; in the language of Scholasticism: *ens* and *unum* do not signify a *res addita*. Let an example explain this more closely. If the word "white" is attached to the word "person" a new determination is as a consequence added to the person; this word "white" signifies an attribute that belongs to the person. But if the word "one" or "existent" were attached to the word "person" the addition (πρό-δεσις) would express no new factual determination. In this sense "person" and "one person" are the same, just as "person" and "existent person" are also the same.[9]

Finally, certain relational words must also be remembered; in their case it is at least open to question whether they signify a *pragma*. To this class belongs, for example, the word "ταυτότης" (identity), when it is used to assert the identity of a thing with itself. It is very doubtful whether the word here signifies a special *pragma*, an actually existent relation additional to the thing itself. Unfortunately, Aristotle only briefly suggests his solution.[10] It would appear that he conceived the origin of this relation as if we treated one and the same thing as if it were two, as if we divided it up, so to say, into two perfectly similar things and then asserted their identity. Thus, the relationship of identity merely consists in the way we treat and approach the thing which is identical with itself.[11]

---

[8] 16b 22—25.   [9] 1003b 22—32.   [10] 1018a 8.

[11] Names for fabulous beings, like, "goat-stag" or "sphinx" constitute a further problem. Strictly speaking these names do not signify a *pragma*, since there are no goat-stags or sphinxes anyway; they belong to non-beings (Physics 208a 31). In spite of this the corresponding names are not meaningless phonetic structures; Aristotle expressly mentions that the word "τραγέλαφος" means something in isolation, even if nothing is asserted about the being or non-being of what is signified. (16a 16).

These limitations clearly show that Aristotle did not regard an over simple interpretation of the relation between language and world as a fitting description of the function of language; for the words just discussed, "being", "entity" and "identity", belong to the so-called transcendental determinations that extend over all categories. Only after striking out the transcendental determinations could the Aristotelian theory be perhaps equated with the thesis that a single peculiar thing corresponded to each categorial expression, to each predicament: *tot praedicamenta, tot res*, as Scholastic philosophy expressed it.

One of the most difficult problems in the whole theory is the question: what is the concept of "thing" underlying Aristotle's thought when he asserts that each predicament signifies a *pragma* of its own.

In the case of words for individual concrete things there is no doubt about the meaning of the expression "thing". But when one comes to examine the words for the remaining categories this is no longer the case. The question thus poses itself in what sense it is possible to speak of a "thing" in the case, for example, of a quality or a relation. Aristotle is clear in his own mind that qualities or relations never have an independent existence but can only occur in connection with independent things and, in general, are only called "things" or "existent" with reference to independent things.[12] Thus, he does not use the term "thing" univocally. On the other hand, expressions are to be found that do indicate that Aristotle did sometimes conceive the existence of attributive determinations as somehow "thing-like". In particular, he does not appear to have freed himself from certain substance conceptions in the ontological interpretation of qualities like sweetness, warmth, blackness etc. Roughly speaking he construes these qualities as if they were ingredients in things.[13] Nor does he entirely deny the character of "*physis*" (essentiality) to relations[14], although he does construe them very a-substantially. It is well known that Aristotle tries to overcome

[12] 1028b 20.
[13] 9a 28—35.
[14] 1088a 23.

these difficulties with the help of an analogous concept of being. According to this concept the expression *"ens"* (ὄν, existent thing, *res*, object etc.) is asserted of different things neither univocally, nor equivocally but *analogically*. In this account the fundamental idea is that the word *"ens"* is used primarily for substance, while the remaining categories, i.e. qualities, relations etc., are called *"entia"* merely because they occur as determinations of substances.[15]

In spite of all modifications the starting point of Aristotle's theory of language is the relation between a substance and a concrete individual thing. Starting with the category of substance he interprets the remaining categories in such a way that even in their case a specific word always signifies a definite "thing", although the expression "thing" changes its meaning analogically. As a result the schema: word—pre-existent thing becomes flexible and makes it possible to give a homogeneous explanation of the signification-function of all categorematic linguistic signs.

Summing up, we can now describe Aristotle's theory of language as follows: in every respect Aristotle maintains an "atomic" conception of the structure of language. The smallest independent phonetic entities are letters and syllables; all higher entities, for example, words and propositions, can be put together summatively out of "phonetic atoms". The semantic functions of language are similarly analysed: the smallest independent symbolic entity is the word; all entities of greater complexity, for example, propositions or inferences can be compounded from words mosaic-wise, in such a way indeed that the signification-function of words remains unchanged in the higher entities. Corresponding to this analysis of phonetic signs and their semantic function is a similar atomic analysis of the *pathemata* that effect the connection between word and thing. The relations between language and the world are also conceived "atomically", or, as we could also say, "brick-wise": the things of the world exist antecedently to and independently of all language: words are names attributed subsequently to things. However, this theory is true only with limitations. Not all words stand

[15] 1003a 33.

for definite things, but only the *categoremata*, and even these do not all designate the same kind of thing. But in spite of these limitations the basic schema remains definitive for the whole interpretation: to the highly articulated multiplicity of pre-existent things corresponds an equally highly articulated multiplicity of linguistic signs. Thus, in essentials, Aristotle maintains a correspondence theory of language, orientated on the atomic model.[16]

(3) In conclusion to this short sketch of the Aristotelian theory of language let us cast a glance at the history of its interpretation, a history which will show to what extent the Aristotelian theory has been transformed and modified in the course of time.

In the more exact analysis of individual kinds of words it was recognised more and more clearly how differently words can function and how difficult it is to interpret the Aristotelian theory adequately from an ontological point of view. The starting point of the discussion was the question how one was to understand the assertion that a single thing corresponded to each categorematic expression. Aristotle attempted to answer this question with the help of an analogical concept of thing: every predicamental expression signifies a thing, but the concept of thing is modified in individual categories. His successors and interpreters were not, however, satisfied with this solution.

So as to have a basis for clarifying the question an effort was particularly made to define more closely the concept of *"res"* in the thesis: *tot praedicamenta, tot res*.[17] For this purpose the *"res absoluta"*

---

[16] The problems arising from Aristotle's approach to the philosophy of language have remained amazingly unchanged until the present day. It would e. g. be interesting to investigate Russell's philosophy of language and that of the early Wittgenstein with respect to their Aristotelian or Scholastic origins. References to this connection between Aristotle and the *Tractatus* are to be found in Urmson (1) p. 58f. In particular he emphasises the analogy between the concept of substance in the *Tractatus* (cf. T. 2.021) and Aristotle's concept of substance.

[17] On the problem: *tot notiones, tot res* and *tot praedicamenta, tot res*, cf. Martin (1) p. 201 ff., 207 ff.

was taken as the starting point, a something able to exist in itself alone, in real separation from other things.

In investigating the problem of whether every predicamental expression signifies a "*res*" in the sense of a "*res absoluta*", the interpreters of Aristotle divided into two schools of thought. For short, we shall call them here "Realism" and "Nominalism".[18] In general, agreement prevailed that substances and qualities were *res absolutae*; even William of Ockham was still interpreting quality as a *res absoluta*. Differences of opinion first arose in connection with the remaining categories: relations, determinations of quantity, place etc. The Realists tried, as far as possible, to make a *res absoluta* correspond to every categorematic expression, while the Nominalists tried to reduce the number of entities and, as far as possible, to retain only individual things and also, perhaps, qualities as independent things.

In what follows we shall often make use of the expressions "Nominalism" and "Realism" to characterise certain positions examined by Wittgenstein. These expressions will always be used in a sense similar to that just described. By "Nominalism" we understand any effort to postulate corresponding objects in the case of as few words as possible, in other words to make do with as few entities as possible in constructing a theory of language. Conversely, "Realism" for us consists in postulating a *res absoluta* as the corresponding entity in the case of as many words as possible, i. e. in trying to multiply the number of entities in the theory of language.

Even a cursory examination of the history of the interpretation of Aristotle's theory of language permits one to see what ontological

---

[18] The contrast between "Nominalism" and "Realism" developed particularly in the discussion of the problem of universals. But this opposition can be transferred to the problem about the being of categories. In this sense, then, Duns Scotus e. g., would belong to the Realists, when he interprets the relation of similarity on the model of quality as an independent thing (Duns Scotus (1) op. ox. II, d. 1, q. 4). Ockham, on the other hand, would count as a Nominalist, insofar as he does not interpret this relation as a *res absoluta* (Ockham (1) p. 140 ff.).

difficulties arise from an interpretation of the thesis: "a definite thing corresponds to every categorematic expression".

Ancient and medieval philosophy did indeed attempt so to modify the simple schema which constitutes the foundation of the atomic model: given thing—subsequent naming, in such a way that it could be used fittingly to interpret the whole of language. However, it never freed itself from this basic schema. Had it done so it might perhaps have solved the ontological problems of the philosophy of language quite differently and with quite different thought-models. This is the point at which Wittgenstein begins. In order to free himself of the atomic model conception Wittgenstein, in the *Philosophical Investigations*, looks for a starting point in the concept of the language-game, i.e. linguistic entities in which linguistic signs, human activity and object constitute a structural unity which cannot be constructed out of its individual elements in an atomic, i.e. in a summative fashion.

III. THE LANGUAGE-GAME AS MODEL-CONCEPT IN WITTGENSTEIN'S THEORY OF LANGUAGE

2. Genesis and development of the term "language-game"

If one wished to illustrate the theory of language in the *Tractatus* comparatively, one would resort to comparisons and images from the spheres of natural science and mathematics: as in the formula for a chemical structure, names for objects combine with each other into elementary propositions through immediate combination; so in the same way elementary propositions combine with each other to form complex propositional structures with the help of logical particles. The words and propositions of this language must, therefore, be "something pure and sharply cut", "no empirical cloudiness or uncertainty can be allowed to affect" its order; it must rather "be of purest crystal" (P. I. 97, 108). Most of the concepts used to determine language in the *Tractatus* originate from mathematics or are constructed on the analogy of mathematical concepts: logical space, truth-argument, propositional variable; language is a picture that pictures the world according to a definite law of projection; all truth functions are the result of successively applying a finite number of truth operations etc.

Quite different notions underlie the concept of language in the late work. One does not need to look very long for a suitable comparison. Wittgenstein himself gives the appropriate image right at the beginning of the *Philosophical Investigations*. Our language, he there says, is like an old town: "a maze of little streets and squares, of old and new houses, and of houses with additions

from various periods; and this surrounded by a multitude of new
boroughs with straight regular streets and uniform houses." (P. I.
18). This picture of language belongs to Wittgenstein's many
appropriate comparisons and images which remain illuminating
even in detail. Our language is a structural growth, not a construction drawn up according to a uniform plan. Just as no uniform
building plan forms the basis of an old town, so neither is our language erected on the outline of a uniform logic or grammar. The
stock of words and grammatical forms, transmitted down the
centuries, is like "the maze of little streets and squares" of the old
town. New technical languages and technical terminologies are like
new annexes and street systems. Finally, the artificial languages
of mathematics and logic can be compared with the modern parts
of the town, built on a uniform plan, sometimes still closely connected, at other times only quite loosely connected to the centre of
the town.

This comparison of language with a town that has gradually
come into existence illustrates one of the most important aspects
of Wittgenstein's conception of language in the *Investigations*. Our
language, with all its forms, modes of application, systems of parts,
is a multiplicity in which there is "nothing firm, given once for all"
nothing closed, no sharp boundaries (P. I. 23). This conception of
language of Wittgenstein's results in his founding all his reflections
in the *Investigations* on the central concept of the language-game.
This concept developed gradually to the form in which it appears
in the late work.

The first signs of Wittgenstein's comparing certain linguistic
phenomena to a game are to be found in the Moore Lectures. Here,
in considering the problem of meaninglessness in propositions, he
says that when we say "This makes no sense" we always mean
"This makes no sense *in this particular game*." The expression "game"
here signifies the specific total context in which the proposition is
used (M. L. II p. 295). This linguistic use is continued in the *Blue
and Brown Books*. Wittgenstein there speaks of a "great variety of
games" that are played with the propositions of our language
(B. B. 67). On occasion he also makes use of the expression "gram-

matical games" to characterise the various ways in which a word is used.

But in addition to this use of the word "game" the expression "language-game" already occurs in the *Blue and Brown Books*, *expressis verbis;* various moments are united in the concept. In the *Blue Book* language-games are "ways of using signs simpler than those in which we use the signs of our highly complicated ordinary language"; they are "primitive forms of language or primitive languages", linguistic forms such as a child uses when it is learning a language and here they even have the "entertaining character of games". They are not incomplete parts of a language, they are rather complete languages in themselves, independent communication systems of human information. In addition to this meaning of the word, another one closely related to it immediately emerges: the use of cards and diagrams, descriptive geometry and chemical symbolism are also "language-games" (cf. B. B. 81).

Wittgenstein employs such language-games in the *Blue and Brown Books* to clarify the problems of truth, the agreement of proposition and reality, the nature of assertion, assumption and question etc. (B. B. 17).[1]

The language-game concept of the *Philosophical Investigations* developed later out of these approaches in the *Blue and Brown Books*. Here also language-games are "primitive kinds of linguistic use", "primitive languages" or even linguistic forms used by the child in language learning (P. I. 5 and 7). In addition to these uses, however, two new meanings of the word are to be found, which are only hinted at in the *Blue and Brown Books*. On one occasion Wittgenstein even calls the whole of language and all the the activities woven into it *the* language-game (P. I. 7), and finally, certain partial systems or individual ways of using fully developed everyday language are called language-games. (Cf. P. I. 23).

[1] On this point Rhees, in his Preface to the *Blue and Brown Books* communicates the following unpublished note of Wittgenstein's from the year 1934: "When I describe certain simple language-games, it is not so as to gradually build up the processes of cultivated language — or of thought, ..., but I put the games as such there, and allow them to radiate their clarifying effect on particular problems." (Rhees (1) VIII.)

Strawson in his review of the *Philosophical Investigations* distinguishes the following meanings of the word: "Wittgenstein uses this phrase to refer to any particular way, actual or invented, of using language (e. g. to a particular way of using a certain sentence, or a certain word; and also 'to the whole consisting of language and the actions into which it is woven')". [2] Stegmüller, on the other hand, suggests a somewhat different division: "Wittgenstein understands by language-games sometimes those methods, mostly playful, by means of which children learn the use of their mother-tongue, but then also simple models of language and finally the whole of everyday language, together with the activities with which it is interwoven, are also so called." [3]

Doing justice to both classifications we accordingly understand by "language-game":

(a) certain primitive and simplified forms of language such as, say, those used by a child when learning a language, or such as can be artificially drawn up.

(b) ordinary everyday language together with all the activities and performances indissolubly belonging to it. (Generally in the locution "*the* language-game.")

(c) certain individual partial language systems, functional entities or applicational contexts that constitute part of an organic whole.

Let us now go more closely into the individual meanings.

(a). In the *Investigations* Wittgenstein frequently uses simplified language-games to represent in simplified form, by means of a model, so to say, relations of our everyday language that are not distinct or transparent. Examples of this kind of language-game are to be found particularly at the beginning of the work; we choose the language-game in No. 2 which is important also for the later investigations.

In order to understand to what extent this language-game is a "primitive" form of language we start from a linguistic situation familiar to us from the use of everyday language: a builder A and

---

[2] Strawson (3) p. 71 Note.
[3] Stegmüller (1) p. 283 Note.

his assistant B are building a house. A gets various building parts brought to him by saying, for example, "Bring me a few tiles" or "I need another stone slab." B brings the objects that are wanted.

In this use of language the partners are linguistically "tuned in" to each other. Locutions of the most varied kind occur; for example, imperatival propositions of the type: "Bring me ..."; concealed imperatival propositions of the type: "I also need ..."; elliptical propositions of the form: "A few more tiles" or simply "tiles" etc. Now, this whole system of communication can be conceived in a very simplified form, say, in a "language" in which there are only a few individual words. This language is intended exclusively for the mutual understanding of the builder A and his assistant B: "A is building with building-stones: there are blocks, pillars, slabs and beams. B has to pass the stones, and that in the order in which A needs them. For this purpose they use a language consisting of the words "block", "pillar", "slab", "beam". A calls them out; B brings the stone which he has learnt to bring at such-and-such a call." (P. I. 2). This, then, is a very simplified "language" containing just so many means of expression as enables A and B to make themselves understood in the manner mentioned, but not for any other linguistic purpose beyond that one. But with respect to a very limited form of communication it achieves exactly the same as our ordinary language and therefore represents, in a very simplified form, a quite definite function of ordinary language. We are here concerned, therefore, with a "language-game". Admittedly it does not occur in this form, but it is built on the analogy of a definite way of using our ordinary language and therefore is able to serve as model for this mode of use. The simplification in this language-game, by contrast to our ordinary language, consists in the fact that, among other things, the builder can only get one thing brought at a time, whereas in our ordinary language the builder can get several objects brought at once. Only by extending the artificial language-game can the achievement realised by the word "several" in our ordinary language be also represented by means of a model, for example, by adding: if A wants one slab he says "slab"; but if he wants several slabs brought he shouts: "slab, slab."

The example shows the purpose of the simplified or artificial language-games; Wittgenstein uses them to demonstrate the various functions and achievements of our ordinary language in a model, so to say. The simplified language-games are *"objects of comparison"*, as Wittgenstein says, "meant to throw light on the facts of our language by way not only of similarities but also of dissimilarities." (P. I. 130).

Wittgenstein frequently uses this language-game method of clarifying the involved relations of our ordinary language in the *Investigations* and in the *Remarks on the Foundations of Mathematics*. Admittedly, the language-games drawn up for this purpose are quite different in character. Often they are strongly reduced forms of our ordinary language, as for example the language-games used at the beginning of the *Investigations* (P. I. 1, 2, 8). Sometimes they are more like mathematical sign-systems, for example, the language-game intended to explain Socrates' dream from the *Theaetetus* (P. I. 48). Frequently the language-games develop into forms which could rather be called intellectual experiments, for example, when one has to think out a language in which there are two different words for negation (P. I. 556).[4]

However, this method contains a danger. The clarification of the complexity and obscurity of many of the functions of our ordinary language might lead to the view that ordinary language is really incomplete and must therefore be reformed and regulated. Such a view would lead once more to something like the theory of language maintained in the *Tractatus* from which Wittgenstein unam-

---

[4] In artificial language-games the connection between the language and life of man is important. We are, thus, for example, to imagine that a definite language-game is the whole language of a tribe (P. I. 6). Or Wittgenstein portrays tribes with quite different forms of life and then investigates the consequences for the language and speech modes of this tribe (say F. M. 43, 105). Wittgenstein says generally in this sense: "It is easy to imagine a language consisting only of orders and reports in battle. — Or a language consisting only of questions and expressions for answering yes and no. And innumerable others. — And to imagine a language means to imagine a form of life." (P. I. 19.)

biguously distanced himself in the late work: "Our clear and simple language-games are not preparatory studies for a future regularisation of language—as it were first approximations, ignoring friction and air-resistance. The language-games are rather set up as *objects of comparison* which are meant to throw light on the facts of our language by way not only of similarities but also of dissimilarities." (P. I. 130). It is conceivable, of course, that language-games might make someone wish to reform ordinary language for a definite practical purpose, say, to avoid misunderstandings. But that is not the function of the philosophical consideration intended by Wittgenstein in the *Investigations*. On the contrary: "Philosophy may in no way interfer with the actual use of language; it can only in the end describe it. For it cannot give it any foundation either. It leaves everything as it is." (P. I. 124).

(b) Wittgenstein also transfers the expression "language-game" to the whole of language: "I shall also call the whole, consisting of language and the actions into which it is woven, the 'language-game'. (P. I. 7). He uses the word "language" mostly in a very wide sense, so that it also includes for him e.g. the sign-systems of logic or mathematics. Admittedly, he attributes primacy to our word-language, as we ordinarily use it; what we call language is primarily the "apparatus of our ordinary language, of our word-language", and then other structures by way of analogy or comparability with it (P. I. 494). When Wittgenstein speaks of "language-game" in this context he means not only language as a system of linguistic signs, but also all the activities belonging to the use of this sign-system.

(c) Finally one must understand under "language-game" certain partial systems or partial functions of language. How these partial systems are to be conceived can best be explained in a series of examples, which we wish to order in four groups.

The first group of language-games includes everything that could be called "linguistic act" or "linguistic performance": ordering, requesting, thanking, cursing, greeting, reporting an event, telling a story, making a joke, lying, telling a dream, admitting the motive of an action (P. I. 23, 249, p. 184, p. 224). On the periphery of this group are such phenomena as singing a round, acting, solving a riddle (P. I. 23).[5]

Under the second group fall language-games which would not really be called linguistic acts, but in which language plays a decisive role: translating, reading, making up a story, acting on order (P. I. 23).

To the third group belong activities in which speaking and the use of language withdraw considerably into the background, though the activity is indisputably bound up with language: constructing an object from a description, indulging in speculations, forming and testing a hypothesis, presenting the results of an experiment in tables and diagrams, making predictions (P. I. 23, 630).

In language-games of the fourth group the system-aspect of a specific linguistic use stands in the foreground.[6] Language-game here always means a definite, often very small, sometimes very large partial system of language; the totality of signs and sign-rules of which a relatively independent partial system of language consists. An example would be, say, the language-game with sense impression words (P. I. p. 180), or the language-game with our colour words, which certainly consists of a very complicated totality of words, uses of words, types of assertion etc. (Here the concept of "linguistic field" becomes significant, a concept about which we shall come to speak later).

But it does not always have to be many words enclosed within one system. Even a single word or a single proposition is in a way embedded in a whole system of different modes of use and, in this

[5] This group can roughly be identified with what Kainz (1) p. 172 calls "achievements of language". It would be possible for this group to be reducible to some few basic categories of linguistic achievements, say to Bühler's three categories: statement, evocation and representation, or expression, call and representation. Cf. Bühler (1). Wittgenstein would, it is true, be opposed to such a classification, since it always contains in itself the danger that the multiplicity of and differences between the individual linguistic achievements would be hidden by a schematic classification. Cf. P. I. 23.

[6] In the first group of language-games the "organon model", in Bühler's sense, in other words the "linguistic action", stands in the foreground, whereas the last group is determined by the "structure model" of language. Cf. Bühler (1) and (2).

respect, constitutes a "language-game". In this way Wittgenstein, on occasion, analyses the language-game with the word "read", for example, (P. I. 156), or in the analysis of the word "game" he speaks of the "language-game with the word 'game'" (P. I. 71). Finally, to this group of language-games may also belong linguistic systems no longer immediately belonging to everyday language, but still standing in close relationship to it: for example, the symbolism of chemistry or the symbolic language of mathematics.

3. The language-game model and its achievements in the analysis of language. The problem of the definability of the term "language-game"

(1) There has been much discussion about why exactly Wittgenstein chose the expression "language-game", even though he by no means construed language as a "mere game".

The strongest criticism of the expression "language-game" was made by Smart. He writes: "Only the operation of a symbolic calculus bears some remote analogy to the playing of a game, and it may well be that his early pre-occupation with symbolic logic tended to encourage Wittgenstein in the erroneous belief that such an analogy could be generalised so as to cover all language, and thus justify coining the phrase 'language-game'". Smart enumerates various reasons against any significant analogies between language and games. Thus, games, in contrast to language, have no function whatever important for life. They serve no serious end; nor do they belong to the "form of life" of a society. Games are thus in no way an "instrument", whereas language is essentially an instrument. Smart finally sums up his criticism in the following way: "Thus one can hardly imagine a more inappropriate linking of terms than the one incorporated in the phrase 'language-game'. Instead of serving any useful or enlightening purpose, it can only tend to confusion and obscurity."[7] In addition to this very sharp and one-sided

[7] Smart (1) p. 233.

criticism there is also a series of positive evaluations. Gahringer[8]
regards the analogy between language and game as illuminating in
many ways. Language and games are similar to each other in that
they are activities based on definite and to some extent arbitrary
rules; contradictory or inadequate rules put an end to both language
and games; finally, language and games are forms of communication
between partners.[9]

We shall not go any further here into the problem of whether the
word "language-game" is happily chosen or not, nor into the
problem of which analogies and differences really exist between
language and games. For our purposes it is much more important
to show clearly those different aspects in the phenomenon of
language which Wittgenstein wished to make evident by means of
language-games. He obviously aims at three important and most
intimately connected factors: namely, (a) that language is an
activity connected with the whole form of life of the linguistic
partners, (b) that insofar as language consists in the purposeful use
of symbols in accordance with definite rules it has an "instrumen-
tal" character and finally, (c) that language is to be conceived as a
structure compounded of very different functional entities. These
factors will be discussed in detail.

(a) When Wittgenstein extends the word "language-game" to the
"whole, consisting of language and the actions into which it is
woven" (P. I. 7), he may well wish thus to emphasise the indissoluble connection of language with human action; language is an
activity penetrating all forms of life and is indissolubly bound up
with other activities that can in no way be separated from these
forms of life and activities; nor can it be regarded as an isolated
structure. Wittgenstein comes repeatedly to speak of this connection, for example: "The word 'language-*game*' is here meant to

[8] Gahringer (1) p. 662ff.
[9] Ryle emphasises another characteristic common to language and games:
"Even more instructive is the analogy which Wittgenstein now came to draw
between significant expressions and the pieces with which games like chess
are played." Ryle draws out in detail the analogies existing here, while not
omitting to indicate the differences.
(Cf. Ryle (1) p. 255ff.)

bring into prominence the fact that the *speaking* of language is part of an activity, or of a form of life." (P. I. 23); or: "What people *say* is right and wrong: and it is in *language* that people agree. This is no agreement of opinions but of forms of life" (P. I. 24). Pole has paraphrased this passage in the following way: "Our linguistic activities are part of that pattern of things that makes us what we are and determines our relations with our fellows. That men have, within limits, similar basic proclivities, that certain patterns of behaviour come naturally to almost all of them, is the condition of the emergence of society and language. It is within that general framework that particular linguistic activities go forward. We do not make things true or false by agreement. It is of particular statements that truth and falsehood are predicated; but it is clear that unless we agreed, not as to particular beliefs but in some fundamental orientation, the language in which the terms 'true' and 'false' occur could never have existed at all."[10] It is above all the concept of form of life which is important as the ultimate basis of all linguistic communication. We cannot penetrate behind the form of life upon which language is founded; we have to accept it as an irreducible ultimate: "what has to be accepted, the given, is—so one could say—*forms of life*." (P. I. p. 226). Or, as a critic expresses it: "'Forms of life' evidently play the role, in Wittgenstein's own language-game, of a metaphysical ultimate in terms of which the functioning of language is to be understood. They must be *accepted*, and they are *given*—that is to say, they are regarded as an indubitable basis, a rock of certainty, like the Cartesian *cogito*."[11]

Wittgenstein does not stand alone in this conception of language. Similar thoughts are to be found both in modern linguistics as well as in modern linguistic philosophy.[12] The same question repeatedly arises: how is language to be regarded so that it does not become an

[10] Pole (1) p. 52.
[11] Smart (1) p. 232.
[12] As, for example, Weisgerber in German linguistic philosophy, whom we shall examine more closely in a moment. In America, particularly Whorf (1), who studied the close relationship between form of life and *Weltanschauung* in North American native languages. For an account of Whorf's ideas, from a philosophical point of view, cf. Black (10).

abstract structure separated from human life and action. L. Weisgerber attacked this problem from the linguistic side and attempted
a solution along the lines of Humboldt's distinction between *ergon*
and *energeia*.[13] In many investigations into language there is a danger
that the language in question will be regarded as a completed structure, as an *ergon*, a "work that had an existence in the sense of what
was closed, resting in itself."[14] But this leads to equating language
with what is laid down in dictionaries and grammars, i.e. to an
"inadmissible objectification", that in no way does justice to the
real "*life*" of language. If one wishes to meet language in its real
existence, if, in other words, one wishes to avoid all false objectification, it cannot be regarded as a completed *ergon*, it must be
conceived as *energeia*, in Humboldt's sense: "We shall best make this
intelligible to ourselves by understanding a language's form of
existence as that of a *reality*. This idea of the reality of a magnitude,
like that of the German language, permits us to see the context in
which its 'life' unfolds: it is the bearer of a web of effects and
therewith of a power having its existence in the life of the total
linguistic community seen as the focal and radiation point of
effects."[15] Language is thus understood as a reality indissolubly
bound up with the total life and action of a linguistic community.

The distinction intended here aimed at between *ergon* and *energeia*
has a certain parallel with the distinction made by de Saussure (1)
between *la langue* and *la parole* : the total phenomenon, language, *la
langue*, can be observed from two completely different standpoints.
Language can be construed as the vocabulary and linguistic possession of a linguistic community or as linguistic performance and
concrete speaking. Language is thus, on the one hand, *la langue* and
on the other hand *la parole*. Although this distinction is in many
respects illuminating, it contains a danger. It is easy to be tempted
to limit *la parole*, speech, to the speech act, to construe the linguistic
performance as a psycho-physical act compounded of an external,
acoustic-motor event and an internal psycho-mental event. By mak-

13 Cf. in this connection, for example, Humboldt (1).
14 Weisgerber (1) p. 15.
15 Weisgerber (1) p. 15.

ing this limitation, however, a whole series of activities disappears which, although containing nothing spoken, would still be described as "linguistic performances" e. g. quietly reading to oneself, or silently preparing a translation.

In addition to this, the speech act is loosened from the whole fabric of activities with which it is most closely bound up. In order to circumvent such one-sidedness Wittgenstein avoids anything that would bring the analysis of language to the level of psycho-physical speech-acts. That does not, of course, mean that he would regard physiological or psychological investigations in connection with language as misguided; it is just that such investigations approach language from a side which is not of primary interest to him. For Wittgenstein the real linguistic performance does not lie in the isolated speech-act but rather in what could perhaps be called "linguistic activity". This includes very much more than the mere uttering of words or propositions. In this sense, linguistic activities also include, for example, writing and reading, where language, although used, by no means has to be spoken. To express it more sharply: according to Wittgenstein, we do not perform any psycho-physical speech-acts, but we cry for help, we wish one another good morning, we tell a joke, we describe the results of an experiment, we read a book; in short, we perform all the many language-games of which language is compounded. The *speaking* of language is, by contrast, only "part of an activity, or of a form of life." (P. I. 23).

(b) As we have seen, the model of the language-game manifests the moment of linguistic activity and form of life. Another moment is closely connected with this and is revealed by this model: the words and propositions of language are instruments of the activity mentioned; "Language is an instrument. Its concepts are instruments." (P. I. 569). This is the basic thesis of what has been called Wittgenstein's "Instrumentalist Theory of Language". Linsky[16] remarks in connection with this: "This instrumentalist view is the centre of gravity of Wittgenstein's philosophy. We can approach it first from a consideration of the idea of a language-game.

[16] Linsky (2) p. 288.

A language-game is the use of language for some purpose." Linsky gives two examples of language-games and then continues: "In these descriptions the view of language as a tool, an instrument, is prominent. The language-game is a whole 'consisting of language and the actions into which it is woven'."[17] As is known, this tool-conception of language has a long history reaching back to Plato, and to this extent is not a new discovery.[18] However, it is not so much the view of language as a tool that makes Wittgenstein's theory interesting. What makes it interesting is the way in which, by means of a comparison of the use of tools and the use of language, he reveals certain moments of language that had not been perceived so clearly before. It is precisely the artificial language-games that are here intended to bring out the tool-like character of linguistic signs. The analogy between tool and linguistic sign is also often emphasised *expressis verbis :* "Think of the tools in a tool-box: there is a hammer, pliers, a saw, a screw-driver, a rule, a glue-pot, glue, nails and screws.—The functions of words are as diverse as the functions of these objects." (P. I. 11). Similarly in the individual analysis of specific words or propositions: "Look at the word 'to think' as a tool." (P. I. 360), or: "Look at the sentence as an instrument, and at its sense as its employment." (P. I. 421). Correlative to the concept of tool is that of the *use* of a tool and correspondingly that of the *use* of language. We "use" words or propositions in the language-games of our language; the artificial language-games are intended to show how one "operates" with words, what one "does" with a word, how one "uses" language. (Cf. P. I. 1). This concept of the use of language, as it emerges from the tool-aspect of language, is one of the most central concepts of the *Investigations* and it will frequently occupy us later. The importance of this con-

[17] For an instrumentalist interpretation of language in Wittgenstein cf. for example, Feyerabend (3) p. 462f. Feyerabend connects this interpretation of Wittgenstein with a certain constructivism: "I am inclined to say — and there is strong evidence in favour of this view—that Wittgenstein's theory of language can be understood as a constructivist theory of meaning, i. e., as constructivism applied not only to the meanings of mathematical expressions but to meanings in general." (Cf. p. 462, Note.)

[18] Cf. for example, Plato, *Cratylus*, 388 a 8.

cept lies, among other things, in the fact that it stands in close connection with that of linguistic *rule*; the use of linguistic symbols follows definite rules that are "use" or "convention" in the linguistic community in question, and that are most closely connected with the whole form of life of the linguistic community.[19]

(c) A further achievement of the language-game model has scarcely received attention in the literature to-date. By creating the concept "language-game" Wittgenstein analyses language into definite concrete entities that can be examined in relative isolation.

Since they first began reflecting on the nature of language, philosophers have sought entities out of which language is compounded. Plato and Aristotle, to whom we owe the first concise investigations on this theme, thought they had found such entities in phonetic elements, in syllables, words and propositions. For example, in the Aristotelian theory of language, which we discussed in detail in the first section, language is built up hierarchically out of these elements: letters join together to form syllables, syllables to form words, propositions can be built out of words according to definite rules, and propositions connect together to form arguments. On the content side, analogous elements correspond to the phonetic elements. Definite representations in the mind or definite objects in the world correspond to individual words; combinations of representations or combinations among things correspond to sentences etc. In the *Tractatus* Wittgensein himself attempts to discover the entities of language by a corresponding logical analysis. But

---

[19] Feyerabend sums up these connections between rule, linguistic usage, praxis and form of life in the following way: "One can only speak of a rule insofar as a sign (the representation of the rule) plays a role in a praxis, in a definite form of life. 'To follow a rule, to make a communication, to give an order, to play chess are *conventions*', and to follow a rule or break it thus amounts to 'taking part in this convention or not taking part'. This convention determines the sense of the expressions that are used in a definite way as essential constituent parts in it, and convention is the reference system, according to which we decide what is meant by an expression, whether something is understood, or whether a rule has been followed. 'What has to be accepted, the given — one could say — are *forms of life*.'" (Feyerabend (1) p. 1031. The reference to sense, suggested here, or the meaning of linguistic signs, will come to be discussed in detail later, cf. 9.)

whereas the classical theories start from perceptible entities, i. e. from audible sounds and combinations of sounds, Wittgenstein arrives at elements (simple names and elementary propositions) that can only be inferred theoretically but can never be exhibited in concrete language.

In his late work Wittgenstein clearly turns away from the views in the *Tractatus*. In the *Investigations* language-games are functional entities that differ in principle from Aristotle's entities and from the entities in the *Tractatus*. The difference between the two views can best be illustrated by a comparison. If language is compared to an organism (which is, of course, only possible in a quite definite respect) then a theory of organism which starts from individual cells as completely isolated entities and which attempts to construct the organism summatively from these individual cells—such a theory corresponds to the *Tractatus* theory. The conception of language in the *Philosophical Investigations*, however, could be compared to a theory of organism which lays down as a foundation the individual functional systems of the organism as entities and construes the cells only as members of a functional system. The individual language-games correspond to the different functional systems of an organism: circulation, respiration, the organ of sight etc. Now, the decisive thing is that, although different moments can be distinguished in an organic functional system, e. g. individual cells, group of cells, the interplay of these groups of cells etc., they cannot exist independently of the functional system. Something similar is true of language-games; here too, different moments can be distinguished: the individual linguistic signs, the rules for the use of linguistic signs, the activities that are indissolubly bound up with use. But none of these moments can be construed as independently existing entities. Of course, individual words or propositions can for certain purposes be isolated from a language-game and examined in separation; but in doing this one must not forget that a linguistic symbol only derives its "life" from its connection with all the other moments of the language-game.

In order to cover all possible constituent moments in a language-game Wittgenstein also includes things, institutions and conventions in language, that would not ordinarily be included. An example: if a carpenter measures various pieces of wood with a meter rod, dictating the measurements to an apprentice who writes them in his notebook, this, according to Wittgenstein, is a definite language-game. The measuring of the pieces of wood, the repeating of the lengths measured, the writing of the apprentice etc., all these individual activities are ordered together into a unified whole. The presupposition of this language-game is the whole institution of measuring, and thus includes, for example, the determination of the original meter, the agreement to refer all measures to this original meter etc.

Here nothing is achieved with a mere speech-act so long as this speech-act is not embedded in a technique, in a total institution. For Wittgenstein much more than momentary speaking, with its physical and mental conditions, belongs to the language-game, to the real use of language; he even includes the original meter and the meter rod, and also tuning forks, measuring instruments, tables, diagrams and such like in the "tools of language" (P. I. 16). The concept of the language-game is intended to include the concrete entities of language as they actually occur in the life of the language, not abstract entities that have been extracted from the totality of a definite linguistic use like a tiny wheel from a watch.

Concrete entities have also for a long time played an important role in modern linguistics. De Saussure (1) had recognised that in conversation individual words are never used but only whole sentences. In contrast to this, isolated words only occur in analytical reflection on language, in dictionaries and grammars, as it were. Following his twofold division of language into linguistic performance and vocabulary, he characterises the proposition as the entity of linguistic performance *(la parole)*, and the word as the entity of vocabulary *(la langue)*. However, if a concrete linguistic performance is analysed, it is easy to see that even the individual sentence is not an entity separable from the total context of the linguistic performance. Of course, from the point of view of phonetics or content, it can be regarded as a relatively independent moment; but it is frequently impossible to discover from the proposition itself what it means. In order to explain what a proposition means, it is necessary to know what the contextual situation of the proposition is: "You travel tomorrow" could, in one particular situation, be a command; in another, a question. Generally, differences like this are recognisable from the tone of voice. But all the possible applications of the proposition have by no means been exhausted "You travel tomorrow" can assume all the nuances from question to supposition to doubt, from wish to order and entreaty. This proposition could be an hypothesis, an example in an English grammar, the refrain of a hit-song, a cry of despair, the point of a joke etc. What the proposition says, i.e. what one may wish, on any given occasion, to say by its means, depends on a wider context, or, as Wittgenstein would say, on the specific language-game in which the proposition occurs at the time.

Thus, even the individual proposition is in a way still an abstraction, an isolated phonetic structure, not bearing its meaning within itself but deriving it from a wider context.

W. Porzig tries to do justice to this fact by regarding the *discourse* as the ultimate entity of language. A discourse can consist of a one word proposition, an ordinary sentence or several sentences. In each case the discourse constitutes a communicational entity, set above the proposition, and made up of all the utterances "serving, in a definite situation, to call forth a reaction from one or more partners."[20] If someone knocks on the door and I call "Come in", this "Come in" is, according to Porzig, a complete discourse. At the same time it is not necessary to the concept of discourse, that two or more people should stand in a mutual relationship. The soliloquy is also a discourse for one confronts oneself as one's own partner in a soliloquy, and by means of one's conversation, one elicits from oneself a reaction, for example, a resolution. Discourses need not always be of an audible nature: a treatise, a telegram is also a discourse. In many respects the concept of discourse is similar to that of "language-game". There are, of course, some illuminating differences. The principle according to which

[20] Porzig (1) p. 95.

an entity is constituted in the case of a discourse consists, basically, in a behaviouristic, stimulus-response schema: one partner
A calls forth a reaction on the part of one or more partners B, C, D,
etc.; these utterances constitute a discourse. In contrast to this,
the principle according to which an entity is constituted in the case
of a language-game consists, in general, in the connection between
language and life-praxis. It is true, many language-games are intended to elicit a reaction on the part of a partner. On the other
hand, many language-games have an entirely different purpose that
can only with difficulty be set in parallel with the concept of discourse. If I measure various pieces of furniture, for example, and
enter their measurements in my notebook so as to be able to compare them later with the measurements of my room, this is a definite language-game; I use the names of the pieces of furniture and
the numerical words in the context of a definite praxis. But one
cannot very well say that when I use language in this way I elicit
a reaction from myself or others. Apart from this, a discourse is in
some way a linguistic utterance: a one word sentence, an ordinary
sentence, many sentences etc. The concept of language-game, however refers to the totality of the linguistic utterance and the activities bound up with it.

The notion that each individual word in isolation has a fixed
meaning for itself alone has been attacked in linguistics from other
directions as well. An attempt has been made to overcome the
atomic conception of the word with the help of the concept "linguistic field."[21]

L. Weisgerber, partly following J. Trier, discusses some examples that illustrate the concept of linguistic field. A linguistic
field is, for example, the scale of values layed down in schools

---

[21] The field-concept was made fruitful for the first time by J. Trier (1) in
his work: *Der deutsche Wortschatz im Sinnbezirk des Verstandes* namely, in the
investigation of words for *Verstand* (understanding) in Middle High German. Porzig (in Porzig (2)), has a somewhat different field-concept to Trier.
Here it is particularly relations like that of "bite" to "teeth", of "blond" to
"human hair" etc. that are intended to be explained by means of the field-
concept.

for evaluating proficiency. Such a scale consists of from four to six predicates (very good, good etc.) that can be further differentiated by additions (quite good). The number of basic predicates is, however, not constant. There are scales with four, five or six basic predicates. That means that a predicate, say the predicate "good", changes in value with the scale used on any specific occasion.[22] In other words, what is said by the word "good" is determined by the linguistic field in which it occurs at the time. This word cannot be taken out of the total context of its field and then examined as an isolated structure. "In itself" i.e., independently of the specific field, the word has no fixed meaning.[23] The words for the event of dying also constitute a linguistic field, even if with a somewhat different structure: die, depart, succumb, perish, fall, fall asleep, pass away, pass over, be killed etc.* This field is characterised by the fact that all the words refer to an event, but they articulate the event from different points of view. Thus "linguistic field" has to be understood as an integral multiplicity of words existing in a mutual relationship of dependence, so that each word derives its specific value from the total context.

The concept of verbal field is not identical with that of language-game. But here also certain analogies are to be found. E.g. the language-game with relationship words corresponds to the verbal field of relationship words; the language-game with achievement

---

[22] Weisgerber (1) I. p. 90.

[23] Another linguistic field is constituted by relationship words: father, mother, son, daughter, brother, sister, grandfather, grandmother, grandson, granddaughter, uncle, aunt etc. These words constitute a whole network of involved relations of mutual dependence. My uncle is e.g. the brother of my mother, and therefore the son of the father of my mother, of my grandfather. My mother is the sister of my uncle, the daughter of my grandfather. One cannot take any individual word out of this field and examine it in isolation with respect to its linguistic content. What a word like "uncle" means, emerges rather from the total context of all relationship words. This field is naturally relative to the language. Other languages arrange the connections between relations in entirely different ways. (Cf. Weisgerber [1] p. 60 ff.)

* Since the German linguistic field of 'death' words does not correspond to the same field in English the death words listed in the translation do not correspond precisely to the German words. (Translator's note.)

predicates corresponds to the verbal field of achievement predicates. The concept of language-game has, among other things, a systematic aspect which makes it possible to compare verbal field and language-game. But the parallel breaks down as soon as the systematic aspect in the concept of language-game recedes and the moment of linguistic activity moves into the foreground, as was for example, the case in the language-game where measurements were being made. It is true, that the linguistic field of numerical words was used in this language-game (each individual numerical word obviously stands in a structured field context with the other words), but here the field aspect of numerical word usage remains in the background. What is emphasised is rather the connection of numerical word usage with certain activities: the handling of the meter rod, the reading of numerical symbols, the writing down of numerical words etc.

The concepts "verbal field" and "language-game" can never be used synonymously, therefore, but only in parallel. They differ from each other in that the concept "verbal field" groups words together into a relatively closed partial system of mutually dependent relationships, whereas the language-game concept emphasises the connection of linguistic usage with definite activities.

(2) By the above investigations into the application of the concept "language-game", and particularly by distinguishing the concept from similar linguistic concepts, we have tried to explain the meaning of this term in Wittgenstein. Our examples showed how various are the entities which Wittgenstein analyses out of the totality of language by means of this concept. The question arises, whether, in the case of such diverse phenomena as the individual language-games one can speak of a homogeneous concept at all; in other words, whether there is a generic definition of the concept "language-game". Wittgenstein is of the opinion that many words cannot be defined by giving *genus proximum* and *differentia specifica*. The words "game" and "number", for example, belong to this class.[24] These words constitute rather a "family" of meanings, as Wittgenstein expresses it (cf. P. I. 67), i.e. they refer to a multiplicity of phenom-

ena that cannot be grouped together into one class by means of one or more predicates, but only through multiple relations of similarity, through "family likeness", as Wittgenstein puts it. Since the term "language-game" was coined analogically to the word "game", the word "language-game" also belongs to that group of expressions that are not determinable by exact definition: "Here we come up against the great question that lies behind all these considerations.—For someone might object against me: 'You take the easy way out. You talk about all sorts of language-games, but have nowhere said what the essence of a language-game, and hence of a language, is: what is common to all these activities, and what makes them into language or parts of language. So you let yourself off the very part of the investigation that once gave you yourself most headache, the part about the *general form of propositions* and of language.' And this is true—instead of producing something common to all that we call language, I am saying that these phenomena have no one thing in common which makes us use the same word for all—but that they are *related* to one another in many different ways. And it is because of this relationship or these relationships, that we call them all 'language' ...... We see a complicated network of similarities overlapping and criss-crossing: sometimes overall similarities sometimes similarities of detail ...... I can think of no better expression to characterise these similarities than 'family resemblances'; for the various resemblances between members of a family: build, features, colour of eyes, gait, temperament, etc. etc. overlap and criss-cross in the same way." (P. I. 65, 66, 67; cf. also 68—80).[25]

[24] Waismann (Waismann (2) p. 162 and 181) has shown that the word "number" is not exactly definable, not even with the help of modern mathematical definitions. He formulates his conclusion thus: "... the word 'number' does not signify a concept (in the sense of Scholastic Logic), but a 'conceptual family'. We mean by this that the individual kinds of numbers are related to each other in manifold ways, without their necessarily agreeing in any one property or character-trait." (p. 182.)

[25] For the details that result from the opposition between words signifying an "essence" and those constituting a family of meanings, cf. for example, Feyerabend (2) and (3) and Khatchadourian (1).

Now, although the expression "language-game" constitutes a family of meanings in the sense mentioned, and is thus not strictly definable, this does not limit its applicability. Its range is even an advantage, because it makes it possible to bring together very different structures under one, single homogeneous expression: "one might say that the concept 'game' is a concept with blurred edges. —'But is a blurred concept a concept at all?'—Is an indistinct photograph a picture of a person at all?—Is it even always an advantage to replace an indistinct picture by a sharp one? Isn't the indistinct one often exactly what we need?" (P. I. 71)[26]. One maxim, significant for all of Wittgenstein's linguistic-analytical considerations, is thus true of the application of the concept "language-game": "We want to establish an order in our knowledge of the use of language: an order with a particular end in view; one out of many possible orders; not *the* order." (P. I. 132).

(3) Our discussions so far of the language-game concept now enable us to see to what extent the concept renders questionable an interpretation of language that starts from the atomic model.

One of the basic presuppositions of the atomic theory of language is the idea that language is a unified structure, interpretable on a single schema, namely: the word—named object schema. The language-game model, by contrast, shows us how various are the structures of which language is compounded, and how little sense there is, therefore, in wishing to interpret all these structures on a single and, in addition, very narrow schema. In the *Investigations* Wittgenstein, therefore, resists any

---

[26] Pole (1) p. 92f., following Strawson (3) p. 72, criticised the vagueness of the Wittgensteinian concept of the language-game: "In the catholicity of Wittgenstein's list of linguistic activities, such things as saying prayers and writing poetry are included; and Mr. Strawson has suggested that reading aloud to send an old man to sleep might equally legitimately find a place. It seems that Wittgenstein's account of language or language-games, each functioning by itself in its own way, leaves him no criterion for disqualifying from this name any system or pattern of activities — or perhaps we may say any involving marks or noises — no matter how remote from the assertion of what may be true or false."

attempt at such an interpretation of language, even his own effort in this connection in the *Tractatus*; following an enumeration of the most varied language-games he remarks: "It is interesting to compare the multiplicity of the tools in language and of the ways they are used, the multiplicity of kinds of word and sentence, with what logicians have said about the structure of language. (Including the author of the *Tractatus Logico-Philosophicus*.)" (P. I. 23). The concept of the language-game helps us, then, to the following insight: "We see that what we call "sentence" and "language" has not the formal unity that I imagined, but is the family of structures more or less related to one another." (P. I. 108).

Closely connected with this is the rejection of the so-called "ideal language", allegedly concealed behind our ordinary language. The individual language-games of which language is compounded are, as actually found in linguistic communication, concrete entities, not some abstraction or subsequently inferred structure: "We are talking about the spatial and temporal phenomenon of language, not about some non-spatial, non-temporal phantasm." (P. I. 108).

Smart in particular has drawn attention to this side of the language-game concept: ". . . . . . one basic reason for using the phrase 'language-game', instead of the word 'language', Wittgenstein seems to suggest, is in order to make it easier to avoid certain serious errors which beset much of contemporary philosophy. One such error, for example, finds embodiment in the concept of an ideal language which once made a strong appeal to the author of the *Tractatus* himself. But just as there are games and games, but no one game *par excellence*, no ideal game examination of which will reveal a supposedly hidden essence of game-as-such, so there is no ideal language answering to pure, unearthly, sublime logic, the very *essence* of thought-as-such."[27]

But the atomic model is by no means refuted with this first criticism. What has still to be shown in detail is how far the language-game model really puts us in a position to describe linguistic functions more suitably than is possible by means of the atomic model.

[27] Smart (1) p. 225.

IV. THE ONTOLOGICAL AND EPISTEMOLOGICAL PRESUPPOSITIONS OF THE SIGNIFICATION FUNCTION

4. *Wittgenstein's critique of the Augustinian learning theory of language*

One of the central problems of the philosophy of language is the question about the relation between language and the world of objects. The fundamental relation existing between a linguistic sign and that which the linguistic sign signifies is generally called the "signification relation". In everyday language it is expressed by the sentence schema: "The word ...... signifies ......"[1] In what follows we shall adopt this linguistic usage and always employ this schema when we want to express a word's signification function.[2] In our discussion of the *Tractatus* and the Aristotelian theory of language we saw how the signification relation between word and object was to be conceived on the basis of the atomic model.

---

[1] It will become clear in the next section that in Wittgenstein a sharp distinction must be made between what a word designates and the *meaning* of the word concerned. The total semantic function of a word can only be suitably described with the help of both concepts. The signification relation used here differs in many respects from the so-called naming relation. An example will best make this clear: one says: "The word 'here' signifies the place indicated by the speaker at the time of speaking"; on the other hand it would be odd if one were to say: "The word 'here' names the place indicated by the speaker at the time of speaking". It would be odd because one uses "to name" in connection with the use of names, whereas "here" is not construed in our ordinary terminology as the name of a place.

[2] Instead of the schema: "The word...signifies..." one can also use the more general schema: "The linguistic expression...signifies...". With this schema one can also then characterise the signification function of more complex expressions (for example, of the type: "The present Prime Minister of England").

According to this model all the words of language (or at least all meaning-bearing words) refer to their objects more or less in the way names for individual things refer to their pre-existent name-bearers. Atomic theories of language, then, tend to see in names and the individual things correlated with them the primary sphere of application of the sentence schema: "The word ...... signifies ......". The question now arises to what extent this interpretational approach of atomic theories is justified, and whether the language-game model, with which Wittgenstein starts, offers a superior possibility of interpretation. Our first investigation (§ 4) is to be devoted to the problem of why it is exactly that the interpretation of the signification function is based on names for individual things in atomic theories. Wittgenstein treated this problem in connection with the question how one learns a language as a child. (Cf. P. I. 1—38). We shall deal with this question first.

(1) Wittgenstein's starts from the quite definite, atomistically orientated conception of infant language learning, according to which a child learns the signification function of words by means of the ostensive explanations on the part of adults. According to this theory infant learning is roughly conceived, in very simplified form, as: adults pointing to objects and saying: "That is called...." or "That is......" etc. The child understands or guesses that the adults mean the object indicated by the word in question and in this way grasps the signification function of words. Wittgenstein thinks he is able to find a concrete formulation of this conception in the *Confessions* of St. Augustine, in a passage where Augustine describes how he learnt language as a child:

> cum ipsi (maiores homines) appellabant rem aliquam, et cum secundum eam vocem corpus ad aliquid movebant, videbam, et tenebam hoc ab eis vocari rem illam, quod sonabant, cum eam vellent ostendere. Hoc autem eos velle ex motu corporis aperiebatur: tamquam verbis naturalibus omnium gentium, quae fiunt vultu et nutu oculorum, ceterorumque membrorum actu, et sonitu vocis indicante affectionem animi in petendis, habendis, reiiciendis, fugiendisve rebus. Ita verba in variis sententiis locis suis posita, et crebro audita, quarum rerum signa essent, paulatim colligebam, measque iam voluntates, edomito in eis signis ore, per haec enuntiabam.

We shall not go into the question whether Augustine really maintains here in detail the learning theory mentioned. Wittgenstein, of course, is not concerned with an historical interpretation or critique of Augustine, but rather with a conception of infant language learning which he could just as well have described in non-historical terms. Thus, although we shall frequently speak in what follows about the "Augustinian Learning Theory", we shall always be aware that it is primarily a theory that Wittgenstein attributes to Augustine.[3] The question now is, on what presuppositions is this "Augustinian Learning Theory" of language built. For the first time Wittgenstein uses the method of throwing light on the obscure relations of our everyday language with the *help of artificial language-games* to clarify this question. He chooses as starting point the language-game with the four main words "slab", "pillar" etc., and makes the assumption that this language-game is the complete language of a tribe: how would the children of this tribe learn language? (P. I. 6).

It is conceivable that the language-teaching consisted of a number of partial exercises; Wittgenstein describes, for example, the following: (a) the teacher says a word aloud and the pupil repeats it after him; (b) the teacher points to objects, and while attracting the child's attention to them, says a word e. g. "slab" aloud, while pointing out the particular object; (c) the learner "names" objects, i. e. he says the word when the teacher points at a definite object. (Cf. P. I. 6 and 7).

[3] The translation quoted in the *Investigations* runs: "When they (my elders) named some object, and accordingly moved towards something, I saw this and I grasped that the thing was called by the sound they uttered when they meant to point it out. Their intention was shewn by their bodily movements, as it were the natural language of all peoples: the expression of the face, the play of the eyes, the movement of the other parts of the body, and the tone of voice which expresses our state of mind in seeking, having, rejecting or avoiding something. Thus, as I heard words repeatedly used in their proper places in various sentences, I gradually learnt to understand what objects they signified; and after I had trained my mouth to form these signs, I used them to express my own desires." (P. I. 1). On the choice of this Augustine passage N. Malcolm informs us: "On the other hand, he (Wittgenstein) revered the writings of St. Augustine. He told me he decided to begin his Investigations with a quotation from the latter's Confessions, not because he could not find the conception expressed in that quotation stated as well by other philosophers, but because the conception *must* be important if so great a mind held it." Malcolm (3) p. 71.

All these partial exercises have a definite similarity to the training of an animal. This is because in this kind of teaching the teacher gives no explanations of any kind, but trains the child to do certain things by gestures, rewards, punishments etc. Hence it is that Wittgenstein chooses the expression "training" for these partial exercises. (P. I. 6)[4] This expression is tainted by its origins. Although one speaks of the "*Abrichtung eines Hundes*", in ordinary German linguistic usage, one does not talk of the "*Abrichtung eines Kindes*".* Admittedly this linguistic usage does not exclude the possibility of there being moments in infant language learning which are largely analogous to animal learning; just as a dog is induced by suitable means to react regularly in a definite way to a particular stimulus, so a child is brought up by example, teaching etc., to perform certain actions; thus, in our example, to repeat words after someone, to point at things and say a word aloud etc. "I am using the word 'trained' in a way strictly analogous to that in which we talk of an animal being trained to do certain things. It is done by means of example, reward, punishment and suchlike." (B. B. 77).

That the mentioned linguistic exercises of a child can best of all be compared to training is seen very clearly from exercise (b), which Wittgenstein calls "ostensive teaching of words" (P. I. 6). This kind of teaching must be sharply distinguished from what Wittgenstein calls "ostensive explanation" or "definition". (Cf. P. I. 6). The difference lies in the fact that *nothing is explained* in ostensive

[4] This distinction between teaching by training and teaching by explanation is to be found frequently in Wittgenstein. Cf. for example, P. I. 86, 198, 206; G. M. 2, 10 etc. Ryle (3) p. 42 makes a similar distinction between "drill" and "training". "Drill (or conditioning) consists in the imposition of repetitions. The recruit learns to slope arms by repeatedly going through just the same motions by numbers. The child learns the alphabet and the multiplication tables in the same way...Training, on the other hand, though it embodies plenty of sheer drill, does not consist of drill. It involves the stimulation by criticism and example of the pupil's own judgement".

* The German word "*Abrichtung*" and the English word "training" are thus not synonymous. The English word "training" may be applied indifferently to animals and children. The fact that Wittgenstein uses the word "*Abrichtung*" to apply to children thus gives those parts of the *Investigations* in question an emphatic and slightly paradoxical flavour absent in the English. (Translator's note.)

teaching; the teacher merely points to an object and calls out a word (say, to establish in the child an "associative connection" between word and object). By contrast, in ostensive explanation the teacher *explains* the signification function of a word; in other words he points, for example, to an object and says: "That is called . . . . . " or "One calls that . . . . . ." etc.

However, this "ostensive teaching" of words does not exist merely in the above mentioned language-game. In order to show this Wittgenstein draws up a new language-game and introduces additional kinds of words: "Let us now look at an expansion of language (2). Besides the four words "block", "pillar" etc., let it contain a series of words used as the shopkeeper in (1) used the numerals (it can be the series of letters of the alphabet); further, let there be two words, which may as well be "there" and "this" (because this roughly indicates their purpose), used in connection with a pointing gesture; and finally a number of colour samples. A gives an order like: "d-slab-there". At the same time he shows the assistant a colour sample, and when he says "there" he points to a place on the building site. From the stock of slabs B takes one for each letter of the alphabet up to "d", of the same colour as the sample, and brings them to the place indicated by A.—On other occasions A gives the order "this-there". At "this" he points to a building stone. And so on. (P. I. 8; the bracket (1) refers to the language-game with the shopkeeper which is not described here, P. I. 1).

It is also possible to imagine exercises in this language-game in which ostensive teaching plays an important rôle: "When a child learns this language, it has to learn the series of 'numerals' a, b, c, ... by heart. And it has to learn their use.—Will this training include ostensive teaching of the words?—Well, people will, for example, point to slabs and count: 'a, b, c slabs'.—Something more like the ostensive teaching of the words 'block', 'pillar' etc. would be the ostensive teaching of numerals, that serve not to count, but to refer to groups of objects that can be taken in at a glance. Children do learn the use of the first five or six cardinal numerals in this way. Are 'there' and 'this' also taught ostensively?—Imagine how one might perhaps teach their use. One will point to places and things—but in this case the pointing occurs in the *use* of the words too and not merely in learning the use.—" (P. I. 9).

In both language-games, therefore, there are different forms of ostensive teaching of words. It is, however, very illuminating that there are still no ostensive *explanations* in these language-games (Cf. P. I. 27). At this level of speaking the child can neither ask about the naming nor understand ostensive explanations. At first sight this is not immediately clear. Wittgenstein, therefore, tries to explain in a somewhat more extended investigation (cf. P. I. 28—36) the specific conditions of ostensive definition.

Let us assume for the moment that the word "two" is to be explained to a child by means of an ostensive definition. One points, then, to two nuts, two apples, two houses etc., and says "That means 'two'". (P. I. 28). The following objection can be made to this procedure: "But how can two be defined like that? The person one gives the definition to doesn't know what one wants to call 'two'; he will suppose that 'two' is the name given to *this* group of nuts." (P. I. 28).

The same objection can naturally be raised against any ostensive definition: even when a proper name is explained ostensively it is possible for the partner to think that one wishes to explain a colour to him, a racial name, or even a compass direction. In *every* case, then, it is possible to interpret the ostensive definition in a number of ways: "Any definition can be misunderstood" (P. I. p. 14, footnote).

One could try to avoid these difficulties with a somewhat different form of ostensive definition. The teacher points to various groups of two things, two nuts, two apples etc., and then says: "This *number* is called 'two'." (P. I. 29). The addition, "this number", explains to the partner how he is to construe the "two" and the groups of two things; as Wittgenstein puts it: the addition indicates the place which the word "two" occupies in our language; the learner is to construe the word "two" as a number word and the groups of two things as examples of two. Of course, for the learner to be able to understand this improved form of ostensive definition he must be familiar with the respective, additional words: "number", "colour", "length" etc. But that again is not to be assumed out of hand. In general, then, a person can only understand an ostensive definition if he somehow already knows how the word which is to be explained is to be construed: "...... the ostensive definition explains the use—the meaning—of the word when the overall rôle of the word in language is clear." (P. I. 30).

As far as infant language learning is concerned this means: for a child to be able to understand an ostensive definition at all it must first of all know in outline the "rôle" of the word in question. Unfortunately, Wittgenstein did not discuss in greater detail how the child arrives at knowledge of this "rôle of the word". But perhaps it is to be conceived in Wittgenstein's sense in the following way: the child first of all learns the typical modes of application of the individual words in certain very primitive language-games, in which no ostensive definitions are given. In this way he gradually acquires an understanding of the typical characteristics of the individual kinds of words, of the "place" of words in the language. (Cf. P. I. 29). Only when he has learned this can he put new words that have been taught him by ostensive definition in the right position in the linguistic context.

The above reflections of Wittgenstein's are valid not only for the understanding of ostensive definitions but also for the question about naming. Of course, a child can only meaningfully ask: "What is that called?" or "What is that?" etc. if it is already familiar with the linguistic framework within which the question about the name of the object referred to is raised: "One has already to know (or be able to do) something in order to be capable of asking a thing's name ......" (P. I. 30). Wittgenstein explains these connections by means of a comparison: "Consider this further case: I am explaining chess to someone; and I begin by pointing to a chessman and saying: 'This is the king; it can move like this, ... and so on.'— In this case we shall say: the words 'This is the king' (or 'This is called the king') are a definition only if the learner already 'knows what a piece in a game is'. That is, if he has already played other

games, or has watched other people playing 'and understood'—
and similar things. Further, only under these conditions will he be
able to ask relevantly in the course of learning the game: 'What do
you call this,—that is, this piece in a game." (P. I. 31).

The question about names and the explanation of names by
means of ostensive definition are thus correlative and together
constitute a separate communication system, a specific *language-
game*, to use Wittgenstein's expression: "In languages (2) and (8)
there was no such thing as asking something's name. This, with its
correlate, ostensive definition, is, we might say, a language-game
on its own. That is really to say: we are brought up, trained, to ask:
"What is that called?"—upon which the name is given." (P. I. 27).

These considerations have been made so far with reference to
artificial language-games; but they also show a generally valid
character. The language-game: "asking the name and being able to
understand ostensive definitions" is not only an artifical language-
game but also occurs in our ordinary language as a definite form
of communication. But here too it can only be played on definite
presuppositions, i.e. it rests on definite linguistic forms and
techniques, e. g. on language-games in which the "place" of the
word to be clarified is articulated etc. However, it was a basic idea
of the "Augustinian Learning Theory" that infant language learning be represented as if the child understood the ostensive definitions of adults right from the beginning and learned the signification
function of words by this means. Taken strictly, this theory thus
interprets infant language learning on the analogy of the language-
game: "understanding ostensive definitions of a word", i. e. on
the analogy of a language-game that itself already presupposes
certain linguistic forms and techniques, and which, consequently,
cannot precede language learning. Wittgenstein gives expression
to these relationships in the following way: "Someone coming
into a strange country will sometimes learn the language of the
inhabitants from ostensive definitions that they give him; and he
will often have to *guess* the meaning of these definitions; and will
sometimes guess right, sometimes wrong. And now, I think, we
can say: Augustine describes the learning of human language as if

the child came into a strange country and did not understand the language of the country; that is, as if it already had a language, only not this one. Or again: as if the child could already *think*, only not yet speak. And 'think' would here mean something like 'talk to itself'." (P. I. 32).[5]

The "Augustinian Learning Theory" is thus constructed on a quite definite presupposition; it starts from the situation of an adult who comes to a foreign country where his mother tongue is completely unknown. There are no dictionaries, no grammars etc. He is already master of a (somehow similarly built) language and is thus in the main familiar with the function of individual kinds of words. He learnt the language-game "asking the name and understanding ostensive definitions" in the same way; he can therefore grasp or guess the explanations that are given him by pointing, gestures and mimicking. The theory takes this case as a model of infant language learning: in other words, the child already knows the function of the individual kinds of words and can, for this reason, understand or guess ostensive definitions.

(2) The question now is, what relevance has this discussion of the "Augustinian Learning Theory" for the problem of the signification function. Strawson attempted an interpretation in his review of the *Philosophical Investigations*: "In the first thirty-seven or thirty-eight paragraphs of Part 1, which are concerned with meaning, Wittgenstein is anxious to make us see 'the multiplicity of kinds of

---

[5] Stegmüller interprets this passage in a similar way: "We are inclined to think of a child's learning its mother tongue on the analogy of an adult learning a language, who already has the use of another language, as if the child had come to a foreign country whose language it did not yet understand, at the same time having already mastered another language (or able to think already). Someone who already speaks a language can be taught words from another language by ostensive definitions. But this is only possible because the place for this word has already been prepared by the wealth of rules, which the learner has mastered in his own language. To think that this is the procedure, in principle, in learning language itself, is as naive as thinking that learning chess as such proceeds in the same way as learning chess with unfamiliar pieces, after having already played chess before, only with different figures." (Cf. Stegmüller (1) p. 287.)

words and sentences' (23). We are prone to assimilate different kinds. In particular, we are prone to work with a certain idea of language as consisting of words each correlated with something for which it stands, an object, the meaning of the word (1). This picture, though philosophically misleading for all words, is better suited to some than to others ...... But there are more complex reasons both for the general tendency and for its particular direction. The central point is this: *the picture with which we are inclined to work derives essentially from the instruction-setting of someone who has already mastered in part the technique of using the language ;* i. e. from the situation in which someone is being taught the place of one word, of which he is ignorant, in a way of using language with which he is familiar (cf. 10, 27, 30, 32). In this situation, the instructor may well proceed by saying something like 'the word x means (is the name of, stands for, signifies, etc.) y' where the place of 'y' is taken by, e. g. 'this', 'this number', 'a number', 'this colour', 'the colour which ......''; or simply by a synonym or translation of the word in question. In some, though not all, cases, he may accompany these words by pointing ...... These procedures may give us the impression of a relation of a unique kind being established between two items, a word and something else ......''[6]

From our interpretational approach these explanations of Strawson's may be understood to mean that Wittgenstein, by his analysis of infant language learning, wished to clarify the problem of why there is a tendency in atomic language theories to interpret the signification function of words on the analogy of the relation between names and pre-existent bearers of names. Obviously, in these efforts at an atomic interpretation, one repeatedly proceeds from a linguistic communication-situation of the kind presupposed as model in the "Augustinian Learning Theory". Here we have the situation of a person who has already to a certain extent mastered language, and to whom names are then explained by means of ostensive definitions, and by whom these explanations are understood or guessed at on the basis of his previous linguistic knowledge. The basic

---

[6] Strawson (3) p. 70f. The numbers in brackets refer to the numbers in the P. I.

structure of this situation is so clear that an effort has been made to transfer it to the whole of language. It is thought that all, or at least most, words must refer to their objects more or less as names referred to their alleged name bearers in the situation mentioned above.[7]

For this reason it is also thought that the primary sphere of application of the sentence scheme: "The word ...... signifies ... ..." is that of proper names; all other kinds of words must be thought of on the analogy of this sphere. The sentence schema thus expresses more or less the same state of affairs in the case of all kinds of words as it expresses when it applies to proper names: i. e. the relation between a name and its pre-existent name bearer, conceived as an individual thing.

A series of semantic and ontological misunderstandings now results from this interpretation of the signification relation or of the sentence schema referred to. Findlay, in his review of the *Philosophical Investigations*, has drawn attention to the connections that exist here; the curious position of precedence attributed to names for individual things, and the fact that there is a tendency to overlook the differences in the usage of words because of the similarity of their sensible appearance, these two factors lead to the *significata* of individual kinds of words being brought into close analogy with concrete individual things: "It is we who are tricked by the unvarying, discrete, thing-like aspect of the words in our language into thinking that they all must stand for unvarying, discrete, thing-like entities of some sort."[8]

---

[7] Wittgenstein's attempted explanation of the tendency to interpret all kinds of words on the analogy of proper names and names for individual things is, as Strawson remarks, not entirely satisfactory: "Wittgenstein does not seek to give a complete explanation of why, among all the kinds of names there are, it is substance-names that tend to be taken as the model of meaning. A suggestion which can perhaps be extracted from the text is that (a) pointing figures largely both in ostensive explanation of words, and in that more primitive training in the naming-game which a child goes through before it actually uses words for any more practical purpose; and (b) pointing is more naturally used to discriminate the individual man or horse than any other kind of item. But there remains a question here." (Strawson (1) p. 71 f.)

[8] Findlay (3) p. 174.

The misunderstandings and deceptions that reveal themselves here lie, according to Wittgenstein, at the root e. g. of Nominalism: "Nominalists make the mistake of interpreting all words as *names*, and so of not really describing their use ......" (P. I. 383). This must presumably be understood to mean that Nominalism is only willing to admit one kind of signification function: the relation between a proper name and its name bearer. Since all words are not, of course, names in this sense, the words left over are interpreted in Nominalism in such a way that they either signify nothing at all or are merely "connotative", "syncategorematic". In this lies established the reductionalist character of Nominalism, which is ultimately willing to admit as real only the *significata* of proper names, i. e. concrete individual things, and to dismiss all other *significata* as "superfluous entities".

Reflections similar to those made here by Wittgenstein on Nominalism also apply to Realism; its semantic approach to the interpretation of the signification function is the same. Realism also starts out from the relation between a proper name and the name bearer; only, in contrast to Nominalism, it tries to interpret as many words as possible as names for things, in the manner of individual things, as names for "*res absolutae*". Admittedly, in order to carry through this interpretation, Realism has also to make a "*res absoluta*" correspond to those words that are not generally construed as names for independent things. This leads to the assumption of "supplementary" entities and therewith to an hypostatising ontology.[9]

The dispute between Nominalism and Realism may thus, in

---

[9] When we talk about "hypostatisation" here and in what follows we always understand this in the sense that a hypostatisation is present if and only if an object is construed as an independent individual thing when it is not an individual thing. We follow a definition of Carnap's on this point: "...a hypostatisation or substantialization or reification consists in mistaking as things entities which are not things. Examples of hypostatization of properties (or ideas, universals, or the like) in this sense are such formulations as 'the ideas have an independent subsistence', 'they reside in a superheavenly place', 'they were in the mind of God before they became manifested in things', and the like..." (Carnap (5) p. 22.)

Wittgenstein's sense, have its ultimate origin in the fact that both schools of thought choose the signification function of proper names as the starting point of their interpretation of language; in other words, they both from the beginning encumber the pro-position schema: "The word ...... signifies ......" with a semantic and ontological interpretation, such as results from the conceptions that dominate the atomic theory of language. As a result, both schools of thought are considerably limited: they neither describe how individual kinds of word function, nor do they succeed in giving a satisfactory ontological interpretation of the corresponding kinds of object.

5. *The signification function of words in the language-game*

So far our investigations have shown that Wittgenstein was opposed to the one sided interpretation of the signification function of words that started from proper names and generic words. Now, in order to explain in what way the kinds of word really function and what types of object they thereby signify on a given occasion, Witt-genstein once more makes use of specific artifical language-games. His intention is to make clear how we are to conceive the significa-tion function of words in the language-games of our ordinary lan-guage. Here also he uses his method of presenting "primitive kinds of linguistic use" (cf. P. I. 5), where the functioning of words can be observed better than in the involved linguistic usages of our everyday language. In using this method the discussion is continu-ally moving at two levels; on the one hand, Wittgenstein draws up artifical language-games and describes the functions of words within these artifical language-games; on the other hand, however, he looks at the function of the words in the natural language-games of our everyday language, intending to illuminate this everyday function by means of the artifical language-games. It is hence indispensible to the understanding of the discussion that these two levels be held separate, while at the same time paying attention to the close parallels which exist between both levels.

(1) We shall limit ourselves to the closer analysis of the artifical language-game (P. I. No. 8) that has already been described in detail above. Our concern is the language-game of the two builders, A and B, which consists of four "main words" ("slab", "pillar" etc.), two "demonstrative pronouns" ("there" and "this"), the letters of the alphabet as "number words" and various colour samples. Although this language-game is also still very simply constructed in comparison with our ordinary language, the difference between the individual kinds of word permits one to see how variously the words of our so much more complex everyday language must function. Wittgenstein says on one occasion: "Think of the tools in a tool box: there is a hammer, pliers, a saw, a screw-driver, a rule, a glue-pot, glue, nails and screws. — The functions of words are as diverse as the functions of these objects. (And in both cases there are similarities.)" (P. I. 11).[10] By means of the language-game mentioned, Wittgenstein now seeks to explain of what kind the signification function of words is, while bearing in mind the variety of word usage. (Cf. P. I. 10—17).

But here a difficulty immediately emerges: how does one know what the words of the language-game signify? To answer this question, let us place ourselves in the position of an observer who does not know the language-game but sees and hears A and B at their activity. He perceives how a word is called out, and how definite activities regularly follow; in other words he observes the *use* of the words in the language-game: "Now what do the words of this language *signify*?—What is supposed to shew what they signify, if not the kind of use they have?" (P. I. 10). The use of the word is

---

[10] In all the language-games discussed by Wittgenstein in this context the interplay of the partners consists essentially in ordering and obeying. In this connection Wittgenstein remarks: "Do not be troubled by the fact that the languages... (the language-games referred to) consist only of orders. If you want to say that this shews them to be incomplete, ask yourself whether our language is complete" (P. I. 18). In spite of this it is a critical point that Wittgenstein in this way moves the action-aspect too much into the foreground and thus neglects all those linguistic activities in which there is no immediate "action".

accordingly the only access to the signification function of the word concerned.

Thus, when A calls out the word "slab" B always brings him a sample of a definite kind of object. Part of the moment of word usage in this case thus consists in the fact that A and B refer to one and the same object, or rather to one and the same kind of object, by means of the word, while speaking and performing definite actions. The observer grasps this moment of reference to an object and describes it with the words: "The word 'slab' signifies a definite kind of object." The formula: "The word . . . . . . signifies . . . . ." is thus, in a way, brought to expression by the use of the word concerned, and indeed one might say that it gives a *shortened* description of the word's usage (cf. P. I. 10).

Observations, similar to those about the word "slab", can also be made in the case of the other kinds of word in the language-game. Closer analysis, however, reveals characteristic differences.

It is also true of the word "this", for example, that a partial moment of its usage consists in the fact that A and B use it to refer in a definite way to a concrete individual thing. But in contrast to the word "slab", reference is only possible in the case of "this" with a gesture of pointing. It is true that "this" signifies for the observer an individual thing, but on each occasion it only signifies that individual thing indicated by the gesture of pointing.

Something similar can also be shewn in the case of the word "there". It is true that A and B refer by means of this word and of a corresponding gesture of pointing to a something; but they now no longer refer to an individual thing but to a particular place.

The differences in the signification functions of the individual words of our language-game emerge most clearly when the usage of the signs "a", "b", "c" etc. are investigated. It is also true that in using the sign "c", for example, A and B refer in a way to "something", only this time not to a particular individual thing or place; they refer rather to a definite group of things, put together with the help of a selective procedure connected with the use of the sign "c". An observer could in other words say that "c" signifies a "number" of things or even simply a "number" determined by the application rules of the sign "c".[11]

Thus, although it is possible to say of all the kinds of words in the language-game that they signify something, their respective signification functions are actually quite different. They are dependent on the total usage of the word concerned in the language-game and are only to be grasped *via* usage. The descriptive formula: "The word ...... signifies ......" articulates a partial moment of the use. If the use is already known, it can be used as a shortened description of it, for example, in the following way: "Of course, one can reduce the description of the use of the word "slab" to the statement that this word signifies this object. This will be done when, for example, it is merely a matter of removing the mistaken idea that the word "slab" refers to the shape of building-stone that we in fact call a "block" — but the kind of "*refering*" this is, that is to say the use of these words, is already known. Equally one can say that the signs "a", "b" etc. signify numbers; when for example this removes the mistaken idea that "a", "b", "c", play the role actually played in language by "block", "slab", "pillar". And one can also say that "c" means this number and not that one; when for example this serves to explain that the letters are to be used in the order a, b, c, d, etc., and not in the order, a, b, d, c." (P. I. 10).

Analysis of the language-game thus shews that the assertion schema: "The word ...... signifies ......" can be applied to the most varied types of word, but that this schema derives its mean-

---

[11] This conception of numerical signs corresponds roughly to a class theory interpretation of numbers. Wittgenstein's interpretation of numbers can only be inferred with difficulty. At any rate, he brings number, numerical sign and numerical sign usage into such close connection that a constructivist theory may be supposed. Cf. in this connection Duthie's review, for example: "Presumably the point is, numbers are not extra things denoted by numerals, nor are they even ways we use numerals; numbers are numerals-with-a-job-to-do... These remarks together with his finitist views on analysis, suggest that he means to accept the intuitionist view of natural numbers..." (Duthie (1) p. 370.) Dummet has drawn attention to the fact that Wittgenstein's Constructivism is much more extreme than that of Intuitionism. (Cf. Dummet (1) p. 341.)

ing and sense, in the first instance, from the total context of the word concerned. Admittedly, this assertion schema does give us a unified descriptive formula for the use of the various types of word, but the differences in use are by no means done away with as a consequence. "But assimilating the descriptions of the uses of words in this way cannot make the uses themselves any more like one another. For, as we see, they are absolutely unlike." (P. I. 10). Granted the variety of individual types of word, such a homogeneous descriptive schema is necessarily very formal. Saying of all words that they signify something no longer says anything very concrete. Wittgenstein makes this situation clear with the following comparison: "Imagine someone's saying: '*All* tools serve to modify something. Thus the hammer modifies the position of the nail, the saw the shape of the board, and so on.'—And what is modified by the rule, the glue-pot, the nails?—'Our knowledge of a thing's length, the temperature of the glue, and the solidity of the box.'—Would anything be gained by this assimilation of expressions?—" (P. I. 14).

This comparison is intended to make clear that the "assimilation of expression" inherent in applying the assertion schema: "the word ...... signifies ......" to all the types of word in the language-game without limitation, brings no substantial gain. The assertion "Every word of the language signifies something" is thus to a large extent empty of content.[12] In spite of this, it can be employed

---

[12] Many Wittgenstein interpreters have construed the just quoted passage in an essentially negative manner, i. e. in the sense of a rejection of the un-limited application of the schema: "The word... signifies..." Thus, for example, Stegmüller: "One only needs to put language with its words in the place of the tool-box with the things in it, and to examine the assertion 'All the words in language signify something' or 'All the words in language have a quite definite meaning', in place of the proposition 'All tools serve to change something', to follow Wittgenstein in drawing the conclusion that it is really meaningless or, to go further, even misleading, to use such locu-tions about signification or meaning." (Stegmüller (1) p. 285.) In contrast to this, the interpretation attempted in what follows tries to do justice both to Wittgenstein's critical tendencies, (which are, without doubt, *the most im-portant*), as also to give a positive interpretation in the sense of an ontological determination.

under certain circumstances to make significant assertions. How this is possible, is shewn by Wittgenstein in the following example: "When we say: 'Every word in language signifies something' we have so far said *nothing whatever;* unless we have explained exactly *what* distinction we wish to make. (It might be, of course, that we wanted to distinguish the words of language (8) from words 'without meaning' such as occur in Lewis Carroll's poems, or words like 'Lillibullero' in songs.)". (P. I. 13).

(2) What Wittgenstein demonstrates here by the model of an artificial language-game, can easily be transferred to the relations of our everyday language. It is possible to give a homogeneous description even of the types of word in our ordinary language by means of the assertion schema: "The word . . . . . . signifies . . . . . .". The following assertions, put together entirely arbitrarily, can for example be constructed: the word "table" signifies a piece of furniture; the word "red" signifies a colour quality; the word "run" signifies an activity; the word "three" signifies a number; the word "equal" signifies the relationship of equality; the word "not" signifies negation; the word "here" signifies the place indicated by the speaker as he says the word; the words *"der"*, *"die"*, *"das"* in German signify the specific gender of a substantive etc.

This account shews sufficiently clearly that we do or can apply the proposition-schema: "The word . . . . . . signifies . . . . . ." in our ordinary language to almost all types of word.[13] Almost any

---

[13] We speak intentionally here of "almost all types of word", since there are types of word that can only with great artificiality be described with the help of the schema mentioned; among them are words like "Liliburlera"; above all, however, "performatory utterances", as they are called, the semantic status of which utterances was first set forth by Austin (cf. Austin (1)). If someone for example says "I christen you to the name. . .", "christen" does not here signify any act of the subject's; far rather is the whole proposition "I christen you. . ." itself a moment of the act of christening. It is true, we do, in addition, employ the word "christen" to signify the act of christening itself, for example in the proposition: "Mrs. X christened the ship yesterday afternoon". In the first case, the application of the proposition-schema: "The word. . . signifies. . ." to the word "christen" is out of place, in the second case, however, altogether fitting.

word one chooses can stand in the position of subject in the schema, and almost any "something" one chooses may function as accusative object. In other words, it is possible to construct both the proposition: "The word 'Socrates' signifies a philosopher" and the proposition: "The word 'not' signifies negation". Both propositions are correctly constructed and both are entirely significant in our ordinary understanding of the words.

It is evident from these considerations, that both Nominalism and Realism, from the standpoint of a specific model case, try to give a homogeneous interpretation of the use of the sentence schema: "The word ...... signifies ......", a use that is in no way limited or determined in our ordinary language. Both schools of thought believe (as we have already explained earlier) that fundamentally the sentence-schema always expresses something similar to the signification relation between proper name and pre-existent individual thing. Following this model-case, Nominalism wishes to limit the application of the proposition-schema to proper names for concrete individual things, and reduces all other cases of the ordinary application of the schema to this case. It would thus, say for example, that the proposition: "The word 'equality' signifies the relationship of equality" is really meaningless and at most is to be construed as an empty *façon de parler*.

Realism, on the other hand, wishes to apply this sentence schema to as many types of word as possible; but, in spite of this, it wishes at the same to construe it as if it represented the relationship between a proper name and a pre-existent individual thing. For this reason it thinks that e. g. in the proposition: "The word 'equality' signifies the relationship of equality" the relationship of equality is an entity existing in itself (a *res absoluta*), of which 'equality' is the proper name.

I think we may say that it is characteristic of Wittgenstein's conception that he leaves to the sentence schema mentioned the whole scope of its ordinary application. In this respect he is unfavourably disposed to reductionalistic Nominalism and holds a position similar to Realism. On the other hand, he wishes to avoid the difficulties of Realism which, while leaving to the sentence schema its scope, is only able to do so at the price of frequent hypostatisation.

In order to understand Wittgenstein's characteristically intermediate position between Nominalism and Realism, between the reduction of entities and the hypostatisation of entities, it is perhaps to the point to insert a short historical excursus.

(3) At the beginning of the Thirties there was a school of logical analysis in England known as "Directional Analysis". Using modern logic, it tried to reduce the "superfluous entities" presupposed in our everyday speech by expressions like "the state", "the average tax payer", "the English Constitution", "numbers" etc.[14] "Directional Analysis" interpreted these expressions as if a non-empirical ontology were already connected with them, as if our ordinary language and its forms of expression thus already implied a transcendental metaphysic. In order to avoid assuming transcendental entities, an attempt was made to translate all locutions in which there was talk about the English Constitution, numbers, the state etc. into equivalent assertions in which these entities were no longer mentioned.[15] In this way it was hoped that it would be possible to exclude the "superfluous entities" presupposed in our language.

Wisdom was the first to turn against this reductionalist programme.[16]

According to Wisdom, "Directional Analysis" is opposed to what could be called "Realism"; by "Realism" is to be understood

[14] Instead of "Directional Analysis" one also spoke of "new-level", "philosophical" and "reductive" analysis. Perhaps the last name best brings out the reductive character of this line of thought (Urmson (1) p. 39). For further details and literature cf. our account in the Introduction.

[15] An example of Urmson's may explain the principle of this procedure: "As a first step in new-level analysis we might transform 'The modern age is materialistic' into something like 'There are many people now living who have materialistic beliefs, and there are few or no people now living who have not materialistic beliefs.' The step would eliminate only the incomplete symbol 'the modern age'; further new analysis would be required to get rid of such an incomplete symbol as 'materialistic beliefs'." (Urmson (1) p. 40.)

any philosophy that operates with "subsistent entities"; in other words, any philosophy that construes propositions about the state or the English Constitution as irreducible propositions about definite entities. (Wisdom here ignores the distinction between a Realism that operates with subsisting entities and a Realism that hypostatises these subsistent entities to the status of independent objects. Apparently, however, Wisdom is only referring to Realism in the first sense.)

Now, in a sense, Wisdom agrees with Realism.[17] It is nothing other than "common sense answers dressed up", i. e. the forms of expression of our ordinary language dressed in the garb of a philosophical theory. If the "plain man", who is taken as the representative of common sense, is asked what the proposition "$2 + 2 = 4$" is about, he would answer: "about numbers", and it is exactly this answer that Realism tries to underpin theoretically when it opposes the attempted reduction of "Directional Analysis": "...... it is apparent that the transcendentalist theories are common-sense answers dressed up. The plain man, when asked what the proposition $2 + 2 = 4$ is about and how we know it, replies 'It is about numbers and we know it in a special way', and 'Red is a colour is about colours'. The transcendentalist replies: 'Both pro-

---

[16] For the following discussions we refer frequently to Pole's account in Pole (1) p. 103 ff. "By Realism Wisdom means a philosophy which works with non-natural qualities, subsistent universals and the like metaphysical entities taken in each case as ultimate." (Pole (1) p. 118.) Wisdom speaks in this context of "realist" and "transcendental theories". (Cf. Wisdom (8) p. 51 and 83 ff.)

[17] Cf. Wisdom (8) p. 84 and 85. Wisdom opposes Realism, it is true, insofar as he represents its theory as if it had discovered special and until then unknown entities. "...Wisdom's position is at once identical with that of the realist metaphysician and worlds removed from it. For the metaphysician believes that in discovering the hitherto undreamt of existence of this realm of transcendental entities, he has come on something striking and strange; whereas Wisdom believes that he has made no discovery more remarkable than that of Polonius, that true madness consists in being mad. For these metaphysical modes of discourse say no more than we all said... The value of Realism for Wisdom is only as a corrective to Reductionism." (Pole (1) p. 119 f.)

positions are about subsistent entities and we know them by intuition' ......"[18]

For this reason Realism is on the same side as what Wisdom calls the "Idiosyncracy Platitude". He describes it in this way: "According to the idiosyncracy platitude every sort of statement has its own sort of meaning, and when philosophers ask, What is the analysis of x-propositions? the answer is that they are ultimate, that 'everything is what it is and not another thing' (Butler, quoted by Moore on the title-page of *Principia Ethica*)."[19]

Widom follows the "Idiosyncracy Platitude" to the extent that for him too every category of linguistic discourse is irreducible; in his opinion, assertions about the state, about numbers etc. always have their own logic and meaning, and are not reducible to any other form of assertion, as "Directional Analysis" wished. Since Wisdom would also appear to hold to the correlation of the categories of linguistic discourse and the categories of being,[20] the "Idiosyncracy Platitude" asserts on the object side that every object (e. g. the state or numbers etc.) "is what it is" and is thus not reducible to any other kind of object.

(4) What Wisdom here raises by way of criticism against "Directional Analysis" is also to be found in related form in Wittgenstein, who likewise expresses himself as opposed to any reductionalist programme in the *Philosophical Investigations*. Wittgenstein thus repeatedly emphasises that the language-games of our ordinary language (these are the counterpart to Wisdom's "category of discourse") are to be accepted and only misinterpretations of these language-games are to be rejected. (Cf. P. I. 124 and 654). Our ordinary language and all its forms of expression is, as he already emphasises in the *Blue and Brown Books*, "all right" (B. B. 28). These expressions speak unambiguously against any reductionalist attempt at translating assertions about some object or other to synonymous assertions in which these objects no longer occur. (Wittgenstein in the same way opposes e. g. Phenomenalism, which

[18] Wisdom (8) p. 85.
[19] Wisdom (8) p. 51.

wishes to reduce assertions about physical objects to assertions about sense-impressions). (cf. P. I. p. 180).

The rejection of all ontological Reductionalism by Wisdom and Wittgenstein also applies, of course, to the interpretation of the sentence schema: "The word . . . . . . signifies . . . . . .". In all its respective uses this schema also has a quite definite, irreducible sense not translatable into any other type of assertion schema. E. g. the proposition: "The word 'equal' signifies equality" is not reducible to a proposition of the kind "The word 'equal' is used in this and this way."

However, Wittgenstein's language-game method, which pushes the use of a word into the foreground, at first gives the impression that all assertions about the signification function of a word could be reduced to assertions about the use of the word concerned. The proposition: "The word 'red' signifies a colour quality" could be reduced, for example, to the proposition "The word 'red' is used in this and this way"; similarly the proposition: "The word 'three' signifies a number" could be reduced to the proposition: "The word 'three' is used in the following way . . . . . ." In other words, this would lead to a position closely related to the Reductionalism of "Directional Analysis".

It is certainly true that in his analyses Wittgenstein brings signification function and word use into the closest relationship: what a word signifies can be derived exclusively from the use of the word concerned. Assertions about use for Wittgenstein thus underlie the application of the sentence schema: "The word . . . . . signifies . . . . . ." But this *binding* of a proposition about signification

---

[20] "But the point of philosophical statements is peculiar. It is the illumination of the ultimate structure of facts, i. e. the relations between different categories of being or (we must be in the mode) the relations between different sub-languages within a language." (Wisdom (8) p. 37.) In connection with this, however, the limiting judgement of Pole's: "As to Wisdom's position, I cannot but suspect that he has not sufficiently earnestly asked himself whether he believes in ontological categories to match his linguistic ones or not. Where he speaks of it [the passage just quoted is in question — Author]. He vacillates easily, even ironically, between talk of 'different sub-language within a language' and ontological talk of 'different categories of being'." (Pole (1) p. 123.)

function to propositions about word usage still does *not* amount
to a *reduction*.

The application of the sentence schema mentioned can be here
brought into close parallel with the "Idiosyncracy Platitude". This,
of course, says: "Every sort of statement has its own sort of meaning, and when philosophers ask, What is the analysis of x-propositions? the answer is that they are ultimate . . . . . ."[21] Transferred
to propositions of the kind: "The word 'three' signifies a number",
"The word 'red' signifies a colour quality" etc. these maxims say
that such propositions are irreducible and assert precisely what
they do assert and not something else. If the "plain man" is asked
what these propositions are about, he will answer that they are
about words and what these words signify.

It is exactly this answer that our interpretation of the assertion-
schema: "The word . . . . . . signifies . . . . ." tries to take account
of. When Wittgenstein describes the various types of word with
the help of this schema he is only following a tendency of ordinary
language which permits the application of this schema in the case of
almost all types of word; i.e. of almost any word one can ask:
"What does this word signify?" and it will always be possible to
answer the question by giving a definite something, whether this
something be a concrete individual thing, a colour quality, a relation or any other something.

Thus, by closely following this everyday usage, Wittgenstein
avoids, on the one hand, the reductionalist character of Nominalism; and on the other hand, by binding the interpretation of the
proposition-schema: "The word . . . . . . signifies . . . . . ." to the use
of the word concerned, he avoids the error of Realism. The analysis of word usage in the language-game clearly shows, of course,
that not all words signify things in the sense of pre-existent
individual things (*res absoluta*).

The contrast between the atomic and the Wittgensteinian conception of the signification function of words can now be described
in the following way: atomic theories of language start from a

---

[21] Wisdom (8) p. 51.

preconceived concept of the relation between a word and its object, more particularly from the relation, namely, between names and pre-existent bearers of names. Thus, Aristotle, for example, constructs the signification function on the model of words indicating substances, and attempts to make this model suitable for other words by modifying the concept of object by analogous modification of meaning. The ontological difficulties, into which the Nominalistic and Realist attempts at interpreting the Aristotelian theory of language fall, are the result of starting from too narrow a concept of the signification function or from too narrow a concept of object. This, however, leads to a definite preliminary ontological decision respecting the *significata* of words and thus hinders an undistorted view of the real semantic function of words.

In contrast to this, Wittgenstein regards the starting point of atomic theories as for too one-sided to do justice to the differences in semantic function of individual types of word. He himself, therefore, starts from the *use of a word in the language-game*; if one wants to know how and what a word signifies one must investigate how it is used in that specific language-game. In describing the usage of the word clarified in this way, Wittgenstein makes use of the sentence schema: "The word . . . . . . signifies . . . . . .", while leaving to this schema the whole breadth of its usual application. At the same time he implicitly presupposes a very wide concept of object involving no preliminary ontological decision. In this way Wittgenstein finds a starting point for his theory of language, a starting point which avoids the ontological difficulties of the atomic theories and at the same time opens up an undistorted view of the actual semantic function of individual types of word.

6. *The possibility of ontological determinations*
   in Wittgenstein's theory of language

(1) Two tendencies have so far revealed themselves in Wittgenstein's semantic observations: first, the unlimited application of the sentence schema: "The word . . . . . . signifies . . . . . ." to almost

all kinds of word and, connected with this, ontological neutrality; second, resistance to the atomic model of language, a model which gives rise to the most varied semantic and ontological misinterpretations.

These tendencies might lead one to think that Wittgenstein addressed himself exclusively to analysing word usage and wished to avoid making any ontological assertions about the *significata*. The consequence of this would be the entire surrender of the ontological approach in favour of the analysis of word usage. Certain remarks of Wisdom, for example, point in this direction; these remarks can be reduced to the formula that Wittgenstein taught philosophers to ask linguistic questions rather than ontological ones.[22]

Admittedly, the question arises whether this was Wittgenstein's intention. Could it not be that, although he was always orientated towards word usage, he nonetheless allows a determination of the object signified, i. e. that he admits the possibility of ontological assertions about the objects occuring in a language-game?

There is a school of interpretation that construes Wittgenstein in the sense first mentioned; in other words, understands him as if he wished to exclude all ontological questions or even to prove them meaningless.

This interpretation would be further supported if Wittgenstein's critique of the name-model were understood to mean that the words normally construed as names were in reality not names at all and that, therefore, such words did not name anything, so that the question about the objective correlates to these words was falsely

---

[22] "Wittgenstein taught philosphers to ask linguistic questions instead of ontological ones, and so doing, Wisdom claims, he marvellously transformed them." (Pole (1) p. 122.) Perhaps the most important passage in Wisdom in this connection is the following: "At last Wittgenstein gave tongue and the quarry went away to the notes of 'Don't ask for the meaning (analysis), ask for the use', and the transformations of the formal mode — transformations such as these: "X in saying that S is P is asserting a general proposition" means "X in saying that S is P is using the sentence 'S is P' generally"; "X in saying that S is P is asserting a proposition about mathematical entities" means "X is using the sentence 'S is P' mathematically"; ..." (Wisdom (8) p. 177f.)

posed. Pole hints at this line of interpretation (admittedly without following it) when he says: "It is very necessary to distinguish Wittgenstein's own views from others that they superficially resemble. Much linguistic philosophy retains a strongly nominalist flavour; the Wittgensteinian story half-told can have no other consequences .... And the argument will broadly be that such terms as 'mind' or 'remember' need have no ontological correlate; for if we examine their functioning we shall see that they do not operate as names. Examples might be multiplied. Words for motives, we are told, do not name mental occurrences; there are no particular events that answer to such terms as 'pride' or 'ambition' .... And all this we see, is arguable on what may seem to be Wittgensteinian lines." (Pole (1) p. 16 f.). Such an interpretation as this is especially suggested when it is connected with the Wittgensteinian thesis that the meaning of a word is not the object for which the word stands but its use (cf. P. I. 43; we shall go into the problem of meaning in detail later) and when this thesis is construed to mean that Wittgenstein wished completely to reject the object-side of linguistic symbols, at least in the case of words that do not signify individual things, and to reduce it to word usage.

Doubtless, some evidence is to be found in the texts. Thus, favouring this interpretation, Wittgenstein on one occasion speaks in the *Blue and Brown Books* in the following way: "We say 'surely the thought is *something*; it is not nothing'; and all one can answer to this is, that the word 'thought' has its *use*, which is of a totally different kind from the use of the word 'sentence'." (p. 7). It is obviously possible so to understand this passage to mean that Wittgenstein wished to reduce the ontological question about the object signified by the word 'thought' to the question about the use of the word. Similar remarks are to be found in the *Philosophical Investigations*.

It is however, possible to interpret this in another way and unambiguous evidence can also be found in its favour. This interpretation starts from the fact that although Wittgenstein always pushes the investigation of word usage into the foreground in his semantical analyses, and avoids understanding word function in terms of a preconceived concept of an "object", yet he does not wish in principle to deny the possibility of ontological assertions about the object signified.[23] The central reference favouring this interpretation is to be found in the *Philosophical Investigations* : "One ought to ask, not what images are or what happens when one imagines anything, but how the word 'imagination' is used. But that does not mean that I want to talk only about words. For the question as to the nature of the imagination is as much about the word 'imagination' as my question is. And I am only saying that this question is not to be decided—neither for the person who does the imagining, nor for anyone else—by pointing; nor yet by a description of any process. The first question also asks for a word to be explained; but it makes us expect a wrong kind of answer."(P. I. 370). Two further remarks of great importance immediately follow this passage: "*Essence* is expressed by grammar." and "Grammar tells what kind of object anything is." (P. I. 371 and 373. Wittgenstein here understands by "grammar" the rules for the use of a linguistic symbol.)

All these passages shew that Wittgenstein did not wish to do away with the correlation of word usage and essence, grammar and kind of object etc. He only wishes to save himself from the mis-interpretations that arise, if one allows oneself to be lead by a very limited concept of object when interpreting this correlation—(as arises, for example, from the atomic name-model); e. g. if one thinks that the word "imagination" signifies an object of the event-type to which one can point.[24] It is for this reason that he warns us against questions like: "What is an imagination?" or "What happens when one imagines something?" etc; for in his opinion these

[23] The possibility of both these interpretations obviously rests on the fact that certain very general structures, say, of a categorial kind, can be described within two different linguistic systems: in the language of ontology, which is directed to objective determination, and in the language of "grammar", which is directed to word usage. ("Grammar" used in Wittgenstein's sense; cf. the discussions that follow). M. Thompson has drawn attention in an illuminating paper to these two language systems and the possibilities of their application. The author speaks in this context of the "ontological idiom" and the "linguistic idiom". (Cf. Thompson (1).)

questions involve a preliminary ontological decision about the type of object in question. In order to avoid such a preliminary decision Wittgenstein recommends attending to the actual use of the word, so as to infer from the "grammar", i. e. from the rules of the word's usage, what kind of object the word concerned signifies. The ontological interpretation and determination of the object would in this way result from word usage. How the ontological determination of an object, starting from word usage, is to be conceived, will be shewn in detail later.[25]

(2) The question whether Wittgenstein wishes to reduce ontological problems to linguistic ones, or whether he does after all hold to the possibility of ontologically determining the object signified, becomes particularly acute in the case of one of the most difficult problems in the *Philosophical Investigations*, namely that of sensation words. Here also there is a series of passages that at first give the impression that Wittgenstein wished to set aside the question about the ontological status of the *significata* of sensation words. On one particular occasion he clarifies e. g. the function of the word "pain" by the following comparison: "Suppose everyone had a box with something in it: we call it a 'beetle'. No one can look into anyone else's box, and everyone says he knows what a beetle is only by looking at *his* beetle.—Here it would be quite possible for everyone to have something different in his box. One might even imagine such a thing constantly changing.—But suppose the word "beetle" had a use in these people's language?—If so it would not be used as the name of a thing. The thing in the box has no place in the

---

[24] When "correlation of word and object" is spoken of here, it is to be sharply distinguished from the Correspondence Theory of language, mentioned at the beginning of our investigation. In the Correspondence Theory a world of objects existing in itself is presupposed to which a multiplicity of linguistic symbols is subsequently subordinated. The Correspondence Theory thus presupposes a very one sided concept of object and a Realist ontology. By contrast, the "correlation of word and object" is only intended to express the fact that, with words of the most varied type, it is possible to ask about word usage and also about the kind of object signified, and that both these lines of enquiry are correlative.

[25] Cf. section VI.

language-game at all; not even as a *something*: for the box might even by empty.—No, one can 'divide through' by the thing in the box; it cancels out, whatever it is. That is to say: if we construe the grammar of the expression of sensation on the model of 'object and designation' the object drops out of consideration as irrelevant." (P. I. 293).

It is possible to construe this passage to mean that Wittgenstein regarded the assumption of a special entity, pain, as the signification of the word "pain", as superfluous; in other words, to mean that he tended towards a kind of linguistic Behaviourism which tried to reduce all propositions about sensations to propositions about the use of the sensation words concerned. According to this theory, sensation words, although they have a definite use, would not name anything. Strawson, in particular, has tried to interpret Wittgenstein's discussions along these lines.[26]

However, the analysis of sensation words in the *Philosophical Investigations* also permits another interpretation, according to which Wittgenstein by no means wished to deny that sensation words name something: he only wished to resolve the difficulties that result from an erroneous determination of the naming relation between sensation word and sensation.

More precise consideration of the relevant passages concerned in the *Philosophical Investigations* first of all reveal that Wittgenstein by no means disputes the fact that sensations can be *named*: "Don't we talk about sensations everyday and give them names?" (P. I. 244). For him the problem lay only in how in this case "the connection between the name and the thing named is set up" (P. I. 244).[27] He is opposed to conceiving this naming as if one gave a name to a "private object" (in other words, to an object accessible only to the experiencing subject and to no one else); i. e. to construing the

---

[26] "Wittgenstein seems to me to oscillate in his discussion of this subject between a stronger and a weaker thesis, of which the first is false and the second true... The stronger thesis says that no words name sensations (or 'private experiences'); and in particular the word 'pain' does not (cf. 293)." (Strawson (3) p. 83f.)

[27] For a similar interpretation cf. for example Malcolm (2) who is sharply opposed to Strawson's interpretation. Also Passmore (2) p. 433.

relation between a sensation word and a sensation as the naming of an "inner thing".[28] This is very clearly shewn when Wittgenstein formulates his analyses in the following antithetical form:" 'But you will surely admit that there is a difference between pain-behaviour accompanied by pain and pain-behaviour without any pain?'—Admit it? What greater difference could there be?—'And yet you again and again reach the conclusion that the sensation itself is a *nothing*.'—Not at all. It is not a *something*, but not a *nothing* either! The conclusion was only that a nothing would serve just as well as a something about which nothing could be said. We have only rejected the grammar which tries to force itself on us here." (P. I. 304). The paradoxical formulation that sensation is not a something but also not a nothing either may be resolved, conformably to the interpretation here offered, in this way: although the sensation is not something in the sense of a "private object", it by no means necessarily follows that it is nothing—provided that the concept of something is suitably determined.[29] Admittedly if it was

---

[28] For this reason Wittgenstein attacks the so-called "private language", by which is to be understood a language by means of which a subject refers to private objects accessible only to himself, and which is consequently intelligible to no one else.

The problem of such a private language belongs to one of the most difficult discussed by Wittgenstein in the *Investigations*. Here we must dispense with a detailed analysis, but we refer to the very extensive literature on this theme: the most important investigations are in: Strawson (3), Malcolm (2), Findlay (3), Ayer (2), Rhees (1), Garver (1), Hervey (1), Hardin (1), Linsky (2), Wellmann (1).

[29] For this interpretation of sensation as a something permiting closer determinations, cf. Hervey (1). This author thinks that, with respect to the ontological status of sensation, Wittgenstein has no "positive thesis" ("Sensations, whatever they are but Wittgenstein gives us no positive thesis on this point...", Hervey (1) p. 68); but she holds firmly to the view that the question about the ontological status of sensation is meaningful, even if, following Wittgenstein, private language is rejected: "Thus, even those who accept Wittgenstein's argument that a private language is impossible because in the absence of external 'criteria' there are no means of recognising and identifying sensations, cannot thereby argue that the notion of a 'private experience' is for this reason satisfactorily dispensed with. In any case, when it *can* be recognised and identified a sensation is still presumably a 'something' and the question still remains what this 'something' is. Whatever this 'something' is, on Wittgenstein's terms it cannot of course be private..." (Hervey (1) p. 78.)

thought that a pain were a "private thing" i. e. a something accessible only to the experiencing subject, then this something, about which nothing could be said in our inter-subjective language, would "drop out of consideration as irrelevant", i. e. would be the equivalent of a nothing. (Cf. P. I. 293). Wittgenstein is only opposed to an erroneous determination of the naming relation between a sensation word and a sensation, but he does not deny that such a relation exists.

Wittgenstein's discussion is also hostile to an ontological misinterpretation of sensation; more precisely to an ontology which interprets sensation on the pattern of an object that is supposed to be internal and private, in contrast to objects that are external and public.

It is probably in this sense that the previously quoted passage is also be understood, the passage (P. I. 293) where Wittgenstein says: "If we construe the grammar of the expression of sensation on the model of 'object and designation' the object drops out of consideration as irrelevant." When Wittgenstein speaks here of an "object", he probably means by it an object in the sense of private object.[30]

Wittgenstein's critique of Behaviourism and Dualism can also be understood in terms of this resistance to a misinterpretation of the naming relation between sensation word and sensation. Behaviourism, to put it crudely, attempts to reduce assertions in which sensation words occur to equivalent assertions about modes of behaviour, in order to dispose of sensations as "superfluous entities". Dualism attempts to interpret assertions in which sensation words occur as if they referred to "private objects", to objects in a "second world" as Wittgenstein expresses it: "At first sight it may appear . . . . . . that here we have two kinds of worlds,

[30] Cf. for example Hardin (1): "I do not think that Wittgenstein would wish to deny that there are, in some sense, 'inner processes', that we can, in certain circumstances, justifiably ascribe pains or after-images to ourselves even though nobody around us happens to have any evidence other than our reports that we are indeed in pain or sensing an after-image. What he does wish to deny is that such experiences can be used as the designata of expressions in a private language." (Hardin, p. 527.)

built of different materials; a mental world and a physical world." (B. B. 47).

Wittgenstein is opposed to both lines of thought. *Behaviourism* says: "Here there is nothing more than ...." and thus "denies the existence of something" (F. M. 63). In contrast, Wittgenstein emphasises: "Why should I deny that there is a mental process?......." (P. I. 306). *Dualism* commits the mistake of construing mental events, denied by the Behaviourist, on the pattern of external occurrences; i. e. they are construed as if they were occurrences like the external occurrences known to us all, except that they are not "external" but "internal" (in other words as if "external" and "internal" occurrences were sub-species of the *genus* "occurrence"). This rejection of Dualism is best expressed in a passage where Wittgenstein defends himself against the objection that he denies mental occurrences: "The impression that we wanted to deny something arises from our setting our faces against the picture of the 'inner process'. What we deny is that the picture of the inner process gives us the correct idea of the use of the word 'remember' ......" (P. I. 305).

Here Wittgenstein is taking up a peculiar, intermediate position between Behaviourism and Dualism, which remains unintelligible so long as one is prone to the opinion that mental words must either signify objects as if they were external objects or, on the other hand, as if they were modes of behaviour.[31] But, once it is recognised that

---

[31] Pole interprets Wittgenstein's position as if for him the difference between mental and physical were merely a "grammatical" difference, as if in other words the corresponding ontological distinction were a misunderstanding: "The rejection of behaviourism, Wittgenstein says, — the denial that pain is a form of behaviour — may have an air of obscurantism; but only because the grammatical discussion is mistaken for an ontological one." (Pole (1) p. 68.) Again: "The problem becomes acute with reference to the two great categories of mental and physical discourse. For Wittgenstein this difference is a grammatical one only." (Pole (1) p. 123, Note.) On the other hand, it is clear that there are obviously difficulties of interpretation here, since Wittgenstein emphasises at several places the correlation of grammar and kind of object: "Grammar, Wittgenstein says, tells us what kind of object anything is; and, of course, there are many kinds of object—sensations as well as physical objects, for example." (Pole (1) p. 94.)

the disjunction mentioned is not complete this difficulty disappears, provided the object concept is suitably determined.

Our interpretation of the passage quoted repeatedly starts from the fact, then, that Wittgenstein is opposed in his analyses to a too narrow or too one-sided concept of object, while holding firmly in principle to the possibility of ontological determinations of objects.

How inner states, sensations, mental occurrences etc. are to be ontologically determined, so as to avoid the difficulties into which Behaviourism and Dualism fall, is a problem whose solution is still outstanding.[32] Wittgenstein's analyses, suitably interpreted, are perhaps adapted to throw light on this problem. But that is a task for further research.

(3) Our investigations into the signification function of words in Wittgenstein's theory of language can now be formulated thus: in order to describe the signification function of words our language has the bi-articulated relation-schema: "The word . . . . . . signifies . . . ." This schema can be applied to the most varied types of word, without any preliminary semantic or ontological decisions

---

[32] In the *Blue and Brown Books* there is a passage which, perhaps, gives some information about how Wittgenstein conceives this solution: "The grammar of the word 'geometrical eye' stands in the same relation to the grammar of the word 'physical eye' as the grammar of the expression 'the visual sense datum of a tree' to the grammar of the expression 'the physical tree'. In either case it confuses everything to say 'the one is a *different* kind of object from the other'; for those who say that a sense datum is a different kind of object from a physical object misunderstand the grammar of the word 'kind', just as those who say that a number is a different kind of object from a numeral. They think they are making such a statement as 'A railway train, a railway station, and a railway car are different kinds of objects', whereas their statement is analogous to 'A railway train, a railway accident, and a railway law are different kinds of objects." (B. B. 64.)

Clearly Wittgenstein wishes to point to the danger that results from construing sense data and physical things as species of the genus 'object', in other words from using a univocal concept of object. They are rather different objects in the sense in which a railway engine, a railway accident and a railway law are objects which do correspond to a non-univocal object-concept. Cf. in this connection also P. I. 571.

having at the same time to be made. However, there is a certain tendency to interpret the schema on the model of the signification function of proper names, in other words to think that every word signifies its object more or less in the way proper names signify name bearers. Such a conception of the signification function leads to many semantic and ontological difficulties. But these difficulties can be circumvented, without having to dispense with the bi-articulate proposition schema: "The word ...... signifies ......" At the same time it is necessary to remember that this schema should not be interpreted on the pattern of the name-model; on the contrary, in applying it one should be unprejudicedly and exclusively orientated towards the use of the words in the language-game; it is from this point of view that one should clarify what the schema specifically asserts in any particular case. In this way *alone* is it possible to recognise from the use of a word how it functions semantically and what kind of object it signifies. It is thus that an ontological determination of the object signified becomes possible.

Taking this interpretation as a basis, it is in a sense right to say that "Wittgenstein taught philosophers to ask linguistic questions instead of ontological ones". But this is not to be understood to mean that he wished to set aside all ontology. It says rather *that for Wittgenstein the investigation of word usage in the language-game has primacy, in other words, that admission to ontological questions is to be won first via "linguistic analysis" i. e. via the analysis of word usage.* In this way the investigation of word usage becomes for Wittgenstein the real starting point of all philosophical reflections: "Grammar tells what kind of object anything is." (P. I. 373).

The previous analyses have been devoted exclusively to the signification relation between word and object. Admittedly it can be asked whether the signification relation suffices fittingly to characterise the semantic function of a word. The sentence schema: "The word ...... signifies ......" is not only used in everyday language to describe the semantic function of a linguistic symbol; in addition one also speaks of "mean" and "meaning" of a word. The further investigations shall now clarify what role the concept of meaning plays in the linguistic philosophy of Wittgenstein.

V. THE ONTOLOGICAL BACKGROUND TO THE PROBLEM OF MEANING

7. *The atomistic theory of meaning*

In the *Philosophical Investigations* Wittgenstein discusses various semantic theories, all more or less orientated on the atomistic model of language. In these discussions Wittgenstein attacks three interpretations of semantic phenomena, namely (a) that meaning is identical with the object signified, (b) that meaning is identical with a mental structure and, (c) that meaning is identical with an ideal entity. He developes his own conception of meaning in the course of discussing these theories.[1]

A preliminary general remark is necessary for the following investigations. In his analyses Wittgenstein wishes to clarify "what meaning is"; to this end he starts out from a concept of meaning such as is used in our ordinary language in locutions like: "having the same meaning", "changing its meaning", "having several meanings" etc.

His investigations are directed against a series of theories that purport to give an explication and interpretation of this ordinary concept of meaning. His criticism is, therefore, not directed against theories that operate with a specially introduced concept of mean-

---

[1] The literature on the problem of meaning has become almost too large to review. We can only mention some of the important writings. The modern discussion of the problem really begins with Mill's *Logic*, Frege's *Über Sinn und Bedeutung* and Husserl's *Logische Untersuchungen* and Meinong's reflections on the theory of objects. One of the best introductions to the whole problem is in Ryle (7). For the linguistic standpoint Ullman (2).

ing that differs *per definitionem* from the ordinary concept (in other words not against e. g. Frege's theory of meaning where "meaning" and "sense" differ and where "meaning" is defined in terms of "object signified", and where no explication of our ordinary language concept of meaning is intended).

Thus, Wittgenstein always presupposes that the theories which he critically discusses use the word "meaning" in our ordinary language sense, in their assertions about meaning. On this presupposition is based his critique which amounts to the view that, although the theories concerned start from our ordinary concept of meaning, they do not suitably explain it.

(1) Wittgenstein first of all discusses an interpretation of meaning which he had himself maintained in the *Tractatus*, namely the assertion that the meaning of a word is identical with the object for which it stands.[2] Wittgenstein refers to this interpretation at the beginning of the *Investigations*, where he says with reference to the Augustine quotation: "In this picture of language we find the roots of the following idea: every word has a meaning. This meaning is correlated with the word. It is the object for which the word stands." (P. I. 2).

He discusses this conception of meaning with the example of proper names, the reason being that the semantic theory of the *Tractatus* is fundamentally orientated on the function of proper names. (Cf. P. I. 37—45). Proper names stand for specific, individual objects. The assertion is so modified that, in the case of names, meaning is identical with the name bearer. (Cf. T. 3.202, 3.203).

However, certain difficulties arise from this simple identification of meaning and name bearer. What happens e. g. if for some reason

---

[2] The most extreme objectification of meaning is to be found in the object theory of Meinong. Meinong writes: "Summing up, then, one can also say: a word means something insofar as it expresses a presenting experience, and the object so presented is the meaning". (Meinong (1) p. 28). Meinong's theory definitively influenced Russell's extremely realist theory of meaning in the *Principles of Mathematics*. (Russell (6).)

the name bearer disappears?[3] Let us, for example, assume with Wittgenstein that someone with the name N. N. dies. The name N. N. would then no longer stand for a really existent person; in other words, would no longer, according to the theory, have any meaning at all and would consequently become a senseless phonetic structure. Nor would it be possible to use this senseless sound to construct a meaningful proposition. The proposition "N. N. is dead" would be senseless and we should no longer express even the fact that N. N. was dead.[4] This consequence of the theory is naturally untenable. If the thesis of the atomic model is construed so that the meaning of a name is identical with the bearer of the name, it leads to difficulties which demand a modification of the thesis.

Logical Atomism attempted such a modification of the simple thesis.[5] Wittgenstein discusses its theory of names in detail in the *Philosophical Investigations*. In doing so he sets himself against his own views in the *Tractatus*, views which, of course, essentially helped to form the theory of Logical Atomism.

The semantic problems that emerged from Mill's distinction between connotation and denotation constitute the starting point of Logical Atomism's theory of names.[6] As is well known, Mill understands by the denotation of an expression the object for which the expression stands, and by the connotation the properties of the

---

[3] An ancient problem of philosophy, already to be found in Plato, shows itself here: namely the problem of how the words in a false assertion are related to reality. In a true assertion, each word, according to Plato, stands for a real something; but for what entities do the words of the corresponding false assertion stand? Cf. in this connection: Plato: *Sophistes* 261 b5—264 d1.

[4] It is tacitly assumed in the argument that the name "Socrates" no longer has any name-bearer once Socrates is dead, in other words once he no longer really exists. The relation between name and name-bearer is thus thought of as a relationship between a word and a really existing object, so that the existence of this relation is dependent on the real existence of the name-bearer. In this respect the name relationship in the argument mentioned differs quite essentially from the signification relationship employed in the previous section. The latter is not bound, namely, to the real existence of the object signified, so that we can indeed still say: the word "Socrates" signifies Socrates, even if Socrates is already dead.

[5] A detailed account of the theory of names in Logical Atomism is to be found in Urmson (1) p. 82 ff.

object connoted by the expression. Thus, the denotation of the expression "The present Prime Minister of England" is e. g. a particular person. The connotation of this expression consists in the property of this person's being the present Prime Minister of England. Now, Mill asserts that proper names have denotation only, no connotation. It is true, difficulties, similar to those discussed above, result from this assertion. If our ordinary proper names were real proper names they would necessarily become meaningless if the corresponding denotations were to disappear. But this is not the case, since the proposition "Socrates is dead" still has a sense, even though the corresponding name-bearer no longer exists. It was concluded from this that the word "Socrates" could not be a real proper name at all, but only a "pseudo-name". Admittedly, the question now arises how it is possible for such pseudo-names to have meaning. In order to explain this, propositions with proper names were submitted to a special logical analysis. This analysis was intended to reveal the concealed semantics both of the proposition concerned and of its constituent parts. E.g. if the proposition "Socrates is dead" is submitted to such an analysis the pseudo-name disappears. On the first analysis the proposition runs something like: "The philosopher who drank the cup of hemlock is dead." Here the pseudo-name "Socrates" has disappeared, but other names have emerged instead e. g. "philosopher" or "cup of hemlock" etc. They can be removed by further analysis. If the analysis is carried far enough these names also disappear, so that one arrives eventually at a form of proposition which is not further analysable, since

---

6 Cf. Mill (1) pp. 35—46. Mill's distinction between denotation and connotation corresponds in many respects to Frege's distinction between "sense" and "meaning". Frege understands by the "meaning" of a symbol what is signified by the symbol, and by "sense" that "in which is contained the kind of being given (signified)". (Frege (1) p. 26.) [The words in brackets are the author's addition]. Mill and Frege differ in respect of their interpretation of the proper name. In Mill, proper names have a denotation only, no connotation, whereas in Frege they have both meaning and sense. We here choose Mill as a starting point because Russell, from whom the whole theory of Logical Atomism ultimately takes its origin, rejects Frege's interpretation of proper names. (Cf. Russell (1).)

each word occurring in it names an actually existent object and is entirely resolvable into this naming function, or, in Mill's language, is now only a denotation. The symbolic entities that are revealed by the analysis are the "real names" out of which the proposition is constituted. Since the proposition "Socrates is dead" is meaningful even after the death of Socrates, the "real names" out of which the proposition is constituted must have definite, really existent name-bearers, even after the death of Socrates. These name-bearers are identical neither with Socrates nor with any of Socrates' properties, which would disappear on his death; the name-bearers must rather be the ultimate unanalysable parts, "logical atoms", from which the configuration Socrates is constituted.[7]

Here we can clearly see how Logical Atomism tries under all circumstances to maintain the thesis that the meaning of a name is identical with the object named, the name-bearer. It admits, it is true, that the meaning of the *pseudo*-name (like "Socrates", for example) is not identical with the name-bearer (with the real Socrates). Logical Atomism wishes to clarify precisely how it is possible for pseudo-names still to have a meaning when the corresponding name-bearers no longer really exist. But in the case of real names, meaning and name-bearer are once more identified, for the meaning of real names consists, according to Logical Atomism, in the logical atoms, name-bearers of simple names.[8] At the same time it is important that Logical Atomism, although introducing the new concepts "real name" and "logical atom", still employs

[7] For a very similar argument cf. for example Russell (2) p. 8 ff. Russell's "Theory of Descriptions" essentially helped to determine Logical Atomism's theory of names.
[8] Russell (2) p. 15: "What pass for names in language, like 'Socrates', 'Plato' and so forth, were originally intended to fulfill this function of standing for particulars, and we do accept, in ordinary daily life, as particulars all sorts of things that really are not so. The names that we commonly use, like 'Socrates', are really abbreviations for descriptions; not only that, but what they describe are not particulars but complicated systems of classes or series. A name, in the logical sense of the word whose meaning is a particular, can only be applied to a particular with which the speaker is acquainted, because you cannot name anything you are not acquainted with."

the concepts "meaning" and "name bearer" unchanged, in their ordinary sense. (Wittgenstein's critique starts at this point, as we shall show later). The basic idea of the thesis thus remains even in the relationship of "real name" to "logical atom": the meaning of a name is identical with the name-bearer.

Wittgenstein presents the reasoning of Logical Atomism by means of the following example: ". . . . . . For one is tempted to make an objection against what is ordinarily called a name. It can be put like this: *a name ought really to signify a simple.* And for this one might perhaps give the following reasons: The word "Excalibur", say, is a proper name in the ordinary sense. The sword Excalibur consists of parts combined in a particular way. If they are combined differently Excalibur does not exist. But it is clear that the sentence "Excalibur has a sharp blade" makes sense whether Excalibur is still whole or broken up. But if "Excalibur" is the name of an object, this object no longer exists when Excalibur is broken in pieces; and as no object would then correspond to the name it would have no meaning. But then the sentence "Excalibur has a sharp blade" would contain a word that had no meaning, and hence the sentence would be nonsense. But it does make sense; so there must always be something corresponding to the words of which it consists. So the word "Excalibur" must disappear when the sense is analysed and its place taken by words which name simples. It will be reasonable to call these words the real names." (P. I. 39).

The representatives of Logical Atomism held entirely different views about what was to be understood by real names and logical atoms. In the *Tractatus*, for example, the "simple signs" of the completely analysed proposition correspond to real names, the "objects" in the "state of affairs" to the logical atoms. The objects are thus the meaning of the names: "The simple signs employed in propositions are called names. A name means an object. The object is its meaning." (T. 3.202, 3.203). Nowhere in the *Tractatus* does Wittgenstein give an example of an object or of a name, so that it is a matter of interpretation what is to be understood by these terms. The function of names can perhaps be best explained by means of certain demonstrative pronouns like, for example, "this" or "that" etc. which stand immediately for an object and become meaning-less if the object disappears. The proposition, for example, "This is red" only has sense as long as the word "this" refers to a definite actually present object; if it no longer does this, the proposition becomes meaningless.[9]

(2) As a counter-move against Logical Atomism's theory of names and consequently by way of criticism of his own views in the *Tractatus*, Wittgenstein draws up a theory of names and meaning that starts from entirely different presuppositions. To this end he first of all engages in some linguistic analytical investigations into the ordinary linguistic usage of the word "meaning", and then explains the outlines of his theory by a series of language-games.

When Wittgenstein investigates the ordinary usage of the word "meaning" he excludes right from the beginning certain ways of using the word as irrelevant to the discussion.[10]

On occasion we speak of "meaning" in non-linguistic contexts, e.g. when we talk about the "meaning of Schiller". This sense of meaning has no rôle to play in the purely linguistically orientated analyses of Wittgenstein. On the other hand, we use the word in connection with linguistic signs. Wittgenstein begins by excluding some of these modes of use as well, all those namely in which there is talk of experiencing meaning, e.g. locutions like: "Hearing or

[9] In this way Russell for example interpreted proper names in the strict sense: "The only words one does use as names in the logical sense are words like 'this' or 'that'. One can use 'this' as a name to stand for a particular with which one is acquainted at the moment... It is an *ambiguous* proper name, but it is really a proper name all the same, and it is almost the only thing I can think of that is used properly and logically in the sense I was talking of for a proper name." (Russell (2) p. 15.)

[10] The limits between the "ordinary use" of the word meaning and the technical use layed down by the new definition cannot always be sharply drawn. For the historical development of the word "meaning" cf. Weisgerber (3) p. 32. The English word "meaning", like the German word "*Bedeutung*", has experienced an abundance of new definitions and semantic modifications. L. Abraham has drawn up the different meanings of the word in a paper. He enumerates 51 different ways of using the word. (Abraham (1). Similarly Gomperz (1).)

experiencing a word in this sense".[11] Having excluded these ways of using the word "meaning", there still remains a large group of contexts in which we use the word, e.g. expressions and locutions like: "having the same meaning", "changing its meaning" etc. Wittgenstein's analyses, to which we here refer, are limited to this group.

Wittgenstein begins by attacking the conception that underlies the whole theory of Logical Atomism, that the meaning of a name must be identical with the bearer of the name. (P. I. 40). We mentioned earlier that, in constructing its theory, Logical Atomism always employed the word "meaning" in its ordinary sense, even when talking about the meaning of simple names. Wittgenstein starts at this point. If the meaning of a simple name were identical with the name-bearer, then the words "meaning" and "name-bearer" would have to be used synonymously. But that is not the case, as the following consideration shows: in the previously mentioned example, if the man with the name N. N. dies, it is possible to say: "The man who bore the name N. N. has died", but one could not say: "The meaning of the name has died". The words "meaning" and "name-bearer" are, therefore, not interchangeable and consequently not synonymous either: "It is important to note that the word "meaning" is being used illicitly if it is used to signify the thing that "corresponds" to the word. That is to confound the meaning of a name with the *bearer* of the name. When Mr. N. N. dies one says that the bearer of the name dies, not that the meaning dies. And it would be nonsensical to say so, for if the name ceased to have meaning it would make no sense to say "Mr. N. N. is dead". (P. I. 40).[12]

[11] Wittgenstein has devoted several special investigations to this meaning of the word "meaning". Cf. P. I. 534 ff., p. 175 ff., p. 181 ff., p. 214 ff. Strawson summarises the result of the Wittgensteinian analysis of the meaning of the word "meaning" in the following way: "In general, the word 'meaning' may be said to acquire a secondary use in connection with all these experiences [experiences of meaning—the author] which are of such significance in relation to the way we *feel* about our language. But this use *is* secondary. Words could still have their meanings, language be used as a means of communication, in the absence of these phenomena." (Strawson (3) p. 82 f. Similarly Findlay (3) p. 179.)

In his review of the *Philosophical Investigations* Strawson drew attention to the fact that Wittgenstein's analysis fails to take account of a definite linguistic fact: "Wittgenstein here gives the wrong reason for objecting to the identification of the or a meaning of a proper name with its bearer, or one of its bearers. If we speak at all of the meaning of proper names, it is only in quite *specialised* ways, as when we say that 'Peter' means a stone, or 'Giovanni' means 'John'. This is not an accident of usage, but reflects a radical difference between proper names and other names. But here, as elsewhere, Wittgenstein neglects the use of 'meaning'."[13] Strawson here emphasises a peculiarity of proper names, which is certainly not to be overlooked.[14] In a certain sense a proper name does actually have "no meaning"; this is the case insofar as its "referring use", i.e. its reference to an object, is not regulated by a general convention,[15] but has to be laid down *ad hoc* for each particular occasion. Any animal, person or ship can be called "Mary"

[12] Xenakis produces similar arguments against identifying name-bearer and meaning: "Some hold that when x is a name the meaning of x is x's bearer. This entails that to say that the meaning of 'Eisenhower' is Eisenhower is to imply that whenever one talks to, plays with, looks at, touches, smells, tastes, hears, pushes, pulls, kisses... Eisenhower, one talks to, plays with, looks at, touches, smells, tastes, hears, pushes, pulls, kisses... a meaning; that as soon as Eisenhower dies, 'Eisenhower' will die too or will become meaningless or at any rate neither meaningless nor meaningful — nor thereby useful? But obviously it is not even grammatical to say any of those things. 'Meaning' or 'a meaning' do not go together in the same sentence with 'pushing', 'pulling', 'kissing', 'dying', and such physical words." (Xenakis (2) p. 55.)

[13] Strawson (3) p. 74. Cf. also Strawson (1).

[14] Xenakis has worked out this peculiarity of proper names still more sharply: "... we ask for the meaning of a name, just in case we have misidentified. As soon as we realise or learn that it is a name, we inquire about its *bearer*. We are no longer tempted to ask, What is the *meaning* of 'Rome'?, but *What (Who)* is Rome?; ... or again, knowing that 'Napoleon' is a name, it sounds appropriate to ask, Whom (What) does 'Napoleon' name?, but queer: What is the *meaning* of 'Napoleon'?, Does 'Napoleon' have any meaning?, what does 'Napoleon' mean? unless of course 'mean' here replaces '(is used to) refer to', and then obviously it means just 'name'... Perhaps the import of all this is merely grammatical, that 'meaning', 'has meaning' etc., do not go together with 'Socrates', 'Plato', 'Abraham', 'Roberto' etc." (Xenakis (2) p. 59f.)

[15] Cf. Strawson (1) p. 45.

without our language having a generally binding convention that regulates this usage in detail. For this reason proper names are not included in dictionaries. However, this fact does not preclude the possibility of proper names having a meaning in another sense. If e.g. a proper name is used in a concrete context to name a definite object, although there are no application rules wich are valid for the total linguistic community and which refer the word unambiguously to this object, yet in spite of this, definite rules, known perhaps only to one person or to a small group of persons, do underlie the application of the word. In cases like this there is no reason for not speaking of the meaning of the proper name concerned. If the word "meaning" were never ever to be used again in connection with proper names, one would be forced to construe proper names either as signs without meaning, i.e. as meaningless series of sounds or ink marks; or one would have to give up the parallelism between "x has meaning—x is a meaningful sign" and "x has no meaning— x is a meaningless sign" i.e. one would have to characterise proper names as "meaningful signs without meaning". Strawson for example does the latter when he says: "......we do not speak of the meaning of proper names. But it won't do to say they are meaningless".[16] Wittgenstein, in contrast, probably wishes to maintain the above mentioned parallelism and accordingly speaks of "meaning" in the case of proper names as well. (Cf. P. I. 40, 43, 55, 79).

The obscurities revealing themselves here obviously rest on the fact that in our ordinary language the use of the words "meaning" and "meaningful" etc. in connection with proper names is not precisely laid down; it is thus to a certain extent an arbitrary matter, whether meaning is to be attributed to proper names or not. Strawson's criticism shows that Wittgenstein had not done suffi-

---

[16] Cf. Strawson (1) p. 45. Xenakis also suggests not using the expression "meaning" in connection with proper names, but instead speaking of the "function" of proper names: "To make a long story short, Don't ask for the meaning of names: ask for their function (but then hammers too have function)." He does not hold the disjunction "meaningful-meaningless" for entirely suitable in the case of proper names: "... so 'Socrates' is meaningless. But is it? Does it make sense to say that it is or that it isn't?" (Cf. Xenakis (2) p. 54 and 60.)

cient justice to this fact. However, the final result of Wittgenstein's investigation may not be affected by this detail, since Logical Atomism in any case speaks of the "meaning of a proper name" and here "meaning" and "name-bearer" are not identical.

(3) Having shown in this way that the thesis of Logical Atomism, that the meaning of a name is the name-bearer, could not be correct, Wittgenstein immediately follows with a further reflection devoted to the problem of how a name can still have meaning, even though the name bearer does not really exist (P. I. 41—44). In this context he develops his own conception of the nature of meaning.

Once more he uses in this passage the language-game method to represent more clearly the relations in our ordinary language. To this end he returns to the language-game in which a builder A and his assistant B communicate with each other. Names also are now introduced into this language-game. Definite figures, say "H" or "N", are printed on the tools which A uses in building. If A shows such a figure to B, by writing it in the sand, for example, B then brings him that tool upon which the figure stands. With respect to their function in the language-game these figures have a strong similarity to our ordinary proper names: A and B use them, on any given occasion, in order to communicate about *one* definite tool. Thus, these signs, like our proper names, refer on a given occasion to precisely one single object; this object is the "bearer" of the sign, the name-bearer, so to say. Let us now assume that one of the tools with the inscription "N" is broken. But B does not yet know about it. A draws the figure "N" in the sand and expects B to bring him the corresponding tool. B does not know, however, what he should now do: the tool with the figure "N" is broken and no agreement has been made for such a contingency. B is then helpless and perhaps he shows A the bits of the tool etc. One could now say that the sign "N" no longer has any meaning in this language-game, because there is no longer an object upon which it stands. No provision has been made in the rules of the language-game for this situation; the game with the figure "N" is idling. But one can easily help oneself by making a new agreement: whenever the tool with the inscription "N" is broken and A gives the sign "N", B shakes his head. Now "N" still has a definite function in the language-game, even when there is no longer any object upon which "N" stands. One could accordingly say that the sign "N" still has a definite "meaning", even though its "bearer" has ceased to exist. (Cf. P. I. 41).

If one asked about the meaning of the sign "N" in this language-game one could explain it in the following way: when A gives the sign "N" he wishes to get B to bring him a definite tool with the inscription "N"; and if the corresponding tool is broken B is to shake his head. The meaning of the sign, clarified in this way, is thus completely independent of whether the tool concerned really exists or not.

This language-game clearly shows in what the meaning of the signs "H" or "N" really consists, according to Wittgenstein. When these signs were introduced into the language-game their use was at first bound to the actual existence of definite objects with the inscription "H" or "N". Thus they only had meaning insofar as they were used with respect to the real existence of the corresponding name bearers. But we then made the usage of the signs independent of the real existence of the name bearers by so modifying the application rules of the signs that they could still be significantly employed, even in the absence of the name-bearers. On the basis of these new application rules for "H" or "N", A and B could still communicate with these signs, even when the tools concerned were broken. "In this way the command 'N' might be said to be given a place in the language-game, even when the tool no longer exists, and the sign 'N' to have meaning, even when its bearer ceases to exist." (P. I. 41).

The meaning of signs is thus obviously most intimately connected with their application rules, with the nature and mode of their usage. Putting it simply, one could say that the meaning of a sign is determined or defined by the rules of its application.

What we have so far studied by means of the language-game model can now, however, because of the strong similarity of the signs "H" or "N" to our ordinary proper names, be easily transferred to the latter. We use, for example, the name "Socrates" even after the death of the name-bearer; i. e. application rules obviously exist in our ordinary language regulating the use of the word "Socrates", even in the contingency of the name-bearer's no longer really existing. Thus, the word has a definite meaning independently of the real existence of the name bearer, and the meaning is attributed to it on the basis of definite modes of application. It can be said here, too, that the meaning of the word "Socrates" is determined by the rules of its use. The connection revealed here between the meaning of a name and its use is reduced by Wittgenstein to the slogan-like formula: "For a *large* class of cases—though not for all—in which we employ the word "meaning" it can be defined thus: the meaning of a word is its use in the language." (P. I. 43).[17]

That part of Wittgenstein's theory of meaning that has so far been portrayed can now be summed up thus: the meaning of a name, insofar as "meaning" is understood in the ordinary sense of the word, is not identical with the name-bearer. It is rather determined by the name's rules of usage. But since it is possible to hold these rules in such a way that the name can still be used even when the object concerned no longer really exists, it thus becomes possible to explain the possibility of a name's having meaning without its name-bearer really existing. The theory of names of Logical Atomism is by contrast encumbered with a series of additional assumptions (e. g. that of logical atoms) which considerably reduces its clarificatory value.

(4) So far we have discussed Wittgenstein's theory of meaning exclusively with reference to proper names, and in doing so we followed Wittgenstein's procedure in the *Philosophical Investi-*

---

[17] We here follow Pole's interpretation: "I take it that the other cases spoken of are those in which we use the term 'meaning' to refer to those distinctive experiences or pictures which, as Wittgenstein says, words often bring with them — that is to intentional meaning..." (Pole (1) p. 18 Note). For another possible interpretation cf. Xenakis (1): "I presume that this is Wittgenstein's way of saying that the meaning of a word is its *established* use not that it is *any* use of it nor therefore just its *use*." (p. 310.)

gations. But the question now arises whether the results gained in the case of proper names can be transferred to other kinds of word as well. Is it possible to distinguish between the object signified and meaning in the case of other kinds of word, and to translate meaning exclusively into rules of usage?

Two fundamentally different lines of interpretation are possible here:

(a) The separation of meaning and signified object is only meaningful in the case of proper names. Other kinds of word only have a meaning, and this meaning is determined by the usage of the word. But there is no additional signified object as well. This interpretation, if it is carried out logically, leads to extreme nominalism: only proper names would signify objects; although other kinds of word would have meaning they would not signify anything. In other words, there "would be" only individual things.[18]

(b) The separation of meaning and signified object can also be carried out in the case of other words. A distinction can also be made between the meaning of the word and the object signified in the case of e. g. colour words. The meaning consists in the special way the colour word is used, the object signified in the corresponding colour quality. This interpretation would also admit other kinds of object in addition to the individual objects.

These two possibilities of interpretation have not been sufficiently expressed in the Wittgenstein literature to date. We are here in favour of the second interpretation. We thus remain in agreement with the analyses in the section on the signification-function of words. We there explained that, with a very wide object-concept as basis, it was possible to say of almost any expression that it signified an object. But there are also other reasons which suggest this interpretation. The separation of meaning and signified object, carried out by Wittgenstein in the case of proper names, can also

[18] Sometimes it seems as if Ryle in particular followed this interpretation of Wittgenstein. Cf. for example Ryle (4) and (7). Ryle's discussions on this point however are not so unambiguous that it is possible to quote it as an example of a logically carried out nominalistic interpretation of Wittgenstein.

be proved in the case of the other kinds of word using exactly the same arguments as were employed by him in the case of proper names. Wittgenstein's argument runs thus: "When Mr. N. N. dies one says that the bearer of the name dies, not that the meaning dies." (P. I. 40). An entirely similar argument can be used in the case of the other kinds of word. E. g. the word "saurian" stands for a species of animal; but this species of animal is not identical with the meaning of the word "saurian". Admittedly one can say: "The species of animal named by the word 'saurian' is extinct". In the same way it is possible to differentiate between the meaning of the word "red" and the colour quality named by the word. One says "Colour blind people cannot see the colour quality signified by the word 'red'". But one does not say: "Colour blind people cannot see the meaning of the word 'red'." These arguments can be generalised: assertions about the object signified by a word obviously follow a quite different logic to assertions about the meaning of the word concerned; the former are empirical or *a priori* assertions about an *object*, the latter are linguistic assertions about a *word* and its use.[19]

The advantage of our interpretation lies first of all in the fact that it does not imply any kind of preliminary ontological decision; thus, in contrast e. g. to the first mentioned interpretation it does not involve any nominalistic limitations of the signification-function or of the sphere of the object. But in the second place our interpretation also avoids all form of hypostatising Realism, since meaning is only determined by the mode of use, while the object signified is not to be understood in the sense of a *res absoluta*.

---

[19] Cf. Strawson (2) p. 189 for a separation of meaning and object signified based on Wittgenstein's theory of meaning: "Sentences and phrases and words have meanings, in virtue of which they may be used to make statements and to refer to things. But the meanings of sentences are not statements they are used to make, and the meanings of words and phrases are not the things they are used to refer to." Strawson is speaking here of referring words in general, not only of proper names. Many other authors make a similar distinction, among others Husserl. (Cf. Husserl (1) Vol. 2, part 1, p. 46 and 54; and our account of Husserl's theory of meaning.)

A further advantage of our interpretation is that it justifies and makes intelligible two different lines of semantic approach. Because of the separation of "meaning" and "object signified" two different but very closely connected questions can be asked in the case of any given word: (a) what meaning does the word have? and (b) what object does the word signify?[20]

Since the meaning of a word is for Wittgenstein determined by the rules of its use the first question can be answered by a description of the way the word is used. i. e. by a linguistic analysis of word usage. Present-day English philosophy, in particular, has turned to this kind of semantic investigation.[21]

The second question is, as we said, most intimately connected with the first, but it aims at quite a different kind of answer; what one wants to know is not only how a word is used, but also what object and what types of object it signifies. Semantics, which applies itself to this task, is not so much linguistically as ontologically orientated. Approaches toward this kind of semantic observation are to be found above all in the writings of Russell, Quine, Carnap, and Goodman, among others. It is no accident that the ontological problems of traditional linguistic philosophy have once more been primarily taken up along these lines.[22]

[20] This distinction corresponds to Quine's distinction between "theory of meaning" and "theory of reference" in Quine (3) p. 130: "The main concepts in the theory of meaning, apart from meaning itself, are *synonymy* (or sameness of meaning), *significance* (or possession of meaning), and *analycity* (or truth by virtue of meaning). Another is *entailment*, or analycity of the conditional. The main concepts in the theory of reference are *naming*, *truth*, *denotation* (or truth of), and *extension*. Another is the notion of *value of variables*."

[21] Primarily the school of thought known under the name "Oxford Philosophy". For a detailed account cf. Weitz (2) and Charlesworth (1); there also further literature. Charlesworth writes: "The main point on which the Oxford philosophers agree is the definition of meaning in terms of linguistic use. The theory of meaning... comes from Wittgenstein, but it has been developed and exploited particularly by the Oxford philosophers so that it has become almost their own distinctive doctrine." (p. 170.)

[22] In this connection cf. for example Russell (1), Quine (1), (2), Carnap (4), (5), (6) and Goodman (1), (2). The fact that in this semantic school the study of formal systems stands in the foreground, whereas in „Oxford Philosophy" the analysis of everyday language predominates, is not of primary importance.

Wittgenstein's position with respect to these two schools of thought should have become clear from our earlier discussions on the signification function and the problem of meaning. On the one hand, Wittgenstein, by his famous maxim "Don't ask for the meaning, ask for the use" revealed the great importance of describing word usage. To that extent Wittgenstein put the centre of gravity of his investigation entirely on the first kind of semantics. On the other hand, it has become clear to us that he by no means neglected the objective side of word usage; on the contrary, grammar, i. e. the use of the word, tells us what kind of object something is. To this extent Wittgenstein admitted the possibility of ontologically and objectively orientated semantics.[23]

8. *Comparison of Wittgenstein's theory of meaning with the Platonistic and psychologistic theories of meaning*

Our first investigation tried to show how Wittgenstein discussed the thesis that the meaning of a word consisted in the object signified. The result of our analysis was that Wittgenstein began by separating "meaning" and "object signified" and transferred meaning entirely to the usage of the word. With the latter conception he moves into opposition to certain other theories of meaning, which, although also distinguishing meaning from object signified, nevertheless regard it as a special object, additional to word usage and signified object.[24]

Various answers have been given to the question what sort of object meaning is. But certain typical, recurring efforts at interpretation can be distinguished. The one school of thought inter-

---

[23] It would go beyond the framework of this study to compare the conceptual pair "signified object" — "meaning", which we have employed in our interpretation of Wittgenstein, with similar conceptual pairs in semantics, say with Frege's distinction of "meaning" and "sense", or Carnap's distinction of "extension" and "intention". Nor can we here go into the difficult problem of whether the Wittgensteinian conceptual pair, derived from ordinary language, is suited to the semantic analysis of formalised languages. Cf. in this connection Frege (1) and Carnap (5).

prets meaning as an ideal entity; the other school of thought interprets it as a mental structure. We shall call them, for short, the
Platonistic and the psychologistic theories of meaning.

(1)   Traces of the *Platonistic theory of meaning* can already be
detected in Plato; but, its purest formulation is found in Husserl.
In his investigations Husserl makes use of an argumentation that
can already be met with in a similar form in antiquity: "If I assert
(truly, and we shall always make this assumption) that the three
altitudes of a triangle intersect at a single point, the fact that I so
judge is naturally fundamental to it .... But is my judging,
which I have here *announced*, also the meaning of the assertion; is it
what the assertion *says* and, in this sense, expresses? Obviously
not. The question about the sense and meaning of the assertion
will scarcely be so understood under normal circumstances by
anybody in the sense that it would occur to him to recur to the
judgement as a mental event. On the contrary, everyone would
answer the question what this assertion says by saying that it is *the
same* irrespective of who it is that affirmatively asserts it, and irrespective of the circumstances and the time of the assertion; and
that which is the same is precisely this: that the three altitudes of a
triangle intersect at a single point, nothing more and nothing less.
'The same assertion' is thus in essence repeated; it is repeated
precisely because it is the only, peculiarly suited form of expression
for what is identical, which is called its meaning ..... The acts of

---

24 In the distinction of meaning and object the "concept" is, incidentally,
lacking. The following is to be noticed in this connection: the word "concept"
is, as Wittgenstein remarks, "altogether too vague" (F. M. 188). In spite of
this he on occasion uses this word, namely, in the sense of: "a word's mode of
use", for example in the following passage: "We are not analysing a phenomenon (e.g. a thought) but a concept (e.g. that of thinking), and therefore the
use of a word." (P. I. 383). For this reason Wittgenstein would not attack talk
about "universals". For him there are universals insofar as, in addition to
words for individual things, there are also words for properties, relations etc.,
and these latter words have a general application. Cf. in this connection the
qualification in Lieb (1) p. 130, Note: "I think Wittgenstein would not say
that a concept is the use of a certain type of word in the language. Instead,
I think he would say that a word is a concept if it is used in a certain way."

judgement are from case to case different. But, *what* they judge,
what the assertion says, is everywhere the same. It is, in the strict
understanding of the word, identical, it is one and the same geometrical truth!"[25] Husserl explains his ideas with the example of
an assertoric proposition. He could have done so with the example
of an individual word; individual words also have a definite meaning, and the meaning is always one and the same, entirely independent of concrete word usage. (Of course there are also words with
more than one meaning; we are not speaking of these here. We shall
go into this later.)

Now, in Husserl's case, a sharp distinction must be made between the meaning of an expression and the object to which the
expression refers. "Every expression not only says something, it
also says something *about* something; it not only has its meaning,
it also refers to some object or other." Similarly: "Indeed, one
frequently hears meanings so spoken of to mean the *objects* signified, a linguistic usage that is difficult to maintain with consistency,
for it is derived from confusion with the real concept of meaning."[26] In penetrating investigations Husserl proves that meaning
is not for example a thought, or representations in the soul,
and is not, therefore, to be confused with mental processes or things
of any kind. Meaning thus has an existence that is relatively independent both of linguistic signs and also of human thought; it is
an ideal object, even if it is not an independent substance in a realm
of ideas beyond.[27] The extent to which Husserl takes the objectification of meaning is shown by an illuminating quotation. "Just
as numbers ...... do not come into and pass out of existence with
the act counting; consequently just as the infinite series of numbers
represents an objectively firm essence of general objects, an
essence that is sharply limited by an ideal legality, an essence
that no one can either increase or diminish; so also it is with the
ideal, purely logical entities, concepts, propositions, truths, in

---

[25] Husserl (1) Vol. 2, Part 1, p. 43 ff.
[26] Husserl (1) Vol. 2, Part 1, p. 46 and p. 54.
[27] Husserl repeatedly defends himself against the objection of "Platonic
hypostatisation". Cf. Husserl (1) Vol. 2, Part 1, p. 101 or (2) p. 48 ff.

short, with logical meanings. They constitute an ideally closed essence of general objects, for which being thought or being expressed is an accidental matter."[28]

Husserl's theory of meaning is introduced here as an example of the Platonistic interpretation of the phenomenon of meaning. The Platonistic theory of meaning must be unconditionally distinguished from Platonism in general. The difference consists in the fact that Platonism interprets the object signified by the word as an ideal entity, whereas the Platonistic theory of meaning in general only construes the meaning of the word as an ideal structure, without wishing to assert anything about the ontological status of the object signified. Platonism would thus interpret e. g. the relation of equality, signified by the word "equality", as an ideal entity, whereas the Platonistic theory of meaning only interprets the meaning of the word "equality" in this way. It is true, this distinction does not come clearly to expression in all platonistic theories of meaning. Particularly in the case of general expressions like e. g. "equal" or "red" etc. the meaning of a word and the object signified are not always sharply separated, so that a semantic Platonism often goes hand in hand with a Platonism of universals. We have here introduced Husserl's theory of meaning because Husserl distinguishes between meaning and signified object, and also takes account of this distinction in constructing his theory.

Whereas for the Platonistic theory of meaning the meaning of a word is an ideal object, the "psychologistic theory of meaning" somehow interprets it as a mental object, as a picture in the soul, as a representation of the object signified by the word, as thought etc. We have already briefly described this position in our discussion of the Aristotelian theory of language. Aristotle starts from the fact that, although different peoples have different languages, yet they are nonetheless able to express the same thing. There must, therefore, be something else in addition to words, which is the same for all peoples and which lends words their identity of meaning.[29] These are the *pathemata* of the soul, the pictures of things that arise

---

[28] Husserl (1) Vol. 2, Part 1, p. 105.

in our souls. The words of language are primarily signs for these *pathemata* and refer to the objects of reality only indirectly, *via pathemata*.[30]

In both Husserl and Aristotle one can see the triple stratification which always occurs when the meaning of words is objectively interpreted. First of all, there is the stratum of words, then, parallel to this, the stratum of meanings subordinated to words, and finally the stratum of objects signified by words indirectly, *via* meanings. The Platonistic and psychologistic theories of meaning differ only in that they give a different, ontological interpretation of the stratum of meanings[31].

What is common and what is peculiar to the two theories will be made still clearer by an example, introduced into the literature by Bröcker and Lohmann. We shall also use this example later to clarify more precisely Wittgensteins attempt to explain the pheno-

[29] The assertion that the differences between languages affects the sphere of meaning only a little or not at all has, incidentally, been much attacked by modern linguistics. If, namely, one studies more closely how different languages give expression to the states of affairs in the world, it becomes clear how various the aspects are, under which the separate linguistic communities approach things with their languages, and how little possible it is to make the semantic spheres of the individual languages overlap. Cf. in this connection for example: Weisgerber (1) Vol. 1. p. 59 ff.

[30] For the different forms of psychologism in the Middle Ages cf. for example Ockham (1) p. 39: "*Illud autem existens in anima, quod est signum rei, ex quo propositio mentalis componitur... aliquando vocatur intentio animae, aliquando conceptus animae, aliquando passio animae, aliquando similitudo rei;...*" Then further: "*Aliqui dicunt, quod non est nisi quoddam fictum per animam. Alii, quod est quaedam qualitas subiective existens in anima distincta ab actu intelligendi. Alii dicunt, quod est actus intelligendi.*" In modern philosophy Locke in particular is regarded as the chief representative of Psychologism. For a detailed critique of Locke's position: Husserl (1) Vol. 1, Part 2, p. 121 ff. especially p. 127 ff.

[31] Because of the "deceptiveness of the concept meaning" (Weisgerber (1) I. p. 103) Weisgerber entirely avoids the schema "word-meaning". Instead he introduces an "intermediate linguistic world" of "mental objects", lying between the phonetic form and the external world. (Weisgerber (1) 1. p. 68 ff.) It is true, this intermediate world has quite a different function to the "sphere of meaning", in Platonistic semantic theories. Also, all thought of hypostatising this intermediate world remains out of the question. It is perhaps a kind of model representation, in order to make the world view of a language empirically comprehensible. (Cf. Weisgerber (1) 1. p. 68 ff. Weisgerber himself speaks in this context of a "basic model" and of "clarificatory models" p. 71 f.)

menon of meaning.[32] A girl makes an agreement with her lover to hang a towel from the window as a sign that she is at home by herself. If, however, the girl happens not to be at home by herself but has only forgotten to remove the towel, an interesting consequence results: the towel has kept its meaning for the lover, although the state of affairs signified by the sign no longer holds.

The Stoics already faced similar problems in their semantic analyses. Therefore, in the case of a linguistic sign (σημαῖνον), they distinguished the real state of affairs to which the sign referred (τυγχάνον) from the λεκτόν or even σημαινόμενον, by which they understood what the sign said or expressed, i.e. what the sign meant. Whereas the state of affairs could change (hence: τυγχάνον), the λεκτόν always remained the same.

We transfer these distinctions to our example. Whereas the towel, on the basis of the agreement, always says or means the same thing, namely the λεκτόν: "I am at home by myself", the state of affairs signified, the τυγχάνον, can change: the girl can be at home by herself, but she can also have visitors etc. From this fact it can be concluded that the meaning of a sign is independent of the real state of affairs. But it is also independent of the choice of sign; for one could, of course, by a corresponding agreement, give the same meaning to a waved handkerchief.

The fact that the meaning remains the same *vis-à-vis* changing signs and changing states of affairs has lead the representatives of the psychologistic and Platonistic theories of meaning to construe meaning as some third thing, existing independently of signs and reality, either as a structure in the soul or as an ideal object.[33]

(2) Critical remarks about the semantic theories mentioned can be found in the most varied passages of Wittgenstein's late work. The criticism of these theories, which is developed in what follows, is kept very general; it results from the basic approach of Wittgen-

---

[32] Cf. Bröcker and Lohmann (1). For the distinction between indication *(Anzeichen)*, sign *(Zeichen)*, and expression *(Ausdruck)* cf. Husserl (1) Vol. 2, Part 1, p. 23ff.

stein's theory of meaning, according to which the meaning of a word is not an independent object at all (neither an ideal entity, nor a mental structure) *in addition* to the word, but is constituted by the rules of word usage alone.[34]

Wittgenstein's critique starts from the fact that both the Platonistic as well as the psychologistic interpretations of meaning are misled by the special grammar of the word "meaning" into supposing that the something signified by the word is an independent object. Since both interpretations are able to substantiate particular arguments for their ontological interpretations, there is no agreement about the actual status of the object. Now, Wittgenstein seeks a way out of this dilemma by asking himself before every ontological determination of meaning how the word "meaning" is actually used in ordinary linguistic usage. As we have already mentioned earlier, he here starts from the presupposition that the representatives of the semantic theories referred to understand by "meaning" only what we call meaning in our ordinary language. He thinks that agreement can be reached about the ontological status of meaning by a penetrating analysis of the use of the word "meaning".

Grammatically, the word "meaning" belongs to the substantives whose basic function is apparently to signify real objects. There can be no doubt that many substantives really do have this function. But there is also a large group of substantives for which no

---

[33] Quine considers various possibilities of explaining the concept of meaning and holds it best to give up entirely the idea that meaning is an entity. He says: "Precise and satisfactory formulation of the notion of meaning is an unsolved problem of semantics. Perhaps the meaning of a word is best construed as the associated 'idea', in some sense of 'idea', which in turn needs to be made precise; (a construction that does not have to lead unconditionally to a semantic Platonism or a semantic psychologism!); or perhaps as the system of implicit rules in conformity with which the word is used... (a position roughly corresponding to the Wittgensteinian solution). Perhaps, indeed, the best treatment of the matter will prove to consist in abandoning all notion of so-called meanings as entities..." (Quine (4) p. 200; the clarificatory remarks in brackets are added by the author.)

[34] For a detailed account of Wittgenstein's critique of Psychologism and Platonism in semantic theory, cf. for example Feyerabend (3) p. 464f.

corresponding object can be found in reality, even when the concept of "real object" is very widely extended. It is true, there is a tendency, in the case of these substantives also, to assume an object which is to be conceived on the analogy of real objects and which thus, for example, has the characteristic of independent existence.

Now, Wittgenstein is of the opinion that the word "meaning" belongs to the latter group of substantives. There is no real independent object that one would call the "meaning of the word x." But, according to Wittgenstein, one is inclined also with this expression to look for an independent object that would correspond to it. He speaks of a "temptation to look about you for something which you might call the 'meaning'." (B. B. 1.). This "temptation" arises from the tendency to look for a corresponding substance in the case of every substantive.[35] "The questions 'what is length?', 'what is meaning?', 'what is the number one?' etc. produce in us a mental cramp. We feel that we cannot point to anything in reply to them and yet ought to point to something. (We are up against one of the great sources of philosophical bewilderment: we try to find a substance for a substantive.)" (B. B. 1).

[35] It is true, the hypostatisation of meaning does not rest *only* on the illusions resulting from the special use of the word "meaning" as a substantive. Wittgenstein explicitly remarks: "We are looking for the use of a sign, but we look for it as though it were an object *co-existing* with the sign. *One* of the reasons for this mistake is that we are again looking for a 'thing corresponding to a substantive.'" (B. B. 5. We have italicised the word "one" — Author). Other grounds for the hypostatisation of meaning arise, for example, from the need to explain how different signs, words of different languages etc., can have one and the same meaning.

Ryle also represents the view that the hypostatisation of meaning has its roots in certain linguistic forms of expression. His arguments sound, it is true, much more radical than the cautious formulations of Wittgenstein: "A host of errors of the same sort has been generated in logic itself and epistemology by the omission to analyse the quasi-descriptive phrase: the meaning of the expression 'x'. I suspect that all the mistaken doctrines of concepts, ideas, terms, judgements, objective propositions, contents, objectives and the like derive from the same fallacy, namely, that there must be *something* referred to by such expressions as: the meaning of the word (phrase or sentence) 'x', on all fours with the policeman who really is referred to by the descriptive phrase in 'our village policeman is fond of football'." (Ryle (1) p. 30.)

Wittgenstein thinks that one can distinguish two possible ways of interpreting this object, meaning. One way is to conceive meaning as a picture in the soul, (in other words psychologistically), or as an independent thing additional to real things (in other words Platonistically). Cf. B. B. 18: "... the idea that the meaning of a word is an image, or a thing correlated to the word." For the Platonistic interpretation cf. B. B. 36: "... we... ask the question 'What is the sense?' And we make of 'it' a shadowy being, one of the many which we create when we wish to give meaning to substantives to which no material objects correspond." Similarly: "... when we perceive that a substance is not used as what in general we should call the name of an object, and when therefore we can't help saying to ourselves that it is the name of an ethereal object." (B. B. 47).

Wittgenstein tries to resist this tendency to interpret the word "meaning" as if it were a substantive referring to a substance. To this end he asks himself whether the word "meaning" really functions in our ordinary language like a substantive indicating a substance, (in other words, in locutions like "having the same meaning", "the meaning changes" etc.). In order more closely to clarify his conception of the actual function of the word, we shall first of all examine a substantive whose semantic function has similarity to that of the word "meaning".

The expression "the purchasing power of money" is frequently used in economics, for example in contexts like "the purchasing power of money is greater today than it was 5 years ago."[36] Now, someone might think that purchasing power was a kind of power, a special independent essence of money, whose increase and decrease can be followed. It is true the word is not generally used in this way. The proposition "The purchasing power of money is greater today than it was 5 years ago" is, of course, intended to say nothing more

---

[36] The idea of explaining certain philosophical problems with the help of economic concepts was used in particular by the English linguistic analysts. Cf. for example Ryle (7) p. 239. Xenakis also clarifies the relation between word and meaning by reference to the relation of money and buying power. Cf. Xenakis (1) p. 321.

than: "One can buy more today with a given sum money than one could 5 years ago." Assertions about the purchasing power of money do not, therefore, refer to some independent essence of money; they are only ways of speaking, to express the fact that the quantity of goods that can be purchased with a definite sum of money varies from time to time. With some caution one could thus say that the expression "purchasing power" is merely a *façon de parler* for expressing certain relationships in our economic life; to that extent it does not signify any independent object additional to money *qua* physical thing, but only a property of money *qua* means of payment.

The expression "purchasing power" is thus a paradigm for *substantiva* that do not signify an independent object and, as such, it has been introduced into the literature.[37]

How does it stand now with the substantive "meaning"? Wittgenstein thinks that the question "What is meaning?" steers the investigation in the wrong direction from the beginning. The form of question "What is ......? leads one to think of a special independent entity, concerning whose existence the question is posed. (Cf. B. B. 1). Accordingly he looks for another way of putting the question. In order to clarify meaning he investigates how one gives the *explanation* of meaning: "What is the meaning of a word? Let us attack this question by asking, first, what is the explanation of the meaning of a word; what does the explanation of a word look like? .... Studying the grammar of the expression 'explanation of meaning' will teach you something about the grammar of the word 'meaning' and will cure you of the temptation to look about for something which you might call the 'meaning'". (B. B. 1. Similarly P. I. 560.)[38]

[37] Cf. Xenakis (1).
[38] With this critique of the hypostatisation of meaning Wittgenstein takes up an old idea. Already Aristotle was resisting the conception that to every substantive there must correspond a substance (cf. for example *De Sophisticis Elenchis* 178b 37). In the Middle Ages it was above all Ockham who was repeatedly drawing attention to false hypostatisations, resulting from the capacity of certain words to be converted into substantives. (Cf. in this connection Martin's account in Martin (1) p. 208.)

To clarify this procedure, let us go back to the example of the girl who hangs a towel at the window. To explain the meaning of the sign: "Towel at the window" one would describe the agreement of the girl with her lover about the way in which the towel was to be used. They lay down the use of the towel by a definite agreement and by so doing they make it into a meaningful sign. Explaining the meaning of the sign amounts accordingly to explaining the use of the sign, its mode of application, the rules of its employment etc. Obviously, then, quite a close connection exists between the meaning of a sign and the rules of its use. The meaning is explained by giving the rules of use.

It is not difficult to show this connection in the case of *linguistic* signs as well; also in the case of the words of our language, meaning is explained by explaining the ways in which they are used. The meaning of some colour word or other is thus explained by e.g. pointing to a colour sample and saying: "This colour is called . . . .". By referring to the colour sample a paradigm is given of all those objects to which the word is applied; the formula "This colour is called . . . . . ." clarifies the linguistic "positional value" of the word to be explained. Paradigm and explanatory formula together clarify the way the colour word concerned is used. Obviously, the meaning of the word does not consist in the colour quality named, nor in the paradigm. That would lead once more to an identification of name-bearer and meaning, which was rejected at the beginning of the investigation. What is true is rather that, in the ostensive explanation of the meaning of the colour word, one *points* to the colour quality named (or to a representative paradigm), but one *explains* the meaning of the word. "And the *meaning* of a name is sometimes explained by pointing to its *bearer*." (P. I. 43). These connections between the explanation of the meaning and the explanation of the modes of use now show a new and interesting aspect of the word "meaning". In many contexts, the expression "meaning" and "mode of use" (or "rules of use") can be interchanged without changing the truth value of the context concerned. The following propositions e. g. are equivalent in this way: "The meaning of the word has changed" = "The way the word is used has changed"; "This word has several meanings" = "This word has several modes of application"; "All these expressions have the same meaning" = "All these expressions are subject to the same rules of usage"; "Someone has understood the meaning of the word" = "Someone has understood the word's rules of usage". These equivalences do not, of course, imply that "meaning" and "mode of use" (or "rules of usage") are in all contexts interchangeable and, consequently, synonymous. But they do suggest interpreting the function of the word "meaning" on the analogy of the function of the expression "purchasing power". Thus, just as the expression "purchasing power" does not signify an independent entity, but is only a *façon de parler* for expressing certain relations of economic life, so also can the word "meaning" be construed as a substantive that does not signify an independent entity, additional to language or the word, but is only a *façon de parler* for expressing a word's rules of usage.[39]

Such an interpretation of the word "meaning" comes near to Wittgenstein's conception. It, of course, also starts from the linguistic fact that for a large class of cases of the use of the word "meaning" it can be explained as: the meaning of a word is its use in the language. (P. I. 43). It is true, there is no passage where Wittgenstein would speak of the word "meaning" being a *façon de parler*. But there can be scarcely any doubt that he must have had some similar conception in mind. This becomes clear from the following:

(a) By means of linguistic-analytical considerations Wittgen-

---

[39] When in what follows we speak of "*façon de parler*" it is always to be construed with some caution. This expression is not intended to say that the word "meaning" signifies nothing at all, that all assertions about the meaning of a word are, in other words, reducible to synonymous assertions about the use of the word concerned. The word "meaning" is however a *façon de parler* to the extent that all propositions in which the word occurs are, in their truth value, dependent on propositions about word usage. Accordingly, meaning is not an independent object additional to the word and independent of it, but a quality of the word which belongs to it *qua* linguistic sign used in accordance with rule. The problem of the precise determination of the expression *façon de parler* in the linguistic-philosophical context has not yet been solved. Important approaches relevant to this are to be found in Quine (5) p. 233—276.

stein wishes to show that the word "meaning" is not a substantive that signifies an independent object. (Cf. B. B. 1, 5, 18, 36, 47).

(b) Although Wittgenstein, on the basis of the close connection between meaning and rules of usage, disputes that the word "meaning" signifies an independent object additional to the rules of usage, he carefully avoids *identifying* meaning with the rules of usage. If meaning and rules of usage were identical, the words "meaning" and "rules of usage" would have to be strictly synonymous, i.e. interchangable in all contexts.[40] This, however, is not the case. "He explained later that he did not mean that the meaning of a word *was* a list of rules; and he said that though a word 'carried its meaning with it', it did not carry with it the grammatical rules that applied to it. He said that the student who had asked him whether he meant that the meaning of a word *was* a list of rules would not have been tempted to ask that question but for the false idea (which he held to be a common one) that in the case of a substantive like 'the meaning' you have to look for something at which you can point and say: 'This is the meaning'." (M. L. I. p. 7).

(c) It can be seen from the above considerations that Wittgenstein admits meaning as an object in a particular respect; an object, namely, which, as Wittgenstein puts it, is "defined", "determined" or "constituted" by its rules of usage, but which is, at all events, not to be separated from the rules of usage. "About the meaning of single words, the positive points on which he seemed most anxious to insist were, I think, two, namely (a) something which he expressed by saying that the meaning of any single word in a language is 'defined', 'constituted', 'determined', or 'fixed' (he used all four expressions in different places) by the 'grammatical rules' with which it is used in that language ......" (M. L. I. p. 6.).

---

[40] For this interpretation cf. also Ambrose: "'Meaning of a word', 'use of a word', these he equates definitionally 'for a large class of cases' (p. 20). It is to be noted that these two phrases do not have exactly the same usage else they would be intersubstitutable. (Wittgenstein shows awarenesss of this in remarking that when one understands a word 'in a flash' the whole use does not come before one's mind. (pp. 54, 79)." (Ambrose (3).) Similarly Xenakis (2) p. 55, who likewise disputes the strict synonymity of "meaning" and "use".

We tried to paraphrase these complex relations between the meaning of a word and the rules of its usage by saying that the word "meaning" was a *"façon de parler"* for expressing the way a word is used.

Looking back it now becomes clear why and how Wittgenstein criticised the psychologistic and Platonistic theories of meaning. Both theories allow themselves to be misled by the special function of the word "meaning" into regarding meaning as an independent object additional to the word, either in the soul or in an ideal thing in itself. In contrast, a more precise analysis of the expression "meaning of a word" shows that this expression is not employed for signifying an independent object, additional to the use of the word concerned; it is only intended to paraphrase certain features of this word-usage.

9.
"Meaning" and "use" in Wittgenstein. Some consequences
and special problems of Wittgenstein's theory of meaning

(1) A theory of meaning like Wittgenstein's, according to which the expression "meaning of a word" is a *façon de parler*, which enables one to make certain assertions about the use of the word concerned, opens up for philosophical linguistic analysis new possibilities of application: assertions about the meaning of a word are equivalent to assertions about the use of a word; consequently the meaning of a word can be explained by purely linguistic-analytical investigations into the use of the word.

For such an investigation to become possible, however, it is necessary to determine in advance what is to be understood by the *use* of a word. Following Wittgenstein's maxim: "Don't ask for the meaning, ask for the use", a distinction between "use" and "usage" has been adopted in contemporary English philosophy, a distinction which can also be seen in certain applications of the German word *Gebrauch*. In German one speaks on occasion of the *Gebrauch eines Wortes* and by it is meant the way it is used (e. g. in the proposition: *"So lernen ja Kinder den Gebrauch der ersten fünf oder sechs Grundzahlwörter*" (P. 1. 9)). Corresponding to this one speaks in English of the "use of a word" ("Children do learn the use of the first five or six cardinal numerals in this way.").

But again the word *Gebrauch* is also used to express the fact that a definite word usage is *normal* and then one speaks for example of the *geltenden Sprachgebrauch* ("accepted linguistic usage") of the fact that *der Sprachgebrauch nicht einheitlich sei, sondern regional schwanke* ("linguistic usage is not homogeneous but varies regionally"). In this context the word "usage" is used in English.

"Linguistic usage" in the second sense determines the specific "use of a word" in the first sense, and makes it possible e.g. that one can use a word correctly or incorrectly, according to whether it is used in agreement with the rules accepted in the linguistic community or not.

The distinction mentioned is to be found for example in Ryle: "Much more insidious ...... is the confusion between a 'use', i.e. a way of operating with something, and a 'usage' ...... A usage is a custom, practice, fashion or vogue."[41]

Wittgenstein, it is true, neglects this distinction, so that his use of the word "use" could be better defined in the following way: first of all, by "use" Wittgenstein does not understand the *totality* of all uses or modes of use of a word within a language. A word can have several meanings while there can, of course, only be *one* totality of all uses.

But nor does "use" mean the specific individual uses of a word. We are continually using the words of our language in new combinations, we are continually constructing new expressions and propositions with them, repeatedly using them in new situations. If one wanted to draw up a list of the uses of a word in this sense, one would have to enumerate an interminable number of propositions and contexts. Wittgenstein obviously does not mean this kind of word usage when he says that the meaning of a word consists of

[41] Ryle (6) p. 174. A similar distinction in Strawson (1) p. 28, Flew (4) p. 7f. Passmore (1) has criticised this distinction insofar as it is not entirely justified by the linguistic usage of the words "use" and "usage".

its use. Otherwise every word would have a multiplicity of meanings corresponding to the immense number of individual uses.

The false and accidental uses of the word must also, of course, be excluded. If one uses a word falsely, this does not constitute a further new meaning of the word. Something similar is true of accidental uses, as for example when a parrot calls out its name.

However, a number of *regular* modes of use can be distinguished among the limitlessly many individual uses of a word or sign; in other words, definite, for the most part implicit, *rules* underlie the various modes of use. In equating meaning and use, Wittgenstein always thinks of the modes of use of a word or sign, laid down by rules, implicit or explicit. Insofar as these modes of use, laid down by rules, are *normal* or *accepted* in a definite linguistic community, one speaks of "linguistic usage", in the second sense distinguished above. But it is not necessary for the constitution of meaning that the rules of usage concerned be normal in the linguistic community; they can also be laid down on occasion by means of dictionaries etc.[42]

In this sense Wittgenstein already says in the Moore Lectures that the meaning of a word in a language is "defined", "determined", "constituted" or "fixed" by the rules, in accordance with which the word is used (M. L. I. p. 6). The locution, current in our ordinary, everday language; "The word ...... has several meanings" thus means for Wittgenstein the same as "The word ...... has several modes of use" or "The word ...... has several sets of rules of use" or suchlike.[43]

What Wittgenstein here understands by "rules of usage" is clarified by some examples which also show how the rules constituting the meaning of a word can be expressed.[44]

(a). The rules for usage can e. g. be formulated in definite descriptive propositions. Thus for the use of the word "blond", say, there is the rule that it can only be ascribed to hair, ripe wheat and certain kinds of tobacco. This rule can be expressed by a correspond-

---

[42] Strawson's equation: "The current usage in which 'use' (of a particular word, phrase, sentence) = (roughly) 'rules for using' = (roughly) meaning" is therefore only correct with certain limitations. (Cf. Strawson (1) p. 28.)

ing descriptive proposition: "The word 'blond' is used for signifying ......" Two rules for the usage of the word "is" can be described in a similar way: "The word 'is' can stand as copula between a subject and a substantival predicate; but it can also stand as copula between a subject and an adjectival predicate." ("Socrates is a person", "Socrates is wise").

(b) Another possible way of describing rules of usage consists in giving propositions, by way of example, in which the word usage becomes clear. If one wished to bring out certain differences in the rules of usage of the words "receive" and "get" one could produce the following propositions by way of example. One can say "A gets a letter" and "A receives a letter". Similarly one can say "A gets a cold" but not "A receives a cold". These illustrative propositions make clear to us a difference in the way the words "get" and "receive" are used, a difference that we admittedly observe in speaking, but the propositions first make us aware of it.[45]

(c) Many rules can only be described by means of an ostensive explanation; as, for example, when one explains the way the word "red" is used by pointing to various red objects and saying "This colour is red".

(d) On occasion, one can give the rule for the use of a word by means of a verbal definition, thus e.g. in explaining the expression "bachelor" by "unmarried man".

---

[43] Most of the words of our ordinary language do not have sharply defined sets of rules and, accordingly, they do not have sharply defined meanings either: "There are words with several clearly defined meanings. It is easy to tabulate these meanings. And there are words of which one might say: They are used in a thousand different ways which gradually merge into one another. No wonder that we can't tabulate strict rules for their use." (B. B. 28). Resulting from this insight is a series of important semantic conclusions for the analysis and determination of everyday linguistic expressions, e.g. the introduction of families of meanings (cf. P. I. 67). The problems of the "vagueness", "porousness" and "elasticity" of our ordinary concepts also have their origin here. In this connection cf. Waismann (5) and (7).

[44] The concept of rule raises great difficulties for philosophical analyses and determinations. The literature on this problem has already become very extensive. Cf. for example: Black (10), Mays and Midgley (1), Ullman (2), Wilson and Martin (1), Abelson (1).

[45] These examples are derived from Leisi (1) p. 51.

(e) Finally there is the further possibility of expressing a linguistic rule by means of what Wittgenstein calls a "grammatical proposition". We shall later discuss in detail what is meant by this. For the time being let an example show the possibility. The rule of usage, expressed by the just mentioned verbal definition of the word "bachelor" could also be rendered by the grammatical proposition: "All bachelors are unmarried men".

It may become clear from these examples what Wittgenstein understands by the rules that constitute the meaning of a word, and what different possibilities we have of giving these rules verbal expression.

(2) The question now arises, however, whence it really is that one knows the rules of usage of words. According to Wittgenstein there is not, in addition to the words and object signified, a third kind of thing: meanings, which can give us information about rules of usage. So far as there are rules of usage for a word they must therefore be derivable from the use of the word alone. Wittgenstein thereby makes exclusive use of a method which we wish to call "immanent reflection on linguistic use"[46], the possibility of which rests on the following fact: as children we are brought up to use the words of the language exactly as they are normally used in the linguistic community. The consequence is that all members of the community really do follow the same rules. Without this homogeneity of linguistic use our language would loose its character as a general method of communication. Now, if, as an adult, one is asked about the rules of linguistic usage one only needs to reflect on how words are used in everyday linguistic practice. One already

---

[46] This method roughly corresponds to what, on occasion, is called in linguistic philosophy "Exhibition Analysis": "I propose to call the philosophical method which aims at the discovery and exhibition of rules for the use of words exhibition analysis." (Körner (1) p. 763ff. Various reservations are also expressed about this method there.) Hare has drawn attention to the fact that propositions about the rules of an activity, that are derivable from reflection on one's own behaviour, have certain characteristics of *synthetic a priori* knowledge; certain analogies with Platonic *anamnesis* also exist... (cf. Hare (1) p. 745f. and p. 749.)

uses words, of course, in accordance with the rules that have been inculcated into one, and one can, therefore, recognise them by reflecting on one's own linguistic usage. This reflection is "immanent" to the extent that one does not need to go beyond what one *already* knows of linguistic use.

In this method the assumption is silently and, in many cases, justifiably made that everybody follows the same rules, so that one's own linguistic usage is also general linguistic usage. This presupposition shows, however, the limitations of immanent reflection. Linguistic usage is by no means so homogeneous as we may at first assume. Within a linguistic community there are many deviations: dialects, technical languages, the linguistic peculiarities of various social strata etc. Besides this, the linguistic rules are not always laid down unambiguously, so that there are possibilities of individual variation. In such cases it is therefore necessary, so as still to be able to make universally valid assertions, to have recourse to other methods, for example, to statistical linguistic investigations.[47]

As was said, Wittgenstein makes exclusive use of "immanent reflection", and thus derives all his assertions about linguistic usage from reflection on his own (i. e. Wittgenstein's own) linguistic usage. The objection could be raised against this procedure that Wittgenstein's analyses merely lead to assertions about his *own* linguistic usage, and cannot, therefore, ever make any claim to universal validity.[48]

This objection is valid, however, only on certain conditions. In his analyses, Wittgenstein is not concerned about research into linguistic usage, in the sense of empirical linguistics. He expressly remarks that his observation of language received "its light, that

---

[47] There is a survey of the literature on the problem of statistical linguistics in Guiraud (1).

[48] This is an objection that is to be found in similar form in Körner: "Lastly, why, if at all, should the rules discovered by some practitioner of exhibition analysis to have been the ones adopted by himself and certain other members of his community be preferred to the rules which some other philosopher has adopted and is proposing for adoption?" (Körner (1) p. 764.)

is to say its purpose, from the philosophical problems." (P. I. 109). To that extent, all his linguistic analyses are merely means to clarifying certain philosophical problems.

There is also a further moment. Wittgenstein's individual investigations have merely *paradigmatic* value: "...... we now demonstrate a method, by examples; and the series of examples can be broken off." (P. I. 133). With respect to these individual examples it is a matter of indifference whether Wittgenstein proceeds from his own linguistic usage or from general linguistic usage. In each case what Wittgenstein wishes to achieve is reached: the paradigmatic discussion of a philosophical problem with the help of knowledge gained by reflecting on the linguistic usage that is thereby presupposed (whether this is his own or general linguistic usage).

(3) A series of special problems result from the equating of "meaning" and "use",[49] only two of which we wish to select here.

Both the Platonistic and the psychologistic theories of meaning repeatedly examine a characteristic of the phenomenon of meaning which seems to them particularly important and in need of explanation: the constancy and identity of meaning in contrast to the various and changing signs which express it. They explain this identity of meaning with the help of a special object: meaning, which has an existence that is independent of the signs, and which, for

---

[49] To these problems belong the phenomenon of "suddenly understanding the meaning" and the question about the "true" meaning. Wittgenstein is of the opinion that the sudden understanding of meaning need not stand in contradiction to the fact that meaning consists in use. The contrary opinion is reached only through construing the understanding of meaning on the analogy of a mental process like hearing, or feeling pain. Cf. P. I. 38—242. For a short account of this discussion cf. Strawson (3) p. 78f. The locution "true" meaning would also have a certain justification for Wittgenstein if the historically earlier use of the word were intended by the expression, or if it expressed how a word *ought*, in fact, to be used. What he is opposed to is the idea that a definite meaning belongs to the word in itself and that one could miss the meaning, if the word were not used in agreement with the meaning attributed to it in itself. Cf. F. M. 6 and P. I. p. 147, Note. For the details of this discussion see in particular Feyerabend (3) p. 469ff.

that reason, can be expressed by the most varied signs, irrespective of whether this object be an ideal structure or an object in the soul.

Naturally Wittgenstein's theory of meaning must somehow take account of this phenomenon. How then is this identity of meaning to be explained on his theory? Let us start with a concrete example, say, with the meaning of signs at one way streets. Let us assume that these signs are replaced by others, e. g. by red and green lines at the beginning and at the end of the street. These signs would have exactly the same meaning as the old ones. But why do they have the same meaning? According to Wittgenstein's theory it is because these new signs are used in the same way as the old ones, in other words, because the red and green lines are introduced at the beginning and end of those streets which may only be used by vehicles in one direction, in accordance with a specific traffic regulation. Thus, the identity of meaning is here ensured by the identity in the mode of use.

What has just been said can be transferred without difficulty to the meaning of linguistic signs. It is in this way that the German *Pferd* must have the same meaning as the English "horse". The Platonistic and psychologistic theories of meaning explain this identity of meaning by means of a third entity, additional to words and things, by means of the ideal or mental object: meaning. According to the Wittgensteinian theory of meaning, on the other hand, both words have the same meaning because they are used in the same way; both words serve to signify a definite species of animal, or an individual of that species. The identity of meaning in the case of other linguistic signs can also be similarly explained by the identity in the mode of use.

But Wittgenstein did not solve the problem of the identity of meaning by this attempt. This theory of meaning only put the problem on a new level of discussion, insofar as his investigations only needed to refer to concrete linguistic practice. The question remains, however, how is it possible for two modes of use to be *identical* at all. (The problem of identity in Wittgenstein will occupy us later.) A *second* question closely connected with this problem is the question of homonymity and synonymity. Unfortunately, Wittgenstein only treated this problem briefly, so that it is difficult to know which solution he had in mind.[50] He discusses the question in a series of examples that have been selected in such a way that it is impossible to say without further ado whether the linguistic sign in question has the same or a different meaning. In the first example he goes into the question of whether the fact that a word has the same or different meaning in different propositions reveals itself to us clearly or not. (P. I. 552 and 553): "Suppose I were to ask: is it clear to us, while we are uttering the sentences 'This rod is one yard long' and 'Here is one soldier', that we mean different things by 'one', that 'one' has different meanings?—Not at all.—Say e.g. such a sentence as 'One yard is occupied by one soldier, and so two yards are occupied by two soldiers.' Asked 'Do you mean the same thing by both 'ones'?' one would perhaps answer: 'Of course I mean the same thing: *one*!' (Perhaps raising one finger.) Now has '1' a different meaning when it stands for a measure and when it stands for a number? If the question is framed in *this* way, one will answer in the affirmative." (The difference between number and measure, to which Wittgenstein refers, is best seen in the following propositions: "This here is a 1d.; there are two 1ds.". Number and measure here come immediately after each other.)

Wittgenstein obviously wishes to draw attention to two points with this example: (a) that whether a word has the same meaning or not does not always show itself and (b) that the judgement whether a word has the same or a different meaning depends, among other things, on how one approaches the question. In the case of one particular approach one reaches the conclusion that the sign "1" has the same meaning in the propositions mentioned. If one starts

[50] Since Aristotle's first determination of the expressions "synonymous" and "homonymous" in the work on the categories, the problem of synonymity, has remained one of the most difficult questions of semantics. The difficulties result, in particular, from the fact that no agreement can be reached about the criteria for the synonymity of two expressions. For an introduction to the modern discussion of the concept of synonymity cf. Stegmüller (1) p. 297ff. For the linguistic standpoint cf. Ullmann (2).

from a rather different standpoint the distinction between number and measure is introduced and the opposite result is reached. In the proposition "This rod is 1 meter long" the "1" can be interpreted as quantity, in other words in the sense of "this rod has the length: 1 meter". In the proposition "one soldier is standing here" the 1 signifies, by contrast, the number. A difference in meaning is thus suddenly revealed here which we would not have seen without the number-measure distinction.

The extent to which judgement about difference and identity of meaning can fluctuate is made clear by Wittgenstein in the following example: "Imagine a language with two different words for negation, 'X' and 'Y'. Doubling 'X' yields an affirmative, doubing 'Y' a strengthened negative. For the rest the two words are used alike.—Now have 'X' and 'Y' the same meaning in sentences where they occur without being repeated?" (P. I. 556). Entirely different answers can be given depending on one's approach to the question. Holding quite strictly to the equivalence of meaning and mode of use one could say: "X" and "Y" have different modes of use and consequently also *different* meanings. But one could also say "X" and "Y" are semantically identical and one could try to establish this in the following way: "X" and "Y" are used in the same way in all essential contexts, their use is taught in the same way etc; therefore they also have the same meaning. That they cannot be interchanged in certain propositions is something incidental, one of those "capricious features of the language" (P. I. 556) which cannot detract from the semantic equivalence of the two words. Again, from a different standpoint the following objection could be made against the complete semantic equivalence: "We connect different images with the two negatives. 'X' as it were turns the sense through 180°. And *that* is why two such negatives restore the sense to its former position. 'Y' is like a shake of the head. And just as one does not annul a shake of the head by shaking it again, so also one doesn't cancel one 'Y' by a second one. And so, even if, practically speaking, sentences with the two signs of negation come to the same thing, still 'X' and 'Y' express different ideas" (P. I. 556).

Here, and also in some other examples in the *Philosophical Investigations*, Wittgenstein shows that not all words have one or more fixed and unambiguous meanings; it is not unambiguously laid down whether "X" and "Y" have the same meaning or not. Arguments for and against can be produced without either argument being decisive. In the last analysis, judgement about the semantic equivalence or difference of these signs depends on which argument one has *decided* to favour. From this fact naturally grew major difficulties for the Platonistic theory of meaning, which took the meaning of a word to be independent of human beings. However, Wittgenstein had a simple explanation applicable to many cases. Many of the expressions of our everyday language are not equipped with unambiguous rules of usage applicable to all possible cases of use. If one wishes to carry the discussion of such expressions further, it is necessary to extend their rules or we must ourselves make the rules precise, a procedure that Wittgenstein, on occasion, paraphrases with the words: "make up the rules as we go along" (P. I. 83).[51] To this group belong also the expressions "to have the same or, as the case may be, different meanings." In a large number of cases it is relatively unambiguously laid down when we say a word has the same or a different meaning. But there are also many borderline cases which we must ourselves so determine that they still have an unambiguous use.

In this connection Wittgenstein gives a further example which has particularly interesting consequences. He poses the question (P. I. 555) whether the number 5 means the same for people whose number-series ended at 5, as it does for us. The numerical sign "5" of these people would have the same use in many contexts as our own sign "5"; for example in the propositions "5 apples are lying there" and "$2 + 3 = 5$". But some rules of usage, determining the use of our ordinary numerical sign 5, would no longer be true for the 5 of these people; e. g. the rule expressed in Peano's Second Axiom that to every natural number there is exactly one successor

---

[51] One could object that this extension of the rules contradicts the Wittgensteinian maxim to leave everything as it is. We shall come to speak in greater detail about the objection later.

which is itself a natural number. Now, do the two numerical signs have the same meaning or not? Again, several conflicting answers are conceivable: (a) both numerical signs have a different use and therefore different meanings. The features that are common to the use of the signs are inessential to the constitution of meaning. (b) Although the use of the two numerical signs differ in some points, fundamentally their function is the same: both signify *the same number*. They, thus, have the same meaning. However, a counterthesis could be set up in opposition to the second interpretation: (c) it is precisely the differences in use of the two signs that show that they do not signify the same number but rather different numbers from entirely different numerical systems. The two numbers thus have different meanings. The decision about the semantic equivalence of the two signs can thus depend, among other things, on certain ontological presuppositions; more specifically it can depend on the ontological interpretation of the objectivity signified by the sign. Here, then ontological differences lead to controversial questions about the semantic similarity and semantic difference of two signs. Wittgenstein's analytical method, on the other hand, preserves the possibility of reaching an agreement about the semantic similarity and difference of two signs merely by means of an agreement between the partners of the conversation to secure unanimity.[52]

(4) What we have shown so far about the problem of meaning in Wittgenstein's investigations, makes it easy to see the connection

---

[52] That certain questions are only to be decided if there is first agreement about linguistic usage, is held by Wisdom, among others, for one of Wittgenstein's most important insights. Our question about synonymity is in this respect like Wittgenstein's famous question "Can one play chess without the queen?", a question which also can only be decided after having previously determined the linguistic usage of "playing chess". In our ordinary linguistic usage, namely, it is not unambiguously laid down whether a "game of chess" without a queen is still a game of chess, or not.

In empirical linguistics one generally helps oneself by so analysing the concepts of "synonymity" and "heteronymity" that one arrives at a many levelled scale, that does justice to all possible cases of synonymity and homonymity. Such a scale is found for example in Ullman (2) p. 108.

between his theory of meaning and his theory of language in general.

According to Wittgenstein, the meaning of a linguistic sign is not an independent object, but only a *façon de parler* with the help of which assertions can be made about the use of linguistic signs. There is, therefore, no third sphere, additional to language and objects, a sphere of meanings that lends life to the whole of language. Rather, language wins its sense and function in Wittgenstein simply from the practice of people, from their action with linguistic signs and objects. Thus, for Wittgenstein semantic analysis amounts to analysis of actual linguistic use and the analysis of its place in human activities. The only approach to the meaning of a word consists in studying the ways it is used in the concrete *language-games* of our language. In this sense, Wittgenstein repeatedly says: "Let the use of words teach you their meaning" (P. I. p. 229).[53]

This naturally signifies a certain relativisation of language to people or to the specific linguistic community concerned. But all our explanations have suggested that this idea of the relativisation of language to people already exists in the concept of the language-game, which Wittgenstein uses as the foundation of his whole theory of language.

[53] "Don't sit and try to think it out abstractly, the author admonishes his readers, but really 'look and see' how a word or phrase is actually used in any given context, and that procedure will reveal what the word or phrase substantially means in that context... the proper, i.e. the empirical way to discover the meaning of the word 'good', for example, is to turn to the various language-games in which it occurs (is used), and upon doing so one finds that in reality it has not just one but a whole family of meanings." (Smart (1) p. 224.)

VI. THE CONSTITUTION OF OBJECTS IN LANGUAGE

So far our investigations have led us to recognise the specific priority attributed to word usage. This was shown both in the chapter on signification, where a close connection between word usage and object type emerged, and also in the chapter on meaning, where meaning and word usage were brought into the closest connection. The position of priority attributed to word usage is the real basis of Wittgenstein's method of linguistic analysis.

But at this point a decisive objection arises, an objection which has been raised in the most various forms against the school of linguistic analysis. This objection shall be examined in terms of an example discussed by Walsh in a paper on the problem of categories in Aristotle and Ryle. For Ryle, assertions about categorial structures are primarily assertions about possible or impossible combinations of propositional factors, in other words, semantic assertions about the use of linguistic symbols in the proposition. "I call a proposition a 'category-proposition' which asserts something about the logical type of a factor or set of factors......Now assertions about the types of factors are, as we have seen, assertions about what sorts of combinations of them with other factors would and what would not produce absurdities. And as only collocations of symbols can be asserted to be absurd or, consequently, denied to be absurd, it follows that category propositions are semantic propositions."[1] Ryle does not deny that such categorial assertions can, in a way, also refer to objects, to the "nature of things". But

[1] Ryle (2) p. 81.

they are primarily assertions about symbols and their belonging to
definite logical types; primarily, they give expression to certain
rules of logic or grammar. With regard to these grammatical or
logical rules Walsh hypothetically maintains the following reservations: "It might be held, indeed, that even rules of this sort must
find their justification in truths about the world: the reason why it
is wrong to confuse substance-expressions with quality-expressions
is that in fact substances and qualities differ. This is in effect to
argue that any linguistic interpretation of Aristotle's doctrine of
categories presupposes an ontological interpretation."[2] The objection, here discussed in connection with the theory of categories,
can easily be transferred to Wittgenstein's linguistic-analytical
approach. The objection maintained that, although the analysis
of the grammar of a word affords access to the structure of the
object signified, the correctness of the grammatical analysis
does not ultimately depend on language but rather on the structure
of the object signified, and only from that source can it derive its
justification. In this way the primacy of grammatical analysis de-
manded by Wittgenstein, became questionable and had to be replaced by priority of the ontological mode of observation.[3]

Closer observation now reveals, however, that the objection
operates from the beginning on the basis of the atomic model of
language; it is tacitly assumed that the objects are there previous to
language, that language is subsequently added and that the rules of
linguistic usage are read off from the objects. Only in this way is it
at all possible to found an investigation of grammar on an investi-

[2] Walsh (1) p. 285.
[3] The commentaries on the *Philosophical Investigations* to-date have discussed this problem but little. Black makes a point that points in this direction:
in the discussion of Whorf's theory of language he comes to speak of the
thesis that the language of a linguistic community is one of the factors determining its world view, its whole philosophy. In the course of the discussion
he mentions various thinkers who have maintained this thesis, among others
Lichtenberg, Humboldt, Cassirer and Wittgenstein. Cf. Black (10) p. 234.
In particular, however, it is Pole's efforts at interpretation that come into
question here (in Pole (1) p. 29ff.). We shall frequently refer to it in what
follows.

gation into the structure of objects. But if, following Wittgenstein, one starts from the model of the language-game, it is questionable whether the objection mentioned can be further maintained. Wittgenstein's language-games are entities made up of linguistic sign, human action and object, and they cannot be united together in the way in which language and world are summatively united together in the atomic model. The question thus arises whether grammatical rules really do merely portray a picture of the structure of objects, as the objection assumes, or whether the relationship between linguistic sign and object must not be conceived as much more complicated.[4]

In the following analyses of the connection between word and signified object in language-games, the concepts of "grammar" and "grammatical proposition", move into the centre of consideration. Apart from the concept of the language-game and linguistic use, these two concepts are the most important in the *Investigations*.

10. *The concepts "grammar" and "grammatical proposition" in Wittgenstein*

(1) Wittgenstein uses the concept of grammar in a fashion that does not coincide with normal linguistic usage. This apparently contradicts his demand that philosophy should in no way interfere with

---

[4] Charlesworth (1) has raised similar doubts in his investigation into the philosophy of the analytic school. It is true that he also emphasises the correlation of linguistic and ontological attitudes, but he still looks for the foundation of the linguistic analysis in the extra-linguistic correlates of language: "Now, whereas the grammatical conditions of any language may be considered in themselves quite apart from any extra-grammatical reference of language, what we have called the necessary conditions of language cannot be considered apart from the extra-linguistic reference of language. Put in Russellian terms, our language does not have a 'logical form' as it has a 'grammatical form'. For, if the necessary conditions of language are those which govern the *meaningful* use of language, they can only be determined, in the last resort, by reference to *what is meant*, that is to say, by reference to the extra-linguistic correlate of language." (p. 217.)

the actual use of language; philosophy must leave everything as it is. (Cf. P. I. 124). On the other hand, however, Wittgenstein certainly permits a "reform" of language "for particular practical purposes, an improvement in our terminology designed to prevent misunderstandings in practice." (Cf. P. I. 132). The maxim just mentioned, that philosophy may not in any way interfere with linguistic usage, obviously does not refer, then, to terminological coinings like Wittgenstein's term "grammar", but only to the drawing up of a complete linguistic system intended to replace our ordinary language, i.e. to the kind of linguistic reform aimed at in the *Tractatus*. The basic concepts coined by Wittgenstein in his late work: "language-game", "grammar" and "grammatical proposition" are to be construed as terminological inventions that do not interfere with the actual use of language; they only represent definite concepts of order and are intended "to establish an order in our knowledge of the use of language: an order with a particular end in view; one out of many possible orders; not *the* order." (Cf. P. I. 132).

It is first of all necessary, then, to explain what is meant by grammar in general, and how Wittgenstein uses the word in particular. Traditional grammar, with its triad of phonetics, accidence and syntax, investigates language primarily with regard to what is spoken as such. This is self-evident in the case of phonetics and accidence, for they simply aim at determining phonetic elements and their forms (declination and conjugation etc.) independently of content. But also in the case of syntax, which in itself occupies a curious intermediate position between phonetic-syntactic and semantic standpoints, the description of phonetic ordered arrangements, independent of semantic content, stands in the foreground.[5]

Traditional grammar as a whole is thus primarily orientated towards the observation of what is phonetic; it has accordingly been described as a "phonetically orientated" grammar (L. Weisgerber). Other authors speak in this context of a "grammar of material" since it is chiefly occupied with the material of linguistic signs.[6]

Clearly, a grammar that limits itself in essence to the investigation of linguistic signs and the laws of their construction cannot grasp all the laws of our language. Consequently, a linguistic study was set up opposite traditional grammar; it was primarily orientated towards the semantic aspect, towards the content of what is said and the regularities resulting therefrom: in other words, opposite the "phonetically orientated" grammar a "content orientated" grammar; opposite the "grammar of material" a "grammar of meaning".[7] Such a grammar of meaning describes all those rules of sign usage that are related to the meaning of the sign and its semantic modes of use. It would correspond essentially to what Wittgenstein would call grammar in the widest sense. Grammar embraces the observation and description of all rules related to sign usage, in its semantic aspect, of course. (P. I. 354, 373, 496). Hence it is that Wittgenstein calls reflections about a particular linguistic usage "gram-

---

[5] On the phonetic orientation of traditional grammar cf. L. Weisgerber's detailed discussion in Weisgerber (1) Vol. 1, p. 97 ff.: "It is true of all linguistic work that its efforts must start at the phonetic side of language. The phonetic form of words, the construction of forms and sentence-plans, everything sensuous in language, is the pre-condition of all linguistic knowledge and, accordingly, it stands at the beginning of the process of making language into something of which we are conscious... Western grammar is in essence characterised by the fact that the phonetic approach operates further in the construction of a phonetically orientated grammar, namely, both in the 'grammatical' (in other words conscious-making, diagnostic) account of vocabulary, and also in grammar in the narrow sense, in other words, in the account of the means of speech arrangement."

[6] So for example J. Schächter (1) p. 19.

[7] Cf. L. Weisgerber (1) Vol. 1, p. 96 f. "This (content orientated) 'grammar' will however differ essentially from the traditional kind of grammatical procedure, insofar as it is content orientated, i. e. is primarily tuned into the ascertaining of linguistic content." W. Porzig determines the matter in very much the same way (Porzig (1) p. 99): "There are only two ways of investigating the inner structure of speech. One can either concentrate exclusively on the phonetical and ask what characteristics of form and articulation are to be discovered in it. Or, in the case of any deviant phonetic form that occurs, one can observe the resultant change in the reactions that follow. The first procedure has been called *structuralism* by the scholars who have developed it, since their attention is directed to the construction, the structure, of the expressions. In the case of the second procedure, which of course brings two phenomena into relationship, emphasis can be laid either on the changing behaviour (*behaviour research*, American English *Behaviourism*), or on the content which is expressed through the changing phonetic forms (*content orientated grammar*)."

matical observations" (P. I. 90, p. 59 note), "grammatical notes" (P. I. 232), "grammatical remarks" (P. I. 574) etc.[8]

In order to clarify the opposition between traditional grammar and grammar in the sense just described an example shall be introduced: at one point in the *Philosophical Investigations* we read: "If there were a verb meaning 'to believe falsely', it would not have any significant first person present indicative." (P. I. p. 190). It is a peculiarity of the word "believe", namely, that although one can say "I believ*ed* ...... falsely" one cannot say "I believe ..... falsely"; on the other hand, one can say "You believe ...... falsely". In other words the word "believe" cannot be connected, under certain circumstances, with the adverb "falsely". We do not hear about this peculiarity of the word "believe" in any traditional grammar; we learn about the conjugation of the verb and its possible position in propositions etc.; i.e. only about the laws that show themselves in the "phonetic-syntactic" aspect. It is only when we pay attention to the meaning of the word, i.e. practice the grammar of meaning, that we first notice the suprising fact that the compound "I believe ...... falsely" is not a meaningful expression at all.

So far we have spoken about grammar as the science of the rules of the usage of linguistic signs. But that is not the only meaning of the word "grammar" in Wittgenstein. By "grammar" is also to be understood the rules of the usage of linguistic signs, the totality of the rules constituting the meaning of a sign. Thus, for Wittgenstein grammar means both the science of the rules of linguistic usage and also the rules themselves (roughly in the way the word "logic" also means both the science of logical structures as well as the structures themselves). In this way Wittgenstein speaks of the "grammar of a word" (the grammar of "mean" P. I.

[8] The relation of the Wittgensteinian concept of grammar to the *meaning* of the linguistic signs and, consequently, to the rules of usage that constitute the meaning, is discussed by all interpreters of Wittgenstein. Cf. for example Schlick (Schlick [2] p. 340): "The meaning of a word or a combination of words is... determined by a set of rules which regulate their use and which, following Wittgenstein, we may call the rules of their *grammar*, taking this word in its widest sense."

p. 18 note; similarly P. I. 187 and 257), of the "grammar of an expression" (P. I. 660), of the "grammar of a proposition" (P. I. 353) and once even of the "grammar of a state" (P. I. 572). But he always means by the term the grammatical structures of a sign or of a sign usage, resulting from the rules of usage.[9]

In this connection Wittgenstein sometimes distinguishes the "surface grammar" of a linguistic sign from its "depth grammar" (P. I. 664). Surface grammar embraces everything "which immediately impresses itself upon us about the use of a word ...... the way it is used in the *construction of the sentence*, the part of its use —one might say—that can be taken in by the ear." Depth grammar, on the other hand, concerns those rules of usage that do not immediately reveal themselves on the "superficial form of our grammar". (F. M. 32).

Two examples shall clarify the distinction: "A plays a game of chess", "A wins a game of chess." The external similarity in the use of the words "play" and "win" misleads one into construing winning as a process similar to that of playing: the surface grammar of "win" makes one think of an activity. If, however, one penetrates into the depth grammar of the word it then becomes clear that "win" does not mean an activity, but rather the result of playing. "Win" is not an "activity word" but rather a "result word".[10]

This distinction between surface grammar and depth grammar is important for Wittgenstein because he sees the origin of many philosophical problems in the fact that the surface grammar of the use of a sign misleads us about the depth grammar of the sign, i.e. about the deep-lying characteristic of the sign's usage.

Wittgenstein is here thinking of all those problems that grow out of the fact that "we do not *command a clear view* of the use of our words", that "our grammar is lacking in this sort of perspicuity"

---

[9] Cf. Pole (1) p. 30 f.: "The reader of the *Philosophical Investigations* comes very frequently on the term 'grammar' used evidently otherwise than in its literal sense. In this extended sense it is part of the grammar of the word 'rod' that a rod must have a certain length... Grammar in Wittgenstein's sense, is the structure of language, or, seen differently, its system of rules."

[10] Ryle calls such words: "got-it-verbs". Cf. Ryle (3) p. 149.

(P. I. 122). He therefore calls such deceptions "grammatical illusions" (P. I. 110. We shall revert to these illusions later).

(2) Now that we have explained the concept of grammar in Wittgenstein, we must now investigate the concept of the *"grammatical proposition"*. This term is one that Wittgenstein specially coined; it occurs for the first time in the Moore Lectures and recurs repeatedly thereafter. Since it is never explained but always presupposed as understood, we are obliged to infer its more precise definition from occasional remarks. Everything that Wittgenstein says indicates that by a grammatical proposition is to be understood a proposition that makes an assertion about an object; but it is a proposition which depends exclusively for its truth value on the rules of usage of the linguistic sign which signifies the object.

In order to explain this concept more closely we shall start with an example from everyday language: if one wishes to draw some-one's attention to the fact that the word "patience" is used only for signifying card-games which one plays by oneself, one can do so by explaining to the person concerned the rules of usage of the word "patience", i.e. by saying, for example, "The word 'patience' only refers to card-games which one plays by oneself." But one can also clarify the word's rules of usage with the help of a grammatical proposition: "One plays patience by oneself." (P. I. 248). This proposition makes an assertion, on the one hand, about a class of card-games, i.e. about particular objects; on the other hand it gives expression to the rules of usage of the word "patience", which signifies these objects.[11]

In the *Investigations* and the *Foundations of Mathematics* Wittgenstein gives some examples of grammatical propositions: "Every rod has length", "my images are private", "only I myself can know whether I am feeling pain", "every body has extension" (P. I. 251, 252), "an order orders its own execution" (P. I. 458), "the class of lions is not a lion, but the class of classes is a class" (F. M. 182).

(The clause of the last proposition: "the class of classes is a class" is complicated by the fact that it can only be fully understood in the light of Russell's Theory of Types. The question is whether, in the case of the class of classes, one may speak at all without further addition of a "class", to avoid falling into the contradictions revealed by Russell's antinomy. If one wishes to avoid these contradictions, one must at least formulate the proposition in the following way: "The class of classes is a class of higher type than that to which the sub-classes of this class belong." It is clear, however, that within the context of the discussion as a whole, Wittgenstein does not regard this detail as decisive "One can say that the word "class" is used reflexively, even if for instance, one accepts Russell's theory of types. For it is used reflexively there too." (F. M. 182). In the case of the grammatical proposition mentioned, then, Wittgenstein is only concerned with contrasting the non-reflexive use of "lion" and the reflexive use of "class"; and to this extent the recognition or non-recognition of the Russellian Theory of Types plays no rôle.)

What is common to all the propositions mentioned is the fact that they all makes assertions about particular objects and, in this respect, they are like empirical-objective propositions. The proposition "every rod has length" is similar to the objective proposition

---

11 A grammatical proposition is neither an assertion *about* a linguistic rule, nor is it a *linguistic rule formulated in words*. An assertion about a linguistic rule would for instance be a proposition like the following: "In south west Germany the word '*wo*' ('where') is used instead of the relative pronoun; at times also this is to be found in literature ('*das schlechteste Messer, wo er hat.*' Hebel. 'the worst knife which he had')". (Cf. H. Paul (1) p. 371.)

A linguistic rule formulated in words would be for example: "The word 'blond' is only asserted of hair, ripe corn and certain kinds of tobacco." A grammatical proposition, on the other hand, is a proposition which makes a concrete assertion, exclusively dependent for its truth value on specific grammatical rules. A similar distinction is to be found in Ayer, who sharply separates *a priori* propositions, derivable from the grammar of a language, both from empirical assertions about linguistic rules, and from these rules themselves: "Just as it is a mistake to identify *a priori* propositions with empirical propositions about language, so I now think that it is a mistake to say that they are themselves linguistic rules. For apart from the fact that they can properly be said to be true, which linguistic rules cannot, they are distinguished also by being necessary." (Ayer (1) p. 17.) In order to understand this passage, it is necessary to know that in Ayer's theory of the *a priori* judgement, all *a priori* propositions are derivable from grammatical rules, and are therefore grammatical propositions in Wittgenstein's sense.

"everybody has a fault". At the same time all grammatical propositions enable one to see a reference to the rules of usage of the expressions occurring in them, a reference which ordinary concrete propositions do not have in this way.[12] This is shown by the following reflection. Empirical propositions depend for their truth value partly on the rules of usage of the words occurring in them, and partly on the empirical data. Thus the proposition "everybody has a fault" could, for example, be falsified both by the fact that there is someone without a fault and also by the fact that the words "person" and "fault" are not used conformably to present-day linguistic usage. On the other hand grammatical propositions only depend for their truth value on the relevant linguistic usage of the words employed, not on the empirical data. The proposition "every rod has a length" would, in other words, only change in truth value if the linguistic use of the words "rod" and "length" were to change in some way, for instance if we were to call an object which had no length "rod". It is inconceivable that any empirical observation of rods could refute the proposition.[13] Because of this close connection between the grammatical proposition and the linguistic rules of the words occurring in it we also use grammatical propositions in everyday linguistic usage to express particular linguistic rules.

[12] In a similar context Carnap speaks of pseudo-object-sentences, in other words, sentences which in their external form sound like object-sentences but in fact are only disguised "syntactical sentences", in other words express syntactical rules. Carnap (3) p. 286 ff. In here setting Wittgenstein's grammatical proposition in parallel with Carnap's "pseudo-object-sentence", attention must be drawn to an important difference. The term "pseudo-object-sentence" harbours the danger of one's thinking that these propositions did not refer to any objects at all. By contrast, the grammatical proposition is to be construed under all circumstances as an assertion, even if not an empirical assertion, about objects.

[13] Grammatical propositions belong to what have been called "incorrigible propositions". Cf. Gasking (1) p. 207. The difference between corrigible and incorrigible propositions lies in the following: "A *corrigible* proposition gives you some information about the world—a completely *incorrigible* proposition tells you nothing. A corrigible proposition is one that you would withdraw and admit to be false if certain things happened in the world. It therefore gives you the information that *those* things… will *not* happen. An incorrigible proposition is one which you would never admit to be false *whatever* happens: it therefore does not tell you *what* happens…." (Gasking (1) p. 208.)

Whether a propositional structure is a grammatical proposition or not cannot always be determined without further ado. Frequently, the expressions occurring in the proposition concerned are "vague" in respect of the way they are used, so that whether the proposition is grammatical or not depends on a more precise determination.[14]

Whether, for example, the proposition "Machines cannot think" is grammatical or not, depends on how one limits the usage of the word "think", a usage which is not precisely fixed in ordinary language. The use of this word is partly bound up with specific achievement-criteria, so that in this respect it is an empirical question whether there are machines or not that satisfy these achievement-criteria. On the other hand, there is from the beginning a tendency to bind the application of the word "think" in ordinary linguistic usage to a particular sphere. Wittgenstein gives in to this tendency when he asserts: "But a machine surely cannot think!—Is that an empirical statement? No. We only say of a human being and what is like one that it thinks." (P. I. 359, 360). Where the word usage is laid down in this way, the proposition "machines cannot think" is naturally a grammatical proposition which cannot be refuted by any kind of experience with machines.

The above quoted examples of grammatical propositions ought also to be examined in the light of these considerations. "One plays patience by oneself" is only true, for instance, when the word "patience" is in fact only used for card-games which one plays by oneself. That this need not always be the case is shown by the so-called games of "double solitaire", which are kinds of patience played by two people.[15]

In recognising grammatical propositions as significant propo-

[14] Waismann (5) and Black (2) in particular have investigated the problem of the "vagueness" of the way in which certain expressions are employed. Instead of "vague concepts", one also on occasion speaks of "open concepts", cf. for instance Pap (4) p. 302. Wittgenstein also repeatedly draws attention to the fact that not all concepts have fixed boundaries (cf. for example P. I. 68), that not every expression has unambiguously definite rules of use. Unfortunately, Wittgenstein did not draw out the consequences that this conception has for the theory of the grammatical proposition.

sitional structures Wittgenstein's late philosophy differs quite essentially from the conceptions of the *Tractatus*. In the latter Wittgenstein declares all those propositions which express internal i. e. necessary properties or relations (for instance the proposition: "1 is a number") for senseless, pseudo-propositions (Cf. T. 4.122—4.1274). In the late work his attitude to this type of proposition had fundamentally changed. He asks for example in the *Remarks on the Foundations of Mathematics* (182): "What *sort* of proposition is: 'The class of lions is not a lion, but the class of classes is a class'? How is it verified? How could it be *used*?—So far as I can see, only as a grammatical proposition. To draw someone's attention to the fact that the word 'lion' is used in a fundamentally different way from the name of a lion; whereas the class word 'class' is used like the designation of one of the classes, say the class of lions." Wittgenstein then continues further on: "Even though 'the class of lions is not a lion' seems like nonsense, to which one can only ascribe a sense out of politeness; still I do not want to take it like that, but as a proper sentence, if only it is taken right. (And so not as in the *Tractatus*.) Thus my conception is a different one here. Now this means that I am saying: there is a language-game with this sentence too."

---

[15] On the other hand there are however also "empirical" propositions whose status is not to be determined with precision because of the expressions occurring in them. Specific universal assertions, in particular, do not always permit an unambiguous decision as to whether they are of grammatical or empirical nature. The proposition, quoted previously as a universal, empirical proposition: "Everybody has a fault" is certainly a grammatical proposition, if the word "fault" is made suitably precise. In the literature, one on occasion gives as examples of empirical, universal assertions propositions of the type "All lemons are sour" (cf. Pap (2) p. 41). This proposition is similarly characterised by the fact that one can only decide whether it is of grammatical nature or not, after determining the linguistic usage. If for example one establishes that one will only call what is, among other things, sour, "lemon", the proposition mentioned can never be falsified and is consequently of grammatical nature. If by contrast one allows that which has all the properties of the sour lemon with the exception of the property "sour" to be regarded as "lemon" then the proposition "All lemons are sour" is an empirical proposition which can be falsified at any time by the discovery of a non-sour species of lemon. Pap also draws attention to this ambiguity in the passage mentioned.

11. *The theory of the grammatical proposition and the constitution of objects*

So far, our observations on the characteristic qualities of the concepts "grammar" and "grammatical proposition" already enable one to see that with these two concepts Wittgenstein implicitly throws up the whole question of the relationship between language and the world, between word usage and the structure of objects.

(1) First of all a close connection has revealed itself between the problem of grammatical propositions and *a priori propositions*. Like *a priori* propositions grammatical propositions refer to reality without being dependent on this reality in their truth value; both types of proposition are valid in strict universality and are consequently necessarily true; their respective opposites are, therefore, inconceivable or unthinkable. It is difficult to say whether Wittgenstein would designate all propositions called *a priori* in traditional philosophy as grammatical propositions, or not. But at any rate, on the basis of the Wittgensteinian determination of the concept, all grammatical propositions are *a priori*; a grammatical proposition does not depend for its truth value on any empirical fact, and it is thus in the ordinary sense of the word *a priori*. In connection with grammatical propositions Wittgenstein himself on occasion speaks of "*a priori* propositions" (P. I. 251). As in the case of the *a priori* proposition so also in the case of the grammatical proposition the basic problem is: How is it possible for a proposition to make assertions about objects without depending on these objects in their truth value? Since Wittgenstein's attempt to clarify this problem is often opposed to an essentialist conception of the *a priori* (say in part I of the F. M.), we shall begin by briefly describing this conception with respect to Wittgenstein's investigations.[16]

---

[16] In the following analyses we shall to a large extent draw on the *Remarks on the Foundations of Mathematics*, since the account there of the theory of the grammatical proposition, to be described, is far more detailed than that in the *Philosophical Investigations*.

An atomic conception of the function of language generally lies at the foundation of the essentialist theory; in addition, objects have an essence independent of language. One knows the properties of the essence through intuition, and since the objects are built up according to their essence, all properties of the essence necessarily belong to them too. Subsequently one gives definite names to the object one finds. One reads off the rules for the use of these names from the objects or their essence; one designates with a *single* name all those objects that partake of one and the same essence. In this way the use of names is laid down in the language. According to this theory, *a priori* propositions are assertions about essence and thus, at the same time, assertions about the objects sharing in the essence.

Hence their truth value can only be determined by reference to the essence.[17] Bachelors, for instance, are there before any naming takes place; one sees in them the essence of the bachelor, and one recognises that to this essence belong the properties, man and unmarried. The bachelor is then named with the name "bachelor" and one can now make an assertion about the essence of a bachelor, e. g. the proposition: "All bachelors are unmarried."

In opposition to this conception Wittgenstein's theory of the *a priori* starts from the language-game model. In this theory, the genesis of *a priori* propositions is to be conceived roughly as follows: the world confronts us only within language-games and is thus already articulated in detail and ordered according to the most diverse principles.[18] In drawing up a new language-game we spontaneously make new group-formations by gathering together objects with definite features or properties. At the same time we introduce a new name so that only the objects of the newly constituted group, i. e. only objects in which such and such features or

[17] The essentialist conception presented here is complicated in Husserl's case by the fact that a constitution theory is at the same time bound up with his theory of essences. In spite of this, what has been said is still true of Husserl too, when one recalls that although in Husserl's case a constitution theory follows, this constitution is entirely independent of language. With Husserl, language has no object-constituting function. Cf. Husserl (2) p. 363ff.

properties occur bear the name. The rules of usage governing the use of the name are therewith laid down. Objects not having these specific properties do not come within the newly formed group and are not called by the name in question. Now, the *a priori* proposition expresses those properties of an object which necessarily belong to it on the basis of the linguistic rules for its name; its truth value thus depends on the way in which we have gathered objects together and on the linguistic rules that are consequently fixed. An *a priori* proposition thus makes an assertion both about the objects and also about the linguistic rules for the name of the objects; for this reason it is a "grammatical proposition".

According to Wittgenstein's theory, then, the origin of the above mentioned proposition: "All bachelors are unmarried" is to be sought in the following fact: there is already a series of language-games with the linguistic signs: "man", "woman", "unmarried" etc. and objects corresponding to these signs. In drawing up the language-game with the word "bachelor", we now gather all those men who possess the attribute of being unmarried into one group, and these objects alone will be called "bachelors"; at the same time we ignore all the other properties of the objects. On the basis of

[18] Wittgenstein's turning away from a realist ontology, described in what follows, has also been noticed by other interpreters, for example Pole: "He (Wittgenstein) sometimes speaks of grammatical forms as 'a mode of representation'. Our grammar, it seems, is the form in which we represent the world; it is like a scheme for a map which for different purposes might be drawn according to different projections." (Pole (1) p. 36.) Pole, with the expression: "mode of representation" refers to P. I. 46: "One predicates of the thing what lies in the mode of representation." A similar turning away from Realism, probably not entirely independent of Wittgenstein, is to be found in Waismann. Its representation is particularly interesting insofar as he opposes himself *expressis verbis* to theories of language which, following the *Tractatus*, maintain a realist ontology. Waismann concludes his long discussion in the following way: "Reality, then, is not made up of facts... rather, if you want a simile, a fact is present, in much the same sense in which a character manifests itself in the face... Just as we have to interpret a face, so we have to interpret reality. The elements of such an interpretation are already present in language without our being aware of it—for instance, in such moulds as the notion of thinghood, of causality, of number, or again in the way we render colour, etc." (Waismann (5) p. 141.)

these linguistic rules every bachelor possesses the property of being an unmarried man. Thus, the *a priori* proposition: "All bachelors are unmarried" simultaneously makes an assertion about the objects, bachelors, and also about the linguistic rules for the use of the word "bachelor". In other words, one does not recognise a bachelor by seeing an essence; rather it is only those objects of which one notices that they possess the properties: man and unmarried, that are called bachelors.

So far, we have explained Wittgenstein's theory with reference to analytic propositions. Since the word "analytic" is generally used vaguely, a more precise determination of this concept is necessary to clarify the notion of the grammatical proposition. Present-day semantics is frequently based on a very strict concept of "analytic".[19] Quine characterises analytical judgements, for example, as propositions which can be transformed into logical truths by substituting synonymous expressions.[20]

Thus, one can, for example, transform the analytical judgement: "No bachelor is married" into a logically true proposition by substituting for "bachelor" the synonym "unmarried man".

According to this definition many grammatical propositions are certainly analytic, e.g. the proposition: "One plays patience by oneself". One only needs to substitute for "patience" the synonymous expression: "card-games that one plays by oneself" to get the proposition: "One plays card-games that one plays by oneself by oneself." And this is a logically true proposition. In addition, however, there are many grammatical propositions that are not analytic in the sense given, for instance: "There is no blueish-orange."[21]

Although Wittgenstein makes only a few assertions about synthetic *a priori* propositions, it is still clear that he admits such pro-

---

[19] In addition to the strict concept of "analytic", employed here, there is also another less strict concept, according to which all those propositions are analytic whose truth rests exclusively on the meaning of the signs used in them. Like many logical empiricists Ayer also employs this concept of "analytic". His definition, here quoted is: "I hold that a proposition is analytic, if it is true solely in virtue of the meaning of its constituent symbols." (Ayer (1) p. 16.)
[20] Quine (3) p. 22f.

positions in principle. Thus, on this point he differs quite essentially from many analytically orientated philosophers who, following the *Tractatus*, are unwilling to admit any synthetic *a priori* propositions at all.

Wittgenstein uses mathematical propositions as examples to explain the synthetic character of certain *a priori* judgements: "It might perhaps be said that the synthetic character of the propositions of mathematics appears most obviously in the unpredictable occurrence of the prime numbers. But their being synthetic (in this sense) does not make them any the less *a priori*. They could be said, I want to say, not to be got out of their concepts by means of some kind of analysis, but really to determine a concept by synthesis . . . ." (F. M. 125 f. similarly F. M. 75: "The proof exhibits a fact of synthesis to us.").

It still remains to be shown that Wittgenstein's attempted explanation of the *a priori* also applies to grammatical propositions of synthetic character.[22] For this purpose we choose the proposition: "one and the same surface is not blue and red at the same time." This proposition is generally recognised as a synthetic *a priori* proposition; nor can it be really analytically derived, of course, because there are no synonyms that verbally define English colour words (cf. the definition of the analytic judgement mentioned above).[23] We start from the question whether the truth value of this proposition is independent of the rules of use of the expressions occurring in it, and to this end we clarify how our ordinary language-

[21] The fact that grammatical assertions about colours cannot be analytic in Quine's sense is founded on the unanalysability of our ordinary colour words. No synonymous expression can be found, for example, for "orange" which would make the proposition: "There is no blueish-orange" into a logically true proposition. It is frequently admitted that with a strict concept of "analytical proposition" many *a priori* propositions are of synthetic nature. Cf. for instance the detailed discussion of *synthetic a priori* propositions in Pap (2) 193 ff., and Pap (3); also Rozeboom (1).

[22] For the following example cf. already T. 6.3751 and the discussions in *Some Remarks on Logical Form*. In this connection the commentary in Waismann (4) and Stenius (1) p. 42 ff.

[23] Waismann's attempt (Waismann (4)) to prove that such propositions about colours are tautologies was *probably* refuted by Pap (Pap (2) p. 196).

game with coloured surfaces functions.[24] In this language-game the coloured surfaces are ordered into definite groups so that all members of one particular group have a different name to that of the members of any other group. Thus, the members of one group are called e.g. "red surfaces" and the members of another group "blue surfaces" etc. What is called a red surface can only be explained ostensively; the individual groups cannot be verbally defined. By determining the rules of use of the expressions: "red surface" and "blue surface" the possibility of a red surface being at the same time a blue surface is excluded. (With a somewhat different determination of the expressions "red surface" and "blue surface" it would be quite possible for a red surface to be at the same time a blue surface. Think of changing surfaces, of mottled surfaces or surfaces with intermediate colours!). The possibility of the *a priori* proposition: "One and the same surface cannot be blue and red at the same time" is based on the fact that, in spontaneously drawing up the language-game with the expressions "red surface", "blue surface" etc. both the articulation and organisation of the colour phenomena is undertaken; the determination of the rules of use for the corresponding linguistic signs in accordance with the articulation is also undertaken. Thus, the quoted proposition asserts something about the object; on the other hand, in the last analysis it merely expresses the grammatical rules for the expressions "red surface", "blue surface" etc.[25] One sees from this example that Wittgenstein's theory may explain synthetic *a priori* judgements on the same principles as analytic judgements: language is not abstracted from objects; but drawing up a language-game creates a new articulation and organisation of the phenomena simultaneously with the intruduction of the new linguistic sign. In this way, a

[24] Schlick discussed this example in detail, probably in part agreement with Wittgenstein. (Cf. Schlick (3)). Schlick's account, however, starts too one-sidedly from linguistic rules without going more closely into the object-side of the matter. As a result the peculiar problem of constitution, which is of great importance in the Wittgensteinian theory of the language-game, escapes him. Only by taking account of the ontological constitution of the object can one follow Wittgenstein in saying, namely: "Grammar tells us what kind of object anything is" (P. I. 373.)

new group of objects is "constituted" in a language-game simultaneously with the new linguistic sign. The *a priori* proposition expresses this unity of linguistic sign and object by simultaneously making an assertion about the objects constituted in the language-game and giving expression to the rules of usage of the words signifying these objects.[26] For this reason, the *a priori* proposition is a "grammatical" proposition, i.e. a proposition describing the grammar of a language-game.

In explaining Wittgenstein's theory we have so far used the expressions: "group", "organisation" and "articulation" to des-

25 Pears (Pears (1) p. 112) in a long investigation into the status of the proposition: "Nothing can be red and green all over" draws attention to the fact that the dispute as to whether this proposition expresses a linguistic rule or a natural necessity rests on too sharp an emphasis on only one side of the complex relationship between language and the world: "... there is something very academic about the fierce debate whether the sentence owes its necessary truth to the way things behave or to the way words behave, to nature or to convention. It would seem more sensible to say that neither of these two answers is quite adequate; rather, that the sentence is necessarily true because the words 'red' and 'green' pick out two classes which just do not overlap. One could say that this lack of overlap is the result of the way in which the two words are used: but since the two words pick out two classes of things, one could say equally well that it is the result of the nature of things. Each of these two answers emphasises one aspect of the truth. But perhaps emphasis on either side is a mistake; perhaps the culprit is neither convention alone nor nature alone." Wittgenstein's theory circumvents these false emphases, by building on the *simultaneity* of the *introduction of linguistic signs* and *organisation into classes*. Lazerowitz has said that the various theories about logically necessary propositions have each emphasised or over-emphasised different aspects of the curious position of this type of proposition, intermediate between linguistic rule and empirical assertion. Cf. Lazerowitz (1) p. 254 ff.

26 When we here speak of the "constitution" of an object, this expression is *naturally not to be so understood as if the object were "produced" by man.* The intention is only to draw attention to the fact that the linguistic activity of man plays a definitive role in the building of classes, i.e. in organising phenomena into ordered wholes. Similar limitations apply here as those made by Waismann in connection with the question to what extent language is involved in the construction of facts. "I would not dream for a moment of saying that I *invent* them (facts); I might, however, be unable to perceive them if I had not certain moulds of comprehension ready at hand. These forms I borrow from language. *Language then contributes to the formation and participates in the constitution* of a fact; which, of course, does not mean that it *produces* the fact. (Waismann (5) p. 141.)

cribe the specifically synthetic achievement of human activity in drawing up a language-game. Wittgenstein himself frequently has recourse to the paradigm-model to illustrate this synthetic achievement.

In Wittgenstein's opinion the use of many expressions is bound to certain models and paradigmata. A good example of such paradigmatic use of signs is e. g. the gauging of measuring rods by re-reference to the original meter (cf. P. I. 50), or the use of particular, special colour words with the help of a colour chart (cf. P. I. 50). Thus, one associates a linguistic sign with a specific "model", say, "1 meter" or "Titian red" and then, by comparison with this model, one separates out certain objects that are similar to the model and to which one applies the linguistic sign concerned. Wittgenstein counts such patterns or models among the "tools of language" (cf. P. I. 16).

Now, the synthetic achievement of the paradigmatic use of signs is founded on the following fact: in introducing a new linguistic sign and binding it to a paradigm, one gives a regulative principle for the organisation of a new group. The paradigm is the model in accordance with which all those phenomena similar to the paradigm are organised into a group, upon which a single name is imposed. Thus, at the same time as a new linguistic sign is introduced, and with it the mode of use indicated by the paradigm, phenomena in reality are organised into groups.[27]

Now, Wittgenstein also transfers this schema to cases where the use of the sign has become independent of an external paradigm and is effected by means of "memory and association" alone (cf. P. I. 53). The use of our ordinary colour words, for instance, is of this kind. In drawing up the relevant sign usage one had admittedly made use of external paradigmata (for colour names can only be ostensively explained), but later the external models had been completely dropped since memory was able to take over the para-

---

[27] The fundamental espistemological problem in connection with the paradigmatic use of signs lies in the question how one is able to recognise the similarity between the paradigm and its copies; we shall come to discuss this problem later, however.

digmatic function by itself. That a paradigmatic sign usage is still always present in such cases can be seen from the fact that both in cases of doubt and also in teaching[28] colour words one falls back upon external paradigms.

Wittgenstein uses the paradigm schema not only in the case of expressions for simple qualities or quantities but also in the case of certain "figure-types" (F. M. 16), easily impressible forms like straight lines or circles, identity (F. M. 69), "pain behaviour" (P. I. 300) etc. In all these cases the use of the corresponding linguistic sign is bound to a model which originally existed in the external world but is afterwards preserved independently in "the memory of the linguistic community".

Linguistic usages effected by means of a paradigm, such as those just mentioned or cases like them, often constitute the foundation of the grammatical propositions which have a synthetic *a priori* character. Wittgenstein clearly recognised this connection and carried it through in terms of an example. For this purpose he chooses the proposition: "White is lighter than black", which can certainly be counted among synthetic *a priori* propositions, since it is neither dependent on experience in its truth value, nor analytically derivable ("white", "black", "lighter" are only definable ostensively). Wittgenstein now continues: "Whence comes the feeling that 'white is lighter than black' expresses something about the *essence* of the two colours?—But is this the right question to ask? For what do we mean by the 'essence' of white or black? We think perhaps of 'the inside', 'the constitution', but this surely makes no sense here. We also say e.g. 'It is part of white to be lighter than ......'. Is it not like this: the picture of a black and a white patch serves us *simultaneously* as a paradigm of what we un-

---

[28] In doing so the teacher produces the paradigm according to the dictates of his memory; not, however, according to the dictates of his own memory alone, for that can, of course, deceive him. (Cf. P. I. 56). Rather does the teacher follow the general linguistic usage which is continually controlling his own memory in everyday linguistic practice. The paradigm, one might metaphorically say, rests in the memory of all members of the linguistic community; it is, to slightly modify a locution of Wittgenstein's, laid down "in the archive of language" (cf. F. M. 78).

derstand by 'lighter' and 'darker' and as a paradigm for 'white' and for 'black'.* Now darkness 'is part of' black *inasmuch as* they are *both* represented by this patch. It is dark *by* being black.—But to put it better: it *is called* 'black' and hence in our language 'dark' too. That connection, a connection of the paradigms and the names, is set up in our language. And our proposition is non-temporal because it only expresses the connection of the words 'white', 'black' and 'lighter' with a paradigm." (F. M. 30 f.). All the essential moments of the Wittgensteinian explanation of *a priori* propositions are contained in this quotation.

According to Wittgenstein, the proposition mentioned expresses an "internal relation" i.e. a connection independent of all empirical circumstances; it is a non-temporal expression (F. M. 30) in contrast to the proposition: "This object is lighter than that one", a proposition which is perhaps still true at this moment but which can in the next moment be false, should the colour of one of the objects change (F. M. 30). On the other hand, it is impossible to think of a change in experience which could falsify the proposition: "White is lighter than black". Thus, in determining the use of the words "white", "black", "lighter" and "darker" with the help of paradigms, certain phenomena are simultaneously organised together into groups so that altogether four groups are constituted, of which two each have the same paradigm in common: all those things that are called "white" are thus also called "lighter" than all those things which, on the basis of the second paradigm, are called "black" and therewith also "darker". These relationships of homogeneity between the groups are constituted by means of the relevant linguistic sign, and thus belong to grammar; for this reason they can also be represented by the grammatical proposition: "All white things are lighter than black things" or: "White is lighter than black". But Wittgenstein's account is incomplete to the extent that the grammar of these linguistic signs is far more complicated than would appear to be the case in Wittgenstein. The sphere of application of the words: "lighter" and "darker" is much wider

* A black and a white square follow in the original text — Author.

than that of the words "white" and "black", so that the two paradigms in the case of "lighter" and "darker" can be applied to much
more extensive group-formations than in the case of "black" and
"white". Not all things that are lighter than certain other things are
as a result also white. This situation does not, of course, alter the
fact that the truth of the grammatical proposition: "White is lighter
than black" is founded on the paradigm-bound rules of usage of
the words "white", "black" and "lighter".

(2) Wittgenstein's theory of the *a priori* bears a strong resemblance
to the conventionalist and pragmatic theories of the *a priori* maintained e.g. by Poincaré, C. I. Lewis, Dingler and others.

Poincaré was the first to draw attention to the conventional
character of *a priori* propositions, for example, of the axioms of
Euclidean geometry.[29]

The following considerations led him to his conception: in the
case of a Euclidean interpretation of physical space, no result of an
empirical investigation is able to refute the interpretation. The
validity of Euclidean geometry will be repeatedly preserved by
introducing supplementary hypotheses which take account of the
empirical findings within a Euclidean theory. If it should, for instance, be shown that in astronomical triangulations one is continually arriving at angle measurements that deviate from 180° one
would not as a result abandom Euclidean geometry; one would
rather introduce physical hypotheses (say that of a distorting force)
to explain this deviation. The question whether physical space has
a Euclidean or a non-Euclidean structure thus becomes a question
that cannot be decided by empirical investigation but only by an
convention; one chooses one or more possible geometries without
making any assertions about their objective validity. The choice of
Euclidean geometry will be suggested, for instance, by its greater
simplicity.

This would mean for the theory of the *a priori* that *a priori* propositions, e.g. Euclidean axioms, are valid by "convention". Their

---

[29] For the following account cf. Poincaré (1) chaps. III and V.

necessity ultimately rests on the fact that they are established by "fiat" and once this is done one does not depart from them.

For this reason Poincaré goes so far as actually to deny to geometrical axioms the status of synthetic *a priori* judgements in general: "Geometrical axioms are thus neither synthetic *a priori* judgements nor experimental facts. They are determinations based on agreement; among all possible determinations our choice is guided by experimental facts; but it remains free and is only limited by the necessity of avoiding any contradiction."[30]

A similar conception of the *a priori* is to be found in C. I. Lewis,[31] who significantly calls his theory "conceptual pragmatism". The human spirit, in a free act, draws up the *a priori* structures of its understanding of reality and holds firm to them because of their pragmatic fruitfulness. These structures also have the character of "fiat" and cannot be refuted by experience because in a way they make experience possible in the first place.

Already in the Moore Lectures Wittgenstein engages in reflections that appear to follow directly from Poincaré and Lewis. In the discussion of mathematical propositions, which he construes as "part of grammar" (in Wittgenstein's sense), he comes to speak about the peculiar status of Euclidean propositions as rules: ". . . . . what Euclid's proposition 'The three angles of a triangle are equal to two right angles' asserts is 'if by measurement you get any result for the sum of the three angles other than 180°, *you are going to say that you have made a mistake*." (M. L. II p. 303). In other words, one holds firm to Euclidean propositions, as to a standard, under all

[30] Poincaré (1) p. 51.
[31] Cf. Lewis (1): "It is given experience, brute fact, the *a posteriori* element in knowledge which the mind must accept willy-nilly. The *a priori* represents an attitude in some sense freely taken, a stipulation of the mind itself, and a stipulation which might be made in some way other if it suited our bent or need... Mind contributes to experience the element of order, of classification, categories and definition. Without such, experience would be unintelligible. Our knowledge of the validity of these is simply consciousness of our own fundamental ways of acting and our own intellectual intent. Without this element knowledge is impossible, and it is here that whatever truths are necessary and independent of experience must be found." (p. 286 and 293.) Also Lewis (2) p. 213.

circumstances, and one interprets empirical propositions in accordance with them. These *a priori* propositions thus have a certain "normative" character; they express a standard separate from all experience because by its means one judges experience in the first place.

Wittgenstein also adheres to this conception of the *a priori* in the late work. He there introduces it into his theory of language and explains grammatical propositions with the help of language-games. One could say in general that Wittgenstein's attempt at explaining the *a priori* proposition is built on the free activity of human beings in drawing up a language-game; according to him, the possibility of *a priori* propositions rests ultimately on the fact that linguistic rules are not derived from objects but that linguistic signs are *spontaneously* introduced by man and this simultaneously completes the constitution of an object.

Wittgenstein several times draws attention to this spontaneous character in the drawing up of a language-game, for instance in the *Philosophical Investigations*: "Something new (spontaneous, 'specific') is always a language-game" (P. I. p. 224), similarly in the *Foundations of Mathematics*: "'We decide on a new language-game.' 'We decide *spontaneously*' (I should like to say) 'on a new language-game.'" (F. M. 120). In what follows we shall take up Wittgenstein's manner of speaking and, borrowing a Kantian term, speak simply of the "spontaneity" of man in drawing up a language-game.

If, in the creation of a language-game, the rules of language are not read off from the objects but are drawn up spontaneously, i.e. somehow freely and without determination, the question arises to what extent this is "arbitrary" or merely a matter of convention. In conventionalism, particularly in its extreme forms, the achievement of human beings in drawing up a theory or a linguistic system is sometimes described as if it depended merely on convention what rules were chosen for the construction of the theory. The question now is: whether Wittgenstein's theory of language is "conventionalist" in this sense.[32] A series of utterances in Wittgenstein would seem to point in this direction, for instance: "...... And this language like any other is founded on convention." (P. I. 355); similarly: "I say, however, if you talk about *essence*—, you are merely noting a convention." (F. M. 23). But these remarks are in need of closer analysis.

Wittgenstein had already taken up the problem of conventionalism in the Moore Lectures in connection with the question whether the rules of grammar are arbitrary or not. He there decides in favour of an intermediate solution, in which grammatical rules are in one respect arbitrary, but in another respect not. Wittgenstein distinguishes two cases:

(a) A grammatical rule is not arbitrary, insofar as one must commit oneself to it for it to be a rule at all. If, for example, one introduces a name for a specific object, then this only has sense if this name is used later as well to signify this object. Thus, if one has introduced a particular rule, one is no longer free, so to say, with respect to it. Introducing a rule has consequences, as Wittgenstein expresses himself: "...... if a word which I use is to have meaning, I must 'commit myself' by its use. .... If I commit myself, that means that if I use, e.g. 'green' in this case, I have to use it in others .... If you commit yourself, there are consequences." (M. L. I. p. 7).

(b) Grammatical rules are *established* rules in the language, i.e. we not only make rules, but we also find rules already in our language, rules which we follow. Wittgenstein explains this in terms of the following example: "........ if we followed a rule according to which 'hate' was an intransitive verb, this rule would be arbitrary, whereas if we use it in the sense in which we do use it, then the rule we are following is not arbitrary." (M. L. II p. 299).

---

[32] Dummett in particular has drawn attention to the conventionalist basis of the Wittgensteinian investigations into the foundations of mathematics. The distinctiveness of Wittgenstein's conventionalism in contrast, say, to the conventionalism of the logical positivists consists, according to Dummett, in the fact that Wittgenstein construes every necessary judgement as the direct expression of a linguistic convention, an expression, in other words, not mediated by inference: "Wittgenstein goes in for a full-blooded conventionalism; for him the logical necessity of any statement is always the *direct* expression of a linguistic convention. That a given statement is necessary consists in our having expressly decided to treat that very statement as unassailable; it cannot rest on our having adopted certain other conventions which are found to involve our treating it so." (Dummett (1) p. 329.)

In accordance with this distinction he now seeks to explain in what sense grammatical rules are *arbitrary*. In his opinion they are arbitrary insofar as one cannot "justify" a grammatical rule, i.e. one cannot give any reasons for following precisely this rule and not some other rule. It is not easy to find a satisfactory interpretation from the brief suggestions that Wittgenstein makes on this point. Moore himself admits to not having quite clearly understood Wittgenstein's reason for his assertion. But Wittgenstein probably wished to express something like the following: If one wished to justify a particular grammatical rule, in other words, to give reasons why exactly one followed it, this justification would have to be effected by means of a description of reality, thus, by means of a series of empirical propositions produced by way of example. But such a justification is not possible since one already presupposes and follows the rules of grammar to describe reality. (Cf. M. L. II p. 299 ff.).

This idea in the Moore Lectures remains essentially unchanged in the *Investigations* and in the *Remarks on the Foundations of Mathematics*: now, as before, Wittgenstein seeks an intermediate solution so that the rules for the use of a word are partly arbitrary and partly not arbitrary. However in the late work he penetrates more deeply into the connections which are of importance in the question about the free spontaneity of a language-game.

So as to clarify these connections he repeatedly starts from a very simple model-case in which the moment of *arbitrariness* comes strongly into the foreground: the language-game of measuring lengths. The question is what role do those propositions play which express the determination of the measuring system e.g. the proposition: "12 ins. = 1 foot" (cf. F. M. 159). To begin with, this proposition is not an empirical proposition; it rather expresses a convention about the use of the words: "inch" and "foot". However, it is closely connected with certain very general empirical facts; there are, for example, objects upon which linear measurements can be carried out; the measuring rods are relatively rigid etc. Similarly the proposition is most intimately interwoven with our technique of linear measurement, in other words, is founded on certain psychological and sociological data etc. Wittgenstein says: "The proposition *is grounded in* a technique. And, if you like also in the physical and psychological facts that make the technique *possible*. But it doesn't follow that its sense is to express these conditions. The opposite of that proposition, "twelve inches = one foot" does not say that rulers are not rigid enough or that we don't all count and calculate in the same way. The proposition has the typical (but that doesn't mean *simple*) rôle of a rule." (F. M. 159,1 and 2). Now, this rule is arbitrary insofar as there are no decisive reasons why we follow precisely it and not some other rule, say the rule: "12 inches = 2 feet". However, to the extent that it both depends on certain, very general natural facts and is grounded in a particular technique and, therewith, in a particular practice of man, to this extent it is not arbitrary.

The linear measuring language-game with inches and feet is thus partly arbitrary and accordingly drawn up in free spontaneity, while, on the other hand, it is conditioned in many ways by the facts of nature and by facts about human beings, all of which limit our spontaneity.

Although the moment of convention and arbitrariness is particularly prominent in this example, nonetheless certain fundamental structures can be seen which are also valid for other language-games, e.g. that with the colour words discussed above in which the grammatical proposition: "A surface cannot be blue and red at the same time" occurred. This proposition results from the linguistic rules for the use of the expressions "red surface" and "blue surface" and thus expresses certain rules of this language-game. This language-game is, on the one hand, intimately connected with certain physical and psychological facts; if, for example, we didn't have *our mode* of colour perception this language-game would never have been drawn up. On the other hand, however, one can imagine language-games which articulated and linguistically formulated the same colour phenomena in an entirely different manner.

Waismann tried to draw up such language-games: in English one normally expresses colour phenomena with the help of adjectives. This conditions an attributive-qualitative conception;

colours are "qualities" which do not exist in themselves but can only inhere in independent things. But that is not the only possibility of linguistic expression. In German one makes use, though not so frequently, of verbs to express colour phenomena in language: "*grünen*" (to green, to become or grow green), "*blauen*" (to blue, to become or grow blue), (the latter, "*blauen*", being however, mostly poetic) etc. Waismann goes on from this linguistic possibility: "There are languages such as Russian, German, Italian, which render colour by means of verbs. If we were to imitate this usage in English by allowing some such form as 'The sky blues', we should come face to face with the question, do I mean the same fact when I say 'The sky blues' as when I say 'The sky is blue'? I don't think so. We say 'The sun shines', 'Jewels glitter', 'The river shimmers', 'Windows gleam', 'Stars twinkle' etc.; that is, in the case of phenomena of lustre we make use of a verbal mode of expression. Now, in rendering colour phenomena by verbs we assimilate them more closely to the phenomena of lustre; and in doing so we alter not only our manner of speaking but our entire way of apprehending colour. We *see* the blue differently now—a hint that language affects our whole mode of apprehension. In the word 'blueing' we are clearly aware of an active, verbal element. On that account 'being blue' is not quite equivalent to 'blueing', since it lacks what is peculiar to the verbal mode of expression. The sky which 'blues' is seen as something which continually brings forth blueness—it radiates blueness, so to speak; blue does not inhere in it as a mere quality, rather is it felt as the vital pulse of the sky . . . . . ." If, in this way, one were to invent a language in which all colour phenomena were exclusively expressed by means of verbs, it appears questionable whether there would be any equivalent in this language for the concept, occurring in our language, of coloured surfaces which can have only one specific colour. This concept is most intimately connected with the attributive conception of colour. For this reason it is questionable whether there would be an equivalent for our grammatical proposition: "One and the same surface is not blue and red at the same time". It is, of course, not easy to imagine the kinds of experience that would correspond to these linguistic forms of expression. Waismann tries to clarify these ways of experiencing for himself by comparison with the impressionistic way of seeing: "perhaps it may help you to liken this mode of expression to the impressionist way of painting which is at bottom a new way of seeing: the impressionist sees in colour an immediate manifestation of reality, a free agent no longer bound up with things."[33]

It is possible within the framework of physical and psychological facts, then, to think out language-games other than those that actually occur in our language. The facts do not oblige the adoption of this or that language-game; they rather leave a definite latitude on any given occasion, within the limits of which the person can "freely" draw up a language-game. It is also for this reason that the rules of a language-game cannot be read off from reality. It is true, they are closely connected with certain facts, but beyond this they are the product of a free spontaneity.

Summing up what has been said so far, the general picture of the relationship between arbitrariness and non-arbitrariness in the drawing up of a language-game is as follows: our language-games are *arbitrary* insofar as the rules constituting them, although drawn up in the closest connection with certain facts of nature, do not result from these facts *by necessity*. For this reason too one cannot say that the rules of a language-game are true or false, that a language-game is right or wrong in the sense that an empirical assertion is.

It is in this way that we are to understand a quotation from the *Foundations of Mathematics* where Wittgenstein makes the following remark about the language-game with numbers and about our language in general: "Then do you want to say that 'being true' means: being usable (or useful) ?'—No, not that; but that it can't be said of the series of natural numbers—any more than of our language—that it is true, but: that it is usable, and, above all, *it is used*." (F. M. 4). Here Wittgenstein is defending himself against the objection of a pragmatic reduction of the concept of truth. This would amount to the truth of a proposition being constituted by

[33] Waismann (5) p. 138.

its usefulness for practical purposes. In contrast to this, Wittgenstein does not touch the normal concept of truth as propositional truth. For him the truth of a proposition does not consist in its usefulness. But he does refuse to transfer this normal concept of truth to language as a whole or to a constituent system of language. Language-games for him are neither true nor false, for they are somehow prior to the truth and falsity of the propositions that can only be constructed in them and by their means. The relation between a language-game and the propositions possible in it is to be conceived, according to Wittgenstein, roughly like the relation between a particular method of measurement and the measurements themselves. (Cf. F. M. 45).

Even though language-games cannot be true or false that does not exclude the possibility of there being certain other criteria for evaluating a language-game. One such criterion is its usefulness; particular language-games fulfill a particular purpose better than certain other language-games. Wittgenstein thus admits pragmatic criteria for language-games as a whole. But in the case of many language-games it is not possible to give any reasons at all for explaining why exactly this language-game is used and not another. For Wittgenstein such language-games justify themselves simply because they are used i.e. they are recognised as binding and are continually being used by the linguistic community concerned. According to Wittgenstein, in such cases, it is a mistake "to look for an explanation where we ought to look at what happens as a 'proto-phenomenon'. That is, where we ought to have said: *'this language-game is played.'*" (P. I. 654).[34]

[34] This conception of Wittgenstein's leads to the consequence that, in cases where entirely different language-games are played, agreement and dispute are no longer possible. Many commentators regard this abolition of discourse between supporters of entirely different language-games as one of greatest deficiencies of Wittgenstein's theory of language. Thus for example Pole (1): "The essence of rational discourse is the search for agreement. Wittgenstein's failure to take account of it, I suggest, prejudices his whole picture of language. Indeed he sees agreement in certain fundamental tendencies — existing conformity — as the basis of discourse, without which it would be impossible; but he fails to see it as an end, as something dynamic." (p. 59.)

In many respects, however, we are *bound* when we draw up a language-game:

(a) Even if the facts of nature leave us a certain latitude, our language-games must still to a certain extent be drawn up conformably to these natural facts; they are bound to certain facts of nature. If these natural facts were other than they are "this would make our normal language-games lose their point." (P. I. 142). The expression "point" occurs very frequently in Wittgenstein in connections like: the point of a language-game, the point of a word, the point of a rule, etc. (e.g. P. I. 62; F. M. 8, 98 etc). In these contexts "point" means something like: salient point, decisive moment, purpose, sense. This would mean for the passage quoted above that our ordinary language-games would loose their purpose and sense if the facts of nature were different.

In another passage Wittgenstein clearly expresses this dual aspect of boundedness and freedom in the drawing up of a language or language-game: "To invent a language could mean to invent an instrument for a particular purpose on the basis of the laws of nature (or consistently with them); but it also has the other sense, analogous to that in which we speak of the invention of a game." (P. I. 492). The analogy with the invention of a game is perhaps intended to suggest the freedom with which the rules are established.

(b) The rules of our language-game are not taken directly from experience but they derive their sense in the first place from experience: "A rule *qua* rule is detached, it stands as it were alone in its glory: although what gives it importance is the facts of daily experience." (F. M. 160).

(c) The fact that a language-game has rules—rules which are rules, however, only insofar as they are recognised and followed—already constitutes a limitation of spontaneity in drawing up a language-game. A language-game is only established under general consent, recognition and agreement.[35]

Wittgenstein speaks in this way, for example, about the language-game with our colour words: "If there did not exist an agreement about what we call 'red' etc. etc. language would stop." (F. M. 96).

Similarly also in the *Philosophical Investigations* : "There is in general complete agreement in the judgements of colours made by those who have been diagnosed normal. This characterises the concept of a judgement of colour." (P. I. p. 227). That naturally means that a rule, once laid down, repeatedly has consequences. Wittgenstein shows this by the following example: "But isn't a rule something arbitrary? Something that I *lay down*? And could I lay it down that the multiplication 18×15 shall not yield 270?—Why not? But then it just hasn't taken place according to the rule which I first laid down, and whose use I have practised." (F. M. 183.)

(d) This quotation points to a final limitation which results from the fact that in drawing up a language-game one finds a wealth of other already existent language-games that simply cannot be ignored. At the same time certain forms of life are given with these language-games, so that it is not every new language-game which is significant and purposeful within our language and form of life. In a passage which is particularly illuminating in this connection Wittgenstein defends himself against the objection that the continuation of a series, (or a particular language-game) once begun is purely arbitrary: "'Then according to you (so runs the objection) everybody could continue the series as he likes; and so infer *any*how!'

---

[35] The boundedness of human activity to general convention in drawing up a language-game, which is expressed here, was formulated by Wittgenstein on one occasion in the following way: "I say, however: if you talk about *essence* —, you are merely noting a convention. But here one would like to retort: there is no greater difference than that between a proposition about the depth of the essence and one about — a mere convention. But what if I reply: to the *depth* that we see in the essence there corresponds the deep need for the convention." (F. M. 23). Pole comments on this passage as follows: "It is we who adopt the convention; but in so doing we may be deeply committed to it too. We feel it or see it as something inward and inescapable. Wittgenstein says that mathematics creates essences; and an essence too, is normally thought of as an inward thing, as something deep. 'How is that to be squared with conventionalism?' it may be asked. That feeling, so Wittgenstein claims, expresses rather the depth of our need for the convention. It is built into the structure of our lives; and indeed we have already seen how the language we use always operates in a wider setting, how it reflects our different interests and needs." (Pole (1) p. 47f.)

In that case we shan't call it 'continuing the series' and also presumably not 'inference'. And thinking and inferring (like counting) is, of course, bounded for us, not by an arbitrary definition, but by natural limits corresponding to the body of what can be called the rôle of thinking and inferring in our life." (F. M. 34).

(3) By defining the "grammatical proposition" as a proposition whose truth value depends only on the linguistic rules of a language-game, not on empirical data, Wittgenstein offers a new theory of *a priori* propositions. A comparison of this theory with the most important traditional views clearly shows that the language-game model has made an entirely new outlook possible in this connection too.

(a) The *empirical theory* attempts to derive *a priori* propositions from experience; admittedly, these propositions are not ordinary empirical propositions, but they are still very general and are felt to be necessary on the basis of associative habituation.—It is clear from our discussions above that Wittgenstein did not share the empirical point of view. The rules of our language-games from which grammatical propositions are derived, are drawn up spontaneously; they are by no means empirical propositions nor are they to be established through experience. It is even, in a way, the other way round: an articulation and ordering of objects is drawn up in our language-games, and it is this which makes empirical propositions first possible. Wittgenstein refers to this point although he does not express it entirely unambiguously. He says: "The limit of the empirical—is *concept-formation*". (F. M. 121 where "concept-formation" is naturally to be understood as the spontaneous drawing up of a new sign or linguistic sign-usage.) Later he explains this as follows: "Yes: it is as if the formation of a concept guided our experience into particular channels, so that one experience is now seen together with another one in a new way." (F. M. 123). Wittgenstein expresses himself with particular clarity on this question when he wishes to clarify the relation of mathematical language-games to experience; for instance: "'It is interesting to know *how many* vibrations this note has!' But it took arithmetic to teach you this question. It taught you to see this kind of fact." (F. M. 173). Similarly: "'To be practical, mathematics must tell us facts.'—But do these facts have to be the *mathematical* fact?—But why should not mathematics, instead of 'teaching us facts', create the forms of what we call facts?" (F. M. 173).

In spite of this, Wittgenstein gives a place to experience in his theory of the *a priori*. Even though "grammatical propositions" are not empirical propositions the linguistic rules expressed by the grammatical propositions are drawn up in close connection with certain natural facts, forms of life and other data. Thus, ultimately the grammatical proposition is naturally, in the end, somewhere connected with "experience"; but it never brings an experience *to expression* and is, therefore, in no way empirically verifiable.

(b) We have already spoken in detail about the differences between Wittgenstein's theory of the *a priori* and the conception in *essentialism*, which interprets *a priori* propositions as assertions about essential structures. Wittgenstein rejects the essentialist theory in general. That does not, however, mean that he would no longer speak of "essence", "essential" and "essential context" etc. On the contrary: he admits this locution and thus remains in agreement with general linguistic usage where expressions like "the essence of the matter", of course, occur. Essentialism equates essence with a special object which exists independently of language and things; in contrast to this conception, essence for Wittgenstein is constituted *only* in language and in the individual language-games with the corresponding linguistic signs, rules of usage and objects: "*Essence* is expressed by grammar" (P. I. 371). According to Wittgenstein's theory, essence is not only *expressed* in grammar, but also constituted in grammar. This is what Wittgenstein says in the *Foundations of Mathematics* with reference to a mathematical proof: "The proof doesn't *explore* the essence of the two figures, but it does express what I am going to count as belonging to the essence of the figures from now on.—I deposit what belongs to the essence among the paradigms of language. The mathematician creates *essence*. (F. M. 12, No. 32).[36] What is here asserted of the achievement of a proof and of the work of the mathematician in general in constituting essence, can in the same way be asserted of the language-games in our ordinary language: in the spontaneous drawing up of a language-game, *one* process both introduces a new linguistic rule with a particular linguistic sign and also organises the phenomena, thus creating the essence. There is an illuminating passage in the *Investigations* on the indissoluble connection between word usage and the constitution of objects: "One ought to ask, not what images are or what happens when one imagines anything, but how the word 'imagination' is used. But that does not mean that I want to talk only about words. For the question as to the nature of the imagination is as much about the word 'imagination' as my question is" (P. I. 370).

(c) One finds certain parallels with Wittgenstein's interpretation of the *a priori* in Kant's solution of the problem.[37] Both theories use human spontaneity to explain the *a priori* nature of certain propositions. For Kant our reason draws up the *a priori* laws of things in a spontaneous act. Since things thus accommodate themselves to our own *a priori* projection, it is possible for *a priori* propositions both to make assertions about things and yet at the same time to depend on our thought for their truth value. In Wittgenstein's theory this moment of spontaneity means that man

[36] The conception, expressed here, of the constitution of essences in mathematics is one that is repeatedly being emphasised by Wittgenstein, for instance F. M. 47: "The mathematician is an inventor, not a discoverer." F. M. 167: "What is done here is not to improve bad mathematics, but to create a new bit of mathematics." F. M. 194: "Mathematics forms a network of norms." Cf. Dummett's paper on the F. M.: "Wittgenstein adopts a version (as we shall see, an extreme version) of constructivism; for him it is the essence of a mathematical statement that it is asserted as the conclusion of a *proof*, whereas I suppose that for a Platonist a being who had *direct* apprehension of mathematical truth, not mediated by inferences, would not be a complete absurdity." (Dummett (1) p. 324.)

[37] Bernays, in his review of the *Remarks on the Foundations of Mathematics* has also drawn attention to the connections between Wittgenstein and Kant: "A certain dependence on Kant's view also exists in Wittgenstein's conception that mathematics determines the character, 'creates the forms of what we call facts'. In this sense, Wittgenstein is expressly opposed to the view that the propositions of mathematics have the function of empirical propositions." (p. 3.)

creates a new linguistic system in language by undertaking a new articulation of the world or a new organisation of objects, while drawing up a new mode of usage for certain linguistic signs.

There is also a second point of agreement between the two theories. Both in Kant and Wittgenstein there is, in addition to the spontaneous projection, a moment of receptivity that sets limits to the spontaneity. In Kant these limits are given by the thing in itself and the immutable character of our knowing mind. In Wittgenstein spontaneity is limited by the fact that certain facts of nature are presented to us, that we already find a language in existence, and that we are bound to certain forms of life.

The connection existing here between Kant and Wittgenstein becomes clearer if we draw on the linguistic philosophy of E. Cassirer, where Kant's fundamental thought is fruitfully applied to a philosophy of language and which stands, as it were, between Kant and Wittgenstein.

First of all, Cassirer takes over from Kant the idea of the "Copernican Revolution", which he describes in the following way: "The 'intellectual revolution' carried out by Kant within theoretical philosophy, rests on the fundamental idea that the relation, generally assumed in the past to exist between knowledge and its object, was in need of a radical change. Instead of starting from the object as the known and given, it is necessary to begin with the law of knowledge, as the only thing truly accessible and primarily assured. Instead of determining the most general properties of being in the sense of an ontological metaphysic, it is necessary that, through the analysis of understanding, the basic form of the *judgement*, as condition of the *postulatability* of objectivity, should be ascertained and determined in all its many ramifications."[38] Cassirer now transfers this fundamental idea of critical philosophy to all the spheres of culture: "In addition to the function of pure knowledge, it is also true of the functions of linguistic thought, religious-mythical thought, and the artistic perception that they be conceived in such a way that it becomes clear how in them is achieved not so much

---

[38] Cassirer (1) Part I. p. 9.

a particular forming *of* the world, as a particular forming *to* the
world, to an objective sense-context and to an objective perceptual
whole. The critique of reason thus becomes a critique of culture.
It seeks to understand how the whole content of culture—to the
extent that it is more than just particular content—presupposes an
original act of mind."[39] Accordingly, *language* also springs from an
"original act of mind", in which a particular "forming to the world"
is achieved. Language is not a mere picturing of what is perceived
through the senses. Rather does "the process of language building"
show "how the chaos of immediate impressions is cleared and
articulated for us by our 'naming' it and thereby penetrating it
with the function of linguistic thought and linguistic expression
. . . . In this way language becomes a fundamental intellectual
means of progressing from the world of mere feeling to the world
of perception and imagination."[40] In another passage Cassirer
works out in detail this fundamental idea of the function of language: "The words of language are not so much the representation
of the fixed particularities of the world of nature and thought as the
indication of the directions and lines of determination . . . . . . Hence,
if it has been asserted of concepts in general that the principle of
their construction is to be characterised not so much as a principle
of *abstraction* as a principle of *selection*—then this is particularly true
of the form of linguistic concept building. Here, it is not the case
that certain existent differences of consciousness given in feeling or
thought are simply fixed and furnished with a particular phonetic
sign, with a mark, as it were; rather are the boundary lines themselves first drawn within the totality of consciousness."[41] Still more
clearly: "Language never simply follows the features of impressions and ideas; it rather confronts them with independent action:
by virtue of this attitude it first differentiates, chooses, sets and
creates certain centres and focal points of objective perception
itself."[42] In the case of Cassirer's linguistic philosophy we are con-

[39] Cassirer (1) Part I. p. 11.
[40] Cassirer (1) Part I. p. 20.
[41] Cassirer (1) Part I. p. 256.
[42] Cassirer (1) Part I. p. 273.

cerned with a theory of language which closely follows Kant's theory of knowledge, from which it borrows the object-constituting, synthesising effect of man's mind; it transfers this to the whole of language.

But it is also easy to see how Cassirer's linguistic philosophy, drawn up in the spirit of Kant, agrees to a large extent with Wittgenstein's theory. The accounts of the organising, ordering and object-constituting function of language given by Cassirer, could also be applied without any further difficulty to spontaneity in the drawing up of a language-game in Wittgenstein's sense.

Unfortunately, Cassirer did not draw the consequences of his theory for *a priori* judgements (or at any rate only by hints). They would have made the connection with Wittgenstein still clearer. What Kant proved in connection with the *a priori* propositions of mathematics and the natural sciences applies to all the *a priori* propositions in Cassirer's and Wittgenstein's theory of language: in their truth value and unconditional necessity they rest on an object-constituting effect of human thought. This reveals itself both in the building of mathematical and scientific theories and also in the spontaneous creation of the linguistic signs of language-games.

(4) The confrontation of the Kantian and Wittgensteinian interpretation of *a priori* propositions permits one to see that Wittgenstein's conception can only be understood on the basis of a quite specific theory of language. This theory which construes the creation of language both as a spontaneous and an object-constituting achievement of man, bears a strong resemblance to the conception maintained in *modern linguistics* that our language undertakes an articulation of the world or a formation of the world.[43] This conception is most clearly stated in L. Weisgerber whose theory we shall briefly compare with Wittgenstein's.

Weisgerber starts from the fact that individual languages not only have different words for things, but that deposited in the

---

[43] For this conception cf. the discussion in Black (10) of the so-called "Sapir-Whorf Hypothesis", where the philosophical implications are discussed in detail. There are also further references. For Whorf's theory cf. Whorf (1).

different words are entirely different ways of looking at things; that the words contain a specific interpretation of the world.

In order to explain this fact he introduces the concept of "mental object" which lies between objective reality and the phonetic form of words and represents the product of the linguistic transformation of reality. There are for instance, various plants, in objective reality; but our division of plants into herbs, weeds, shrubs and vegetables etc. is a specific product of our mother-tongue, which by no means exists in other languages.* Our mother tongue organises particular phenomena of the plant-world into groups by means of the words "herbs", "weeds" etc. and in this way creates the "mental objects", weeds, herbs, shrubs etc. Thus, between objective reality and the phonetic form of words there is an intermediate strata of objects that only exist in language so to speak. On the basis of this conception of the formative power of language Weisgerber also arrives at a critical position respecting a naive interpretation of naming: "*Naming* appears to the naive consciousness as a simple adding of a phonetic designation to a 'thing', to an 'object' in the external world: this structure here in my hand:—I name it *rose*. But is it such a simple matter to bind a linguistic element to an object, to bind it to a thing? . . . . . . Obviously not, for with *rose* I by no means refer to what is present before my eyes in its uniqueness; I am not giving this structure a *proper-name*, but I express it with one *word*, applicable with as much justification to thousands and millions of other individual structures, one word whose function is certainly not exhausted by saying that it, as 'phonetic mark', is somehow stuck on to a 'thing'".[44] Thus, Weisgerber also thinks that naming is not performed in the way assumed by the atomic model of language; it is not simply the add-

---

* The exact reproduction of the German classification of plants cannot be given in English without some circumlocution. The deviation between the original German and the English translation is of no philosophical importance in this passage, though the difficulty in reproducing the German classification in English does illustrate the philosophical point being made by the author. (D. E. W.)

[44] Weisgerber (1), I p. 50f.

ing of a word to an already tailor-made object. On the contrary, all acts of naming contain "extensive mental transformations" i. e. they organise groups into new unities, establish connections and perform acts of articulation etc.

Weisgerber thus sees in language a mental power at work, in which we not only absorb but also order and form: "What linguistic research is recognising more and more clearly is nothing other than the fact that human language is fundamentally a power, by means of which man opens up an approach to the world. Nor can this approach be understood as a simple registering of the world, but only as an *appropriation of the world within the framework of human possibilities*, in other words, fundamentally a transformation of being into human consciousness, as a linguistic opening-up of the world . . . . . . Everything contained in this 'humanisation' may remain indeterminate; the locutions, *transform*, *open up*, *change* being, hint at the possible lines of approach."[45]

The parallels between Wittgenstein's conception of language and that of Weisgerber can be seen without difficulty. There is one difference however: Weisgerber presupposes an "external world", an "objective existence" which we appropriate to ourselves in a linguistic transformation: "This 'external world' appears throughout as a fixed presupposition of what is linguistic, as approach and as end; and in this sense, linguistic activity reckons with it throughout as something given in advance, something already existing independently of language."[46] In Wittgenstein also, this "objective being" is only linguistically accessible i. e. only given and attainable in language-games. "There are", so to say, only objective objects of reality in the language-game with the corresponding linguistic signs: "objective object", "reality" etc.

Naturally, this is a critical point in Wittgenstein's theory of language. Wittgenstein's analyses always start at a particular linguistic level i. e. at a level of linguistic development in which certain language-games and, hence, certain spheres of objects already

[45] Weisgerber (1) II p. 33.
[46] Cf. Weisgerber (1), I p. 44, 45, 49.

exist. But that immediately raises the question of the first language-game. How is the relation between linguistic "forming"
and linguistic "stuff" to be conceived in the first language-game,
so that something like: object or: something, is made clear to
man?[47]

This is a problem that every constitution theory is confronted
with. These theories start at a certain level of object-articulation
and from this position they explain the relation of spontaneity and
receptivity. They then transfer the results obtained to the lowest
level and thus eventually arrive at a completely unarticulated "primitive matter", where one can no longer speak even of objects or of
something.[48]

Even Wittgenstein does not satisfactorily solve this problem.
It is true that he speaks of the facts of nature and of the physiological data upon which all drawing up of language-games must rest,
but they too, of course, are only revealed linguistically.

One probably has to assume that Wittgenstein presupposed a
certain strata of data pre-existing language, but that he held it for
impossible to determine these data from our linguistic level.[49]

The critique of Wittgenstein's theory of language can start at
another point: i.e. Wittgenstein's fundamental idea that simultaneously with the introduction of a new sign usage, man undertakes
a new organisation of objects into groups, according to certain
points of view or paradigms. It is precisely here that there is a
decisive philosophical problem: organising objects into groups

[47] Pole also asserts that one can speak in a certain sense of "linguistic form"
and "linguistic content" in Wittgenstein: "At least this much is clear, first that
Wittgenstein distinguishes in some sense between the structural apparatus and
the content of language." (Pole (1) p. 37.)

[48] The problem of this primitive matter is posed in Kant, for instance, with
the question about affection; in Husserl with the introduction of the "sensual
hulé". (Cf. Husserl (2) p. 207 ff.)

[49] Pole (1) has discussed the problem of these data in Wittgenstein. He is
opposed to construing organisation into groups according to a paradigm as a
choice from what is given. According to Pole, what is given consists of an
infinite multiplicity of possible forms; and to choose from an infinite multiplicity of possibilities means to create the forms. Cf. Pole (1) p. 43 ff.

according to specific points of view presupposes that one can recognise the identical moments in these objects; but the question,
how this knowledge is possible, is one of the most difficult problems
of philosophy.

Wittgenstein tried on many occasions to give an answer to the
question; in the *Foundations of Mathematics* he produces two illuminating examples; the language-game: "to bring the *same*—to
bring something *else*" functions under the agreement of all those
taking part. In spite of this, the same is not "what all or most human
beings with one voice take to be the same." "For of course I don't
make use of the agreement of human beings to affirm identity.
What criterion do you use, then? None at all. To use the word
without a justification does not mean to use it wrongfully." (F. M.
184). The same applies to the agreement of a colour with a colour
sample: "What right have I to say: 'Yes, that's red'? Well, I say
it; and it cannot be justified. And it is characteristic of this language-game as of the other that all men consent in it without question."
(F. M. 184).

Obviously Wittgenstein wishes to make clear by means of
these examples that there is no justification for the use of the word
"same"; in other words, that the question about knowledge of
identity cannot be answered. If need be, one can say that one just
sees the sameness of objects or the identity of colours. But that, of
course, is not a justification, only the observation of a fact.

We have arrived at one of those points where Wittgenstein breaks
off the question because all reasons and explanations have been exhausted for him: "If I have exhausted the justifications I have
reached bedrock, and my spade is turned. Then I am inclined to
say: 'This is simply what I do'. (Remember that we sometimes
demand definitions for the sake not of their content, but of their
form. Our requirement is an architectural one; the definition a kind
of ornamental coping that supports nothing)". (P. I. 217).

This attitude of Wittgenstein's is connected with the fact that
he does not admit metaphysical explanations but holds them for
"a kind of ornamental coping that supports nothing." As a result,
he naturally from the beginning denies his theory the possibility

of giving metaphysical interpretations in those cases where the problems cannot be solved along analytical lines.

We shall go more closely into Wittgenstein's view of the purely analytic method in philosophy in the following section.

12. *Wittgenstein's determination of the function of philosophy*

At the beginning of this chapter the problem was raised, how investigation into word usage i. e. grammatical analysis, could constitute the chief access to the structure of the object signified.

Our investigations into the construction and function of language-games have now shown the following: a language-game is a totality in which linguistic sign, object and human activity constitute an indissoluble unity, so that an object-constitution is undertaken simultaneously with the drawing up of the rules of the linguistic sign. The rules of the language-game, its grammar, simultaneously determines both the use of the linguistic sign and the essential features of the object. Wittgenstein expresses it thus: "Grammar tells what kind of object anything is." (P. I. 373). This result contains the solution of the problem referred to and the real justification of the linguistic-analytical method: since the rules of word usage are not read off from the structure of the object, but vice versa, word usage in a way determines the structure of the object; the analysis of word usage represents the primary access to the structure of the object and it requires no reasons for its truth or justification apart from those already contained within itself.

That is one of the key positions to Wittgenstein's philosophical method and hence one of the key positions to his conception of philosophy in general.

In traditional philosophy investigating the different kinds of object and their respective structure belongs to the function of ontology. Generally, the methodological foundation of ontology is effected without reference to language. The ontological structures of objects are either there entirely independently of man or they are constituted by human reason. In both cases, however, they have primarily nothing to do with language. Rather is language first added subsequently to the objects, which either exist in themselves or are previously constituted by consciousness.

The former position is expressed in its purest form in Aristotle. For him the objects are there before language, as was shown in our discussion of his theory of language; ontological knowledge thus refers to object structures, independent of language. Since language with its words names objects, the rules of the linguistic signs are derived from the objects, and, although linguistic-analytical considerations can facilitate access to ontological knowledge, the ultimate standard of all knowledge of objects remains the non-linguistic object.

The second position is to be found for instance in Kant and Husserl.[50] Here, ontological knowledge of objects always amounts to grasping the structural system of appearances drawn up by the understanding or by consciousness. Language, however, remains outside ontological consideration. The appearances are admittedly constituted by people but this constitution is effected before language. Thus, the fundamental ideas of the atomic model, according to which things exist before language, prevail both in Aristotle's realist ontology and also in constitution theories. In both approaches, ontological knowledge refers to a non-linguistic objectivity and for this reason requires no justification or substantiation of an extra-linguistic nature.

In Wittgenstein, by contrast, we are concerned with a constitution theory in which the constitution of objects is effected within and by means of the language or the linguistic actions of man; the ontological structure of the object is fixed in the spontaneous drawing up of a language-game simultaneously with a specific sign usage.

---

[50] Cf. the famous passage in the "Critique of Pure Reason": "... and the proud name of an Ontology that presumptuously claims to supply, in systematic doctrinal form, *synthetic a priori* knowledge of things in general... must therefore, give place to the modest title of a mere Analytic of pure understanding." (*Critique of Pure Reason* A 247, N. Kemp Smith's translation.) For Husserl's conception Cf. Husserl (2) p. 362 ff.

Ontological knowledge[51] in Wittgenstein thus, from the beginning, refers to an objectivity that is constituted by language. It has its methodological basis in the investigation into the structures of objects which are fixed by a specific linguistic usage; in other words, it has its basis in the analysis of the "grammar" of a language-game. In this way, with the help of "grammatical analysis" Wittgenstein finds a new, methodologically assured approach to the problems of ontology.

In the traditional definition of the function of ontology the systematic investigation of the individual spheres of objects and their inter-relationships stand in the foreground. Such a systematic study of the spheres of objects is conceivable in any ontology, whether it be realistically orientated (as in Aristotle for instance), or whether it sees itself as a constitution theory (as in Kant and Husserl).

A systematic ontology is conceivable also within a linguistic constitution theory like Wittgenstein's. It would consist of a complete as possible investigation into and explanation of the individual language-games in which the constitution of objects is effected; (thus, for instance, of the investigation of the language-game with the expression "physical object". Cf. P. I. p. 180). The investigation could not be definitively terminated because new language-games would be drawn up with the development of our ordinary and scientific language, and consequently new spheres of objects would be constituted. But that would not in any way alter the idea of a systematic ontology along linguistic-analytical lines.

Now, it is characteristic of Wittgenstein's conception of philosophy that he never considered a systematic study of language-games and the objects constituted in them.[52] It is rather philosophical *problems* that stand in the foreground of his determination

---

[51] When we here use the expression "ontology" any suggestion of speculative metaphysics should be excluded. Ontology, as it is understood here, means a discipline which investigates the fundamental features of the formal and general structures of objects, of the different kinds of objects and of the different spheres of objects. In contrast, a speculative ontology would be an ontology which put up metaphysical entities and sought to determine them.

of the function of philosophy. (Cf. P. I. 109). For Wittgenstein, insofar as philosophical problems cannot be clarified by any decision procedure from the special sciences, they have quite a different character to individual scientific problems. Philosophical problems "are, of course, not empirical"; they are not solved "by giving new information, but by arranging what we have always known." (P. I. 109). Wittgenstein expressed this with particular clarity in reference to logic and mathematics: philosophy "leaves everything as it is. It also leaves mathematics as it is, and no mathematical discovery can advance it. A 'leading problem of mathematical logic' is for us a problem of mathematics like any other." (P. I. 124).

Philosophical problems thus breed a special form of helplessness: "A philosophical problem has the form: 'I don't know my way about." (P. I. 123).

According to Wittgenstein the genesis of philosophical problems is to be seen in the fact that certain analogies exist between various language-games, particularly in their external grammatical form, and these analogies lead to a misinterpretation of the specific objectivity constituted in the individual language-games.[53]

Some of Wittgenstein's remarks at first sound as if philosophical problems were *only* linguistic misunderstandings.[54] But such an interpretation would overlook the fact that in language-games a corresponding object constitution is simultaneously bound up with a specific linguistic usage. Thus Wittgenstein's remarks are probably

[52] Warnock (3): "It was certainly held by Wittgenstein that description of language finds its whole *purpose* in the dissolution of antecedent philosophical problems; and hence, presumably, that it need not be further pursued than seems necessary if that purpose is to be achieved." (Warnock (3) p. 149.)

[53] The thesis that philosophical problems arise out of certain erroneous analogies between different linguistic forms of expression has become one of the most important foundations of linguistic analysis in England. Cf. Flew's introduction to the collection *Logic and Language* (First Series) p. 6 ff.

[54] For a similar interpretation of Wittgenstein's thesis cf. for instance Warnock (3) p. 89: "It is necessary here to add that Wittgenstein of course does *not* suggest that philosophical problems are all 'about language'? Of course they are not; they are about knowledge, memory, truth, space and time, perception and innumerable other things. What he suggests is that, though thus not *about* language, they spring *from* language.

to be understood to mean that philosophical problems are really ontological in nature, but arise from erroneous linguistic analogies.

This conception of the nature and genesis of philosophical problems is of course very one-sided, because Wittgenstein never considered the idea of a *systematic* investigation of language-games and the objectivity constituted in them. As a result he fails to notice all those problems, for instance, which pose themselves in the systematic investigation of a sphere of objects and which are by no means always insoluble.[55]

Wittgenstein's determination of the function of philosophy starts from that group of philosophical problems which have their origin in the obscurity of our language. (Cf. P. I. 122). The aim of philosophy, as he understands it, should be the solution of these philosophical problems.

The method of this essentially analytically orientated philosophy consists in clarifying the structure of the individual language-games i.e. their grammar, and in revealing the erroneous analogies that have led to misunderstandings about the ontological status of the objects developed in the language-games. (Cf. P. I. 109, 122, 126, and 127).

Wittgenstein attaches great value to this method. In his opinion it is capable of solving those philosophical problems which had not yet been solved with the means of traditional philosophy. The individual investigations in the *Philosophical Investigations* are also to be construed in this respect: they do not pursue any systematic aim but are intended to demonstrate *paradigmatically* how philosophical problems can be clarified with the help of grammatical analysis. This is probably what Wittgenstein means when he says: "The real discovery is the one that makes me capable of stopping doing philo-

---

[55] Thus also Strawson (3) p. 78: "Yet there are at least two different directions in which it (Wittgenstein's conception of philosophy) may seem unduly restrictive. First, there is the idea that the *sole* purpose of the distinctions we draw attention to, the descriptions we give of the different ways in which words function, is to dispel particular metaphysical confusions; and, associated with this, an extreme aversion from a systematic exhibition of the logic of particular regions of language..."

sophy when I want to.—The one that gives philosophy peace, so
that it is no longer tormented by questions which bring *itself* in
question.—*Instead, we now demonstrate a method, by examples: and
the series of examples can be broken off.*" (P. I. 133.—Dr. Specht has
italicised the last sentence himself.)

However, the following remarks ought to be made in connection with the purely analytic function of philosophy.

(a) It is true that in many passages Wittgenstein expresses himself decisively in favour of an exclusively analytically orientated
philosophy; but there are other passages which refer to the possibilities of philosophising, as, for example, when he asserts of
certain metaphysical theories that they have taught us a new *way
of looking* at things. (Cf. P. I. 400 and 401). Strawson drew attention
to this point in his review. Phenomenalism, for example, seeks to
construct objects out of sense data and relates the things of the
external world to sense perceptions, something which one had not
previously seen in this form.[56]

(b) Wittgenstein's determination of the function of philosophy
as a clarificatory analysis of language for disposing of philosophical problems does not agree with his own procedure in
the *Investigations* and in the *Foundations of Mathematics*. His theory of
language, which we have studied in some detail, is e. g. a general
theoretical outline which goes far beyond what could have been
discovered by analytic description. The fundamental concepts of
this theory: language-game, grammar, grammatical proposition
etc. are derived neither from everyday language nor from some

[56] The recognition of metaphysics, which reveals itself here, can also be
found in other analytically orientated philosophers, e. g. in Waismann (8), who
seems in his later years to have moved a long way from the radically anti-
metaphysical position of the Vienna Circle. Similarly Strawson who expresses
the view in his Wittgenstein review: "We might make room for a purged
kind of metaphysics, with more modest and less disputable claims than the
old." (Strawson (3) p. 78.) Strawson's book *Individuals*, which he himself
calls an "essay in descriptive metaphysics", shows best of all what form such a
"purified metaphysics" could assume. Cf. Strawson (4). The illuminating
discussion between various Oxford philosophers about the sense and value of
metaphysics in Pears (3) ought also to be mentioned in this context.

previously existent technical language; they are terms newly coined by Wittgenstein. And not only that: they are connected with a whole theory of language which, although it rests in many places on analytically won insights; yet, apart from this, it is a plan that could not have been discovered merely by analysis. Thus, when Wittgenstein demands: "...... we may not advance any kind of theory. There must not be anything hypothetical in our considerations. We must do away with all *explanation*, and description alone must take its place." (P. I. 109)—when Wittgenstein makes this demand, then, every individual point in it runs counter to his own conception of language, which is a *theory* that has *hypothetical moments* and is used to *explain* certain phenomena.

If one looks back at Wittgenstein's philosophy as a whole from the stand point of these critical remarks, an objection can be raised against the late work which had already been raised in a similar form against the *Tractatus*. In the *Tractatus*, namely, there is a striking discrepancy between the determination of the function of philosophy and the theory as actually stated. The theory is constructive and metaphysical, whereas philosophy is determined as analytical and critical. A similar discrepancy runs through the late work. Again Wittgenstein determines the function of philosophy as analytical and critical. But his actual *philosophical* plan is, by contrast, synthetic in its fundamental conception, constructive and hypothetical in its fundamental thesis. This can only mean for the interpretation of Wittgenstein's late work that one ought not to hold exclusively to his determination of the function of philosophy. It may be one-sided and narrow. Greater stimulation and more fruitful ideas are to be found in his actual philosophising.

BIBLIOGRAPHY

The bibliography, which makes no claim to completeness, was terminated in 1959; individual entries were added in 1960. For a comprehensive bibliography on analytical philosophy cf. for example Ayer (4), Feigl and Sellars (1) and Black (7).

The numbers in round brackets are the numbers used in quotations. Where a reprint is given the pagination of the reprint has been used in quotations.

I. The Works of Ludwig Wittgenstein

Logisch-Philosophische Abhandlung. Annalen der Naturphilosophie 14, 1921.

Tractatus Logico-Philosophicus. With an introduction by B. Russell. London 1922. (Translated by C. K. Ogden.)

Some Remarks on Logical Form. Proceedings of the Aristotelian Society. Supplementary Volume 9, 1929.

Philosophische Untersuchungen. Philosophical Investigations. Oxford 1953. (Translated by G. E. M. Anscombe.)

Bemerkungen über die Grundlagen der Mathematik. Remarks on the Foundations of Mathematics. Edited and prepared by G. H. von Wright, R. Rhees, G. E. M. Anscombe. Oxford 1956. (Translated by G. E. M. Anscombe.)

Preliminary Studies for the Philosophical Investigations. Generally known as *the Blue and Brown Books.* Oxford 1958.

Schriften. Tractatus logico-philosophicus. Tagebücher 1914 bis 1916. Philosophische Untersuchungen. Frankfurt 1960.

Schriften/Beiheft. Mit Beiträgen von I. Bachmann, M. Cranston, J. F. Mora, P. Feyerabend, E. Heller, B. Russell, G. H. von Wright. Frankfurt 1960.

Moore, G. E.

Wittgenstein's Lectures in 1930—33. Pt. 1—3. *Mind* 63, 1954. 64, 1955.

Two Corrections. *Mind* 64, 1955. (To G. E. Moore: Wittgenstein's Lectures in 1930—33.)

Costello, H. T. (Ed): Ludwig Wittgenstein: Notes on Logic. September 1913. *The Journal of Philosophy* 54, 1957.

II. Literature on Wittgenstein and General Literature

Abbagnano, N. (1) L'ultimo Wittgenstein. *Revista di Filosofia* 44, 1953.

Abelson, R. (1): Meaning, Use and Rules of Use. *Philosophy and Phenomenological Research* 18, 1957.

Abraham, L. (1): What is the Theory of Meaning About? *The Monist* 46, 1936.

Albritton, R. (1): On Wittgenstein's Use of the Term 'Criterion'. *The Journal of Philosophy* 61, 1959.

Aldrich, V. C. (1): Pictorial Meaning, Picture-thinking, and Wittgenstein's Theory of Aspects. *Mind* 67, 1958.

Allaire, E. B. (1): Tractatus 6.3751.
Analysis 19, 1958.

Ambrose, A. (1): Are There Three Consecutive Sevens in the Expansion of π? Michigan Academy of Science, Arts and Letters, 1936.

(2): Finitism and the Limits of Empiricism. *Mind* 44, 1937.

(3): L. Wittgenstein: Philosophical Investigations, *Philosophy and Phenomenological Research* 15, 1954.

(4): Wittgenstein on Some Questions in the Foundations of Mathematics. *The Journal of Philosophy* 52, 1955.

(5): L. Wittgenstein: Remarks on the Foundations of Mathematics. *Philosophy and Phenomenological Research* 18, 1957.

(6): Proof and the Theorem Proved. *Mind* 68, 1959.

Ammonius (1): In Aristotelis De interpretatione commentarium. Ed. A. Busse, Berlin 1897.

(2): In Aristotelis Categorias commentarium. Ed. A. Busse, Berlin 1895.

Anderson, A. R. (1): Mathematics and the "Language Game". *The Review of Metaphysics* 11, 1958.

Anscombe, G. E. M. (1): Wittgenstein. *World Review*, January 1952.

(2): Note on the English Version of Wittgenstein's *Philosophische Untersuchungen*. *Mind* 62, 1953.

(3): What Wittgenstein Really Said. *The Tablet*, April 17th, 1954.

(4): *An Introduction to Wittgenstein's Tractatus*, London 1959.

(5): Mr. Copi on Objects, Properties and Relations in the Tractatus. *Mind* 68, 1959.

Antonelli, M. T. (1): A propósito del último Wittgenstein: observaciones sobre el convencionalismo. *Crisis* 3, 1956.

Aristoteles (1): *Aristotelis opera*. Ed. Acad. Reg. Bor. Berlin 1831.

Augustinus (1): *Opera omnia*. Editio Parisina altera. Paris 1836—1839.

Austin, J. L. (1): Other Minds. *Proceedings of the Aristotelian Society*. Supplementary Volume 20, 1946. (Reprinted in: A. Flew: *Logic and Language*. Second Series, Oxford 1953.)

(2): A Plea for Excuses. *Proceedings of the Aristotelian Society* 55, 1956.

Ayer, A. J. (1): *Language, Truth and Logic*. Fourth impression of second edition. October 1948. London 1948.

(2): Can There Be a Private Language? *Proceedings of the Aristotelian Society*. Supplementary Volume 28, 1954.

(3): *The Revolution in Philosophy*. London 1956.

(4): (Ed). *Logical Positivism*. Glencoe, Illinois 1959.

Baier, K. (1): The Ordinary Use of Words. *Proceedings of the Aristotelian Society*. 52, 1951.

Barone, F. (1): Il solipsismo linguistico di Ludwig Wittgenstein. *Filosofia* 2, 1951.

(2): Wittgenstein inedito. *Filosofia della scienza* IV. Torino 1953.

(3): L. Wittgenstein: Philosophical Investigations. *Filosofia* 4, 1953.

(4): Philosophical Investigations, *Giornale Critico della Filosofia Italiana* 33, 1954.

Berkeley (1): *The Works of George Berkeley, Bishop of Cloyne*. Ed. A. A. Luce and T. E. Jessop. London 1948.

Bernays, P. (1): Betrachtungen zu Ludwig Wittgensteins *Bemerkungen über die Grundlagen der Mathematik*. *Ratio* 1, 1959.

Black, M. (1): Is Analysis a Useful Method in Philosophy? *Proceedings of the Aristotelian Society*. Supplementary Volume 13, 1934.

(2): Vagueness. *Philosophy of Science*, 1937. (Reprinted in: Black (6).)

(3): Relations Between Logical Positivism and the Cambridge School of Analysis, *Erkenntnis, Journal of Unified Science* 8, 1938.

(4): Russell's Philosophy of Language. In: P. A. Schilpp: *The Philosophy of Bertrand Russell*. Evanston 1946.

(5): Wittgenstein's Tractatus. In: Black (6).

(6): *Language and Philosophy*. Ithaca 1949.

(7): (Ed.). *Philosophical Analysis*. Ithaca 1950.

(8): Necessary Statements and Rules. *The Philosophical Review* 67, 1958.

(9): Notes on the Meaning of 'Rule' *Theoria* 24, 1958.

(10): Linguistic Relativity: The Views of Benjamin Lee Whorf. *The Philosophical Review* 68, 1959.

Bochénski, I. M. (1): *Ancient Formal Logic*. Amsterdam 1951.

(2): *Formale Logik*.

Freiburg and München 1956.

Broad, C. D. (1): The Local Historical Background of Contemporary Cambridge Philosophy. In: C. A. Mace: *British Philosophy in the Mid-Century*. London 1957.

Bröcker, W. and Lohmann, J. (1): Vom Wesen des sprachlichen Zeichens. *Lexis* 1, 1948.

Bühler, K. (1): *Sprachtheorie. Die Darstellungsfunktion der Sprache.* Jena 1948.

(2): Der dritte Hauptsatz der Sprachtheorie. Anschauung und Begriff im Sprachverkehr. *Onzième Congrèß International de Psychologie. Rapports et comptes rendus*, 1938.

Burnheim, J. (1): L. Wittgenstein: Philosophical Investigations. *Philosophical Studies* 4, 1954.

Butler, R. J. (1): A. Wittgensteinian on "The Reality of the Past". *The Philosophical Quarterly* 6, 1956.

Campanale, D. (1): *Studi su Wittgenstein.* Bari 1956.

(2): Il problema dei fondamenti della matematica nella critica di Wittgenstein. *Ressegna di Science filosofiche* 12, 1959.

Carnap, R. (1): *Der logische Aufbau der Welt,* Berlin 1928.

(2): Überwindung der Metaphysik durch logische Analyse der Sprache. *Erkenntnis* 2, 1932.

(3): *Logische Syntax der Sprache,* Vienna 1934. *Logical Syntax of Language.* London and New York 1937 (English translation with additions).

(4): *Introduction to Semantics.* Cambridge, Mass. 1942.

(5): *Meaning and Necessity: A Study in Semantics and Modal Logic.* Chicago 1947.

(6): Empiricism, Semantics and Ontology. *Revue Internationale de Philosophie* 11, 1950 (Reprinted in: L. Linsky: *Semantics and the Philosophy of Language.* Urbana 1952).

Cassirer, E. (1): *Philosophie der symbolischen Formen.* Berlin 1923.

Charlesworth M. J. (1): *Philosophy and Linguistic Analysis.* Louvain 1959.

Chiodi, P. (1): Essere e linguaggio in Heidegger e nel Tractatus di Wittgenstein. *Rivista di Filosofia* 52, 1955.

Chisholm, R. M. (1): Philosophers and Ordinary Language. *The Philosophical Review* 60, 1951.

Christensen, N. E. (1): A Proof that Meanings are neither Ideas nor Concepts. *Analysis* 17, 1956.

Collins, J. (1): L. Wittgenstein: Remarks on the Foundations of Mathematics. *The Modern Schoolman* 35, 1957.

Colombo, G. C. M. (1): Introduzione al Tractatus Logico-Philosophicus. In: L. Wittgenstein: *Tractatus Logico-Philosophicus*. Testo originale, versione italiana a fronte, introduzione critica e note a cura di G. C. M. Colombo S. J. Milano, Rome 1954.
(2): Epilogue on Wittgenstein. *Monat* 18, 1957.

Copi, I. M. (1): Objects, Properties and Relations in the Tractatus. *Mind* 67, 1958.

Cranston, M. (1): Bildnis eines Philosophen. *Monat* 4, 1951.
(2): Ludwig Wittgenstein. *World Review*. December 1951.
(3): Vita e morte di Wittgenstein. *Aut Aut*, Maggio 1952.

Daitz, E. (1): The Picture Theory of Meaning. *Mind* 62, 1953.

Daly, C. B. (1): Logical Positivism, Metaphysics and Ethics, 1; Ludwig Wittgenstein. *The Irish Theological Quarterly* 23, 1956.
(2): Wittgenstein's "Objects". *The Irish Theological Quarterly* 23, 1956.

Davie, I. (1): L. Wittgenstein: Philosophical Investigations. *The Downside Review* 72, 1954.

Deledalle, G. (1): L. Wittgenstein: The Blue and Brown Books. *Les Etudes Philosophiques* 14, 1959.

Delius, H. (1): Was sich überhaupt sagen läßt, läßt sich klar sagen. Gedanken zu einer Formulierung Ludwig Wittgensteins. *Archiv für Philosophie* 8, 1958.

Drudis Baldrich, R. (1): Ludwig Wittgenstein y su obra filósofica. *Theoria* 1, 1952.
(2): Consideraciones en torno a la obra de Wittgenstein. *Revista de Filosofia* (Madrid) 17, 1958.

Dubois, P. (1): Natureza da filosofia segundo as «Investigacoes filósoficas» de Wittgenstein. *Revista Portuguesa di Filosofia* 15, 1959.

Dummett, M. (1): Wittgenstein's Philosophy of Mathematics. *The Philosophical Review* 68, 1959.

Duns Scotus (1): *Opera omnia*. Paris 1891—1895.

Duthie, G. D. (1): L. Wittgenstein: Remarks on the Foundations of Mathematics. *The Philosophical Quarterly* 7, 1957.

Evans, E. (1): Tractatus 3.1432. *Mind* 64, 1955.

Evans, J. L. (1): On Meaning and Verification. *Mind* 62, 1953.

Farrell, B. A. (1): An Appraisal of Therapeutic Positivism. *Mind* 55, 1946.

Feibleman, J. K. (1): Reflections after Wittgenstein. *Sophia* 23, 1955.

(2): *Inside the Great Mirror:* A Critical Examination of the Philosophy of Russell, Wittgenstein, and Their Followers. The Hague, 1958.

Feigl, H. and Brodbeck, M. (1) (Eds.): *Readings in the Philosophy of Science,* New York 1953.

Feigl, H. and Sellars, W. (1) (Eds.).: *Readings in Philosophical Analysis.* New York 1949.

Ferrater Mora, J. (1): Wittgenstein oder die Destruktion. *Monat* 4, 1951.

(2): Wittgenstein genio della distruzione. *Aut Aut*, Maggio 1952.

(3): Wittgenstein, a Symbol of Troubled Times. *Philosophy and Phenomenological Research* 14, 1953.

Feyerabend, P. (1): Ludwig Wittgenstein. *Merkur* 8, 1954.

(2): Wittgenstein und die Philosophie. *Wissenschaft und Weltbild* 7, 1954.

(3): Wittgenstein's Philosophical Investigations. *The Philosophical Review* 64, 1955.

Ficker, L. (1): Rilke und der unbekannte Freund. *Der Brenner*, 1954.

Findlay, J. N. (1): Time: A Treatment of Some Puzzles. *The Australasian Journal of Psychology and Philosophy*, 1941. (Reprinted: in: A. Flew, *Logic and Language*. First Series. Oxford 1952.)

(2): Wittgenstein's Philosophical Investigations. *Revue Internationale de Philosophie* 7, 1953.

(3): Wittgenstein: Philosophical Investigations. *Philosophy* 30, 1955.

(4) Some Reactions to Recent Cambridge Philosophy. *The Australasian Journal of Psychology and Philosophy*, 1940.

Flew, A. G. N. (1): (Ed.). *Logic and Language*. First Series. Oxford 1951.

(2): (Ed.): *Logic and Language*. Second Series, Oxford 1953.

(3): (Ed.): *Essays in Conceptual Analysis*. London 1956.

(4): Philosophy and Language. In: A. Flew: *Essays in Conceptual Analysis*. London 1956.

Frege, G. (1): Über Sinn und Bedeutung. *Zeitschrift für Philosophie und philosophische Kritik* 100, 1892.

Gabriel, L. (1): Logische Magie. Ein Nachwort zum Thema Wittgenstein. *Wissenschaft und Weltbild* 7, 1954.

Gahringer, R. E. (1): Can Games Explain Language? *The Journal of Philosophy* 56, 1959.

Garver, N. (1): Wittgenstein on Private Language. *Philosophy and Phenomenological Research* 20, 1960.

Gasking, D. A. T. (1): Anderson and the Tractatus Logico-Philosophicus: an Essay in Philosophical Translation. *The Australasian Journal of Philosophy* 27, 1949.

(2): Mathematics and the World. *The Australasian Journal of Psychology and Philosophy*, 1940. (Reprinted in: A. Flew: *Logic and Language*. Second Series. Oxford 1953.)

Gellner, E. (1): *Words and Things*. An Examination of, and Attack on, Linguistic Philosophy. With an Introduction by B. Russell. London 1959.

Glinz H. (1): *Die innere Form des Deutschen*. Bern 1952.

Gomperz, H. (1): The Meaning of "Meaning". *Philosophy of Science* 8, 1941.

Goodman, N. (1): *The Structure of Appearance*. Cambridge 1951.

(2): On Likeness of Meaning. In: L. Linsky: *Semantics and the Philosophy of Language*. Urbana 1952.

Goodstein, R. L. (1): L. Wittgenstein: Remarks on the Foundations of Mathematics. *Mind* 66, 1957.

Grant, C. K. (1): On Using Language. *The Philosophical Quarterly* 6, 1956.

Grice, H. P. (1): Meaning. *The Philosophical Review* 66. 1957.

Guiraud, P. (1): *Bibliographie critique de la statistique linguistique*. Utrecht 1954.

Gullvag, I. (1): Criteria of Meaning and Analysis of Usage. *Synthese* 9.

Hadot, P. (1): Réflexions sur les limites du langage à propos du «Tractatus logico-philosophicus» de Wittgenstein. *Revue de Métaphysique et de Morale* 64, 1959.

Hall, E. W. (1): *What is Value?* New York: London 1952.

Hamilton, R. (1): L. Wittgenstein: Philosophical Investigations. *Monat* 11, 1954.

Hardin, C. L. (1): Wittgenstein on Private Language. *The Journal of Philosophy* 56, 1959.

Hare, R. M. (1): Are Discoveries about the Use of Words Empirical? *The Journal of Philosophy* 54, 1957.

Hawkins, D. J. B. (1): Wittgenstein and the Cult of Language. The Aquinas Society of London. *Aquinas Paper* 27. London 1957.

Heath, P. L. (1): The Appeal to Ordinary Language. *The Philosophical Quarterly* 2, 1952.
(2): Wittgenstein Investigated. *The Philosophical Quarterly* 6, 1956.

Heinemann, F. H. (1): L. Wittgenstein: Philosophical Investigations. *The Hibbert Journal* 52, 1953.

Henle, P. (1): Do We Discover Our Uses of Words? *The Journal of Philosophy* 54, 1957.

Hervey, H. (1): The Private Language Problem. *The Philosophical Quarterly* 7, 1957.

Hintikka, J. (1): Tutkimus filosofiasta. Suomalainen Suomi 1955. (An Investigation into Philosophy; to L. Wittgenstein's *Philosophischen Untersuchungen*.)
(2): Tutkimus Kielestä. Suomalainen Suomi 1955. (An Investigation into Language; to L. Wittgenstein's "Philosophischen Untersuchungen".)
(3): On Wittgenstein's "Solipsism". *Mind* 67, 1958.

Humboldt, W. v. (1): *Gesammelte Schriften.* Herausgegeben von der Berliner Akademie der Wissenschaften. Berlin 1903—1918. Bd. 7.

Husserl, E. (1): *Logische Untersuchungen.* Bd. 1—3. 2. umgearbeitete Auflage. Halle 1913.
(2): *Ideen zu einer reinen Phänomenologie und phänomenologischen Philosophie.* Neue, erweiterte Auflage. The Hague 1950.

Hutten, E. H. (1): L. Wittgenstein: Philosophical Investigations. *The British Journal for the Philosophy of Science* 4, 1953.

Jackson, A. C. and Gasking, D. A. T. (1): Ludwig Wittgenstein. *The Australasian Journal of Philosophy* 39, 1951.

Kainz, F. (1): *Psychologie der Sprache.* Bd. 1. Stuttgart 1941.

Kant, I. (1): *Kants gesammelte Schriften.* Herausgegeben von der Königlich Preußischen Akademie der Wissenschaften. 1900 bis 1923.

Kenny, A. (1): Aquinas and Wittgenstein. *The Downside Review* 77, 1959.

Khatchadourian, H. (1): Common Names and "Family Resemblances". *Philosophy and Phenomenological Research* 18, 1957.

Klibansky, R. (1) (Ed).: *Philosophy in the Mid-century. A Survey.* Vol. 2. Metaphysics and Analysis. Florence 1958.

Körner, S. (1): Some Remarks on Philosophical Analysis. *The Journal of Philosophy* 54, 1957.

Kraft, V. (1): Ludwig Wittgenstein. *Wiener Zeitschrift für Philosophie, Psychologie, Pädagogik* 3, 1951.

(2): *Der Wiener Kreis. Der Ursprung des Neopositivismus. Ein Kapitel der jüngsten Philosophiegeschichte.* Vienna 1950.

Kreisel, G. (1): L. Wittgenstein: Remarks on the Foundations of Mathematics. *The British Journal for the Philosophy of Science* 9, 1958.

Kretzmann, N. (1): Maupertuis, Wittgenstein, and the Origin of Language. *The Journal of Philosophy* 54, 1957.

Lazerowitz, M. (1) Tautologies and the Matrix Method. *Mind* 46, 1937.

(2): *The Structure of Metaphysics.* London 1955.

Leisi, E. (1): *Der Wortinhalt.* Heidelberg 1953.

Lewis, C. J. (1): Wittgenstein. Remarks on the Foundations of Mathematics. *Thought* 32, 1957.

Lewis, C. L. (1): A Pragmatic Conception of the A Priori. *The Journal of Philosophy* 20, 1923. (Reprinted in H. Feigl and W. Sellars: *Readings in Philosophical Analysis.* New York 1949.)

(2): *Mind and the World Order.* New York 1929.

(3): The Modes of Meaning. *Philosophy and Phenomenological Research* 4, 1944. (Reprinted in L. Linsky: *Semantics and the Philosophy of Language.* Urbana 1952.

Lewis, H. D. (1): (Ed). *Contemporary British Philosophy.* Third Series, London 1956.

Lieb, I. C. (1): Wittgenstein's Investigations. *The Review of Metaphysics* 8, 1954.

Linsky, L. (1): (Ed). *Semantics and the Philosophy of Language.* Urbana 1952.

(2): Wittgenstein on Language and Some Problems of Philosophy. *The Journal of Philosophy* 54, 1957.

Locke, J. (1): *The Works of John Locke.* Tenth Edition. London 1801.

Macdonald, M. (1): The Philosopher's Use of Analogy. *Proceedings of the Aristotelian Society* 38, 1937. (Reprinted in: A. Flew, *Logic and Language*, First Series. Oxford 1951.)

(2) (Ed).: *Philosophy and Analysis.* Oxford 1954.

(3): Introduction to: M. Macdonald (2).

Mace, C. A. (1): (Ed). *British Philosophy in Mid-Century.* London. New York 1957.

Malcolm, N. (1): Philosophy and Ordinary Language. Erroneously under the title: Philosophy for Philosophers. *The Philosophical Review* 60, 1961.

(2): Wittgenstein's Philosophical Investigations. *The Philosophical Review* 63, 1954.

(3): *Ludwig Wittgenstein : A Memoir.* Oxford and New York 1958.

(4): Knowledge of Other Minds. *The Journal of Philosophy* 55, 1958.

Martin, G. (1): *Wilhelm von Ockham.* Berlin 1949.

Mays, W. (1): Note on Wittgenstein's Manchester Period. *Mind* 64, 1955.

Mays, W. and Midgley, G. C. J. (1): Symposium. Linguistic Rules and Language Habits. Proceedings of The Aristotelian Society. Supplementary Volume 29, 1955.

MacIver, A. M. (1): Do Words Mean Anything? *Actes du XIe Congrèß International de Philosophie V.*

McBrien, V. O. (1): L. Wittgenstein: Remarks on the Foundations of Mathematics. *The New Scholasticism* 32, 1958.

McGuinness, F. (1): Pictures and Form in Wittgenstein's Tractatus. *Archivio di Filosofia* 1956.

Meinong, A. (1): *Über Annahmen*. 2. umgearbietete Auflage. Leipzig 1910.

Melden, A. I. (1): "My kinaesthetic sensations advise me..." *Analysis* 18, 1957.

Meyer, H. (1): La philosophie de Ludwig Wittgenstein. *Algemeen Nederlands Tijdschrift voor Wijsbegeerte en Psychologie* 48, 1955.

(2): Zin en onzin volgens Ludwig Wittgenstein. *Allgemeen Nederlands Tijdschrift voor Wijsbegeerte en Psychologie* 48, 1956.

Mill, J. S. (1): System der deduktiven und induktiven Logik. Translated by J. Schiel. Braunschweig 1877.

Moore, G. E. (1): An Autobiography. In: P. A. Schilpp: *The Philosophy of G. E. Moore*. Evanston 1942.

Muirhead J. H. (1): (Ed). *Contemporary British Philosophy*. First Series. London 1924.

Nakhnikian, G. (1): L. Wittgenstein: Philosophical Investigations. *Philosophy of Science* 21, 1954.

Neurath, O. (1): Soziologie im Physikalismus. *Erkenntnis* 2, 1931.

Nielsen, H. A. (1): Wittgenstein on Language. *Philosophical Studies* 8, 1958.

Ockham, W. v. (1): *Summa Logicae*. Pars Prima. Ed. Ph. Boehner. Louvain 1951.

Ogden, C. K. and Richards, I. A. (1): *The Meaning of Meaning*. London 1949.

Paci, E. (1): Negatività e positività di Wittgenstein. *Aut Aut*, Maggio 1952.

Paler, H. (1): The Other Logical Constant. *Mind* 67, 1958.

Pap, A. (1): *Elements of Analytic Philosophy*. New York 1949.

(2): *Analytische Erkenntnistheorie*. Vienna 1955.

(3): Once More: Colours and the Synthetic A Priori. *The Philosophical Review* 66. 1957.

(4): *Semantics and Necessary Truth*. An Inquiry into the Foundations of Analytic Philosophy. New Haven 1958.

Passmore, J. (1): Professor Ryle's Use of "Use" and "Usage". *The Philosophical Review* 63. 1954.

(2): *A Hundred Years of Philosophy*. London 1957.

Paul, G. A. (1): Wittgenstein. In: A. J. Ayer: *The Revolution in Philosophy*. London 1956.

Paul, H. and Stolte, H. (1): *Kurze deutsche Grammatik*. 2. vermehrte Auflage, Tübingen 1951.

Pears, D. F. (1): Incompatibilities of Colours. In: A. Flew: *Logic and Language*. Second Series. Oxford 1953.

(2): Logical Atomism: Russell and Wittgenstein. In: A. J. Ayer: *The Revolution in Philosophy*. London 1956.

(3): (Ed). *The Nature of Metaphysics*. London 1957.

Peduzzi, O. (1): Wittgenstein in Inghliterra. *Aut Aut*, Maggio 1954.

Peursen, van, C. A. (1): Edmund Husserl and Ludwig Wittgenstein. *Philosophy and Phenomenological Research* 20, 1959.

Plato (1): *Platonis opera*. Rec. I. Burnet. Oxford 1899—1906.

Poincaré, H. (1): *Wissenschaft und Hypothese*. Deutsch von F. und L. Lindemann. 2. Auflage. München 1906. (Translation of: *Science et l'Hypothèse*.)

Pole, D. (1): *The Later Philosophy of Wittgenstein*. A Short Introduction with an Epilogue on John Wisdom. London 1958.

Porzig, W. (1): Wesenhafte Bedeutungsbeziehungen. *Beiträge zur Geschichte der deutschen Sprache und Literatur* 58, 1934.

(2): *Das Wunder der Sprache*. 2. Auflage. Bern 1957.

Proctor, G. L. (1): Scientific Laws and Scientific Objects in the Tractatus. *The British Journal for the Philosophy of Science* 10, 1959.

Putnam, H. (1): Red and Green All Over Again: A Rejoinder to Arthur Pap. *The Philosophical Review* 66, 1957.

Quine, W. V. O. (1): Designation and Existence. *The Journal of Philosophy* 36, 1939. (Reprinted in: H. Feigl and W. Sellars: *Readings in Philosophical Analysis*. New York 1949.)

(2): On What There Is. *Review of Metaphysics* 2, 1948. (Reprinted in: W. V. O. Quine: *From a Logical Point of View*. Cambridge, Mass. 1953 and in Linsky: *Semantics and the Philosophy of Language*. Urbana 1952.)

(3): *From a Logical Point of View*. Cambridge, Mass. 1953

(4): *Methods of Logic*. New York 1955.

(5): *Word and Object*. New York and London 1960.

Ramsey, F. (1): Critical Notice of Wittgenstein's Tractatus Logico-Philosophicus. *Mind*, 1923. (Reprinted in: Ramsey (2).)

(2): *The Foundations of Mathematics and Other Logical Essays*. London 1931.

Rhees, R. (1): Can There Be a Private Language? *Proceedings of the Aristotelian Society*. Supplementary Volume 28, 1954.

(2): Preface to the "Blue and Brown Books". In: L. Wittgenstein: *The Blue and Brown Books*. Oxford 1958.

(3): Miss Anscombe on the Tractatus. *The Philosophical Quarterly* 10, 1960.

Rozeboom, W. (1): The Logic of Colour Words. *Philosophical Review* 67, 1958.

Russell, B. (1): On Denoting. *Mind* 14, 1905.

(2): The Philosophy of Logical Atomism. *The Monist*, 1918—19. (Reprinted by the University of Minnesota. o. J.)

(3): *Introduction to Mathematical Philosophy*. 2nd Ed. London 1920.

(4): Introduction to the Tractatus. In: L. Wittgenstein: *Tractatus Logico-Philosophicus*. London 1922.

(5): Logical Atomism. In: J. H. Muirhead. *Contemporary British Philosophy*. First Series. London 1924. (Reprinted in: A. J. Ayer: *Logical Positivism*. Glencoe 1959.)

(6): *The Principles of Mathematics*. 2nd. Ed. London 1937.

(7): L. Wittgenstein. *Mind* 60, 1951.

(8): Philosophical Analysis. *Zeitschrift für philosophische Forschung* 12, 1958.

Russell, B. and Whitehead A. N. (1): *Principia Mathematica* Vol. 1. Cambridge 1910.

Ryle, G. (1): Systematically Misleading Expressions. *Proceedings of the Aristotelian Society* 32, 1931. (Reprinted in: A. Flew: *Logic and Language*. First Series. Oxford 1951.)

(2): Categories. *Proceedings of the Aristotelian Society* 38, 1937. (Reprinted in: A. Flew: *Logic and Language*, Second Series. Oxford 1953.)

(3): *The Concept of Mind*. London 1949.

(4): Meaning and Necessity. *Philosophy* 24, 1949.

(5): Ludwig Wittgenstein. *Analysis* 12, 1951.

(6): Ordinary Language. *The Philosophical Review* 62, 1953.

(7): The Theory of Meaning.
In: C. A. Mace: *British Philosophy in the Mid-Century*.
London 1957.

Sánchez-Mazas, M. (1): La ciencia, el lenguaje y el mundo según Wittgenstein. *Cuadernos Hispanoamericanos*, 1953.

Saussure, F. de (1): *Grundfragen der allgemeinen Sprachwissenschaft* (Cours de linguistique général). (Translated by H. Lommel. Berlin und Leipzig 1931.)

Schächter, J. (1): *Prolegomena zu einer kritischen Grammatik*. Vienna 1935.

Schiavone, M. (1): Il pensiero filosofico di Ludwig Wittgenstein alla luce del "Tractatus Logico-Philosophicus". *Rivista di Filosofia Neo-Scolastica* 47, 1955.

Schilpp, P. A. (1): (Ed.) *The Philosophy of Bertrand Russell*. Evanston 1946.

(2): (Ed.) *The Philosophy of G. E. Moore*. Evanston 1942. 2nd imp. 1952.

Schlick, M. (1): Positivismus und Realismus. *Erkenntnis* 3, 1932. (Reprinted in: M. Schlick (4).)

(2): Meaning and Verification. *The Philosophical Review* 44, 1936. (Reprinted in: M. Schlick (4).)

(3): Gibt es ein materiales *A priori?* In: M. Schlick (4). (English translation in H. Feigl and W. Sellars: *Readings in Philosophical Analysis*. New York 1949.)

(4): *Gesammelte Aufsätze, 1926—1936*. Vienna 1938.

Scholz, H. (1): L. Wittgenstein: Philosophische Untersuchungen. *Philosophische Rundschau* 1, 1953.

Science, Language and Human Rights. Papers for the Symposia Held at the Annual Meeting, at the College of the City of New York, December 29—31, 1952. Philadelphia. 1952

Sellars, W. (1): Some Reflections on Language Games. *Philosophy of Science* 21, 1954.

Shalom, A. (1): L. Wittgenstein: Remarks on the Foundations of Mathematics. *Les Etudes Philosophiques* 12, 1957.

(2): Wittgenstein, le langage et la philosophie. *Les Etudes Philosophiques* 13, 1958.

Shorter, M. (1): Meaning and Grammar. *The Australasian Journal of Philosophy* 34, 1956.

Smart, H. R. (1): Language-games. *The Philosophical Quarterly* 7, 1957.

Stebbing, L. S. (1): The Method of Analysis in Metaphysics. Proceedings of the Aristotelian Society 33, 1932.

Stegmüller, W. (1): *Das Wahrheitsproblem und die Idee der Semantik.* Vienna 1957.

Stenius E. (1): *Wittgenstein's Tractatus. A Critical Exposition of its Main Lines of Thought.* Oxford 1960.

(2): Upphyggnaden av Wittgensteins Tractatus logico-philosophicus. *Ajatus* 19.

Stolpe, S. (1): Ludwig Wittgensteins väg. *Credo* 36, 1955.

Strawson, P. F. (1): On Referring. *Mind* 59, 1950. (Reprinted in: A. Flew: *Essays in Conceptual Analysis*. London 1956.

(2): *Introduction to Logical Theory*, London 1952.

(3): Philosophical Investigations. By Ludwig Wittgenstein. *Mind* 63, 1954.

(4): *Individuals. An Essay in Descriptive Metaphysics*. London 1959.

Swanson, J. W. (1): A Footnote to Mrs. Lazerowitz on Wittgenstein. *The Journal of Philosophy* 56, 1959.

The Times (1): Ludwig Wittgenstein. Obituary. Wed. May 2, 1951.

Thompson, M. (1): On Category Differences. *The Philosophical Review* 66, 1957.

Trier, J. (1): *Der deutsche Wortschatz im Sinnbezirk des Verstandes.* Heidelberg 1931.

Ullman, S. (1): Laws of Language and Laws of Nature. *Modern Language Review*, 1943.

(2): *The Principles of Semantics*. Glasgow 1951.

Urmson, J. O. (1): *Philosophical Analysis. Its Development between the Two World Wars.* Oxford 1956.

Waismann, F. (1): Logische Analyse des Wahrscheinlichkeitsbegriffes. Erkenntnis 1, 1930.

(2): *Einführung in das mathematische Denken*. Vienna 1936.

(3): The Relevance of Psychology to Logic. *Proceedings of the Aristotelian Society. Supplementary Volume* 15, 1936. (Reprinted in: H. Feigl and W. Sellars: *Readings in Philosophical Analysis*. New York 1949.)

(4): Was ist logische Analyse? *Journal of Unified Science*. 1939—1940.

(5) Verifiability. *Proceedings of the Aristotelian Society. Supplementary Volume* 19, 1945. (Reprinted in: A. Flew: *Logic and Language*. First Series. Oxford 1951.)

(6): Analytic-Synthetic. *Analysis* 10, 11, 13. 1949—53.

(7): Language Strata. In: A. Flew: *Logic and Language*. Second Series. Oxford 1953.

(8): How I See Philosophy. In: H. D. Lewis: *Contemporary British Philosophy*. Third Series. London 1956.

Walsh, (1): Categories. *Kantstudien* 45, 1953.

Warnock, G. J. (1): *Berkeley*, London 1953.

(2): Metaphysics in Logic. In: A. Flew: *Essays in Conceptual Analysis*. London 1956.

(3): *English Philosophy*. London 1958.

(4): The Philosophy of Wittgenstein. In: R. Klibansky: *Philosophy in the Mid-Century* II. Firenze 1958.

Wasmuth, E. (1): Ludwig Wittgensteins Tystna. Om 'Det mystica'; Tractatus Logico-Philosophicus. *Credo* 36. 1955. (The silence of L. Wittgenstein. On the mystical in the Tractatus Logico-Philosophicus.)

Weiler, G. (1): On Fritz Mauthner's Critique of Language. *Mind* 67, 1958.

Weinberg, J. R. (1): *An Examination of Logical Positivism*. London 1936.

Weisgerber L. (1): *Vom Weltbild der deutschen Sprache*. 1. Halbband. Die inhaltsbezogene Grammatik. 2. Aufl. Düsseldorf 1953. 2. Halbband. Die sprachliche Erschließung der Welt. 2. Aufl. Düsseldorf 1954.

(2): Die Bedeutungslehre — ein Irrweg der Sprachwissenschaft? *Germanisch-Romanische Monatsschrift* 15, 1927.

(3): Sprachwissenschaft und Philosophie zum Bedeutungsproblem. *Blätter für deutsche Philosophie* 4, 1930—31.

Weitz, M. (1): Philosophy and the Abuse of Language. *The Journal of Philosophy* 44, 1947.

(2): Oxford Philosophy. *The Philosophical Review* 62, 1953.

Wellman, C. (1): Wittgenstein and the Egocentric Predicament. *Mind* 68, 1959.

Wells, R. (1): Meaning and Use. *Word* 10, 1954.

Whorf, B. L. (1): *Language, Thought and Reality*. Edited with an Introduction by John B. Carrol. New York, London 1956.

Wilson, N. L. and Martin R. M. (1): What is a Rule of Language? In: *Science, Language and Human Rights*. Philadelphia 1952.

Wisdom, J. (1): Logical Constructions. (In 5 Parts) *Mind* 40, 41, 42, 1931—33.

(2): Ostentation. *Psyche* 13, 1933. (Reprinted in: Wisdom (8).)

(3): Is Analysis a Useful Method in Philosophy? *Proceedings of the Aristotelian Society. Supplementary Volume* 13, 1934. (Reprinted in: Wisdom (8).)

(4): Philosophical Perplexity. *Proceedings of the Aristotelian Society* 37, 1936. (Reprinted: in Wisdom (8).)

(5): Philosophy and Psychoanalysis. *Polemic* 4, 1946. (Reprinted: in Wisdon (8).)

(6): Ludwig Wittgenstein, 1934—1937. *Mind* 61, 1952.

(7): *Other Minds*. Oxford 1956.

(8): *Philosophy and Psychoanalysis*. Oxford 1957.

Wisdom, J. O. (1): Esotericism. *Philosophy* 34, 1959.

Wollheim, R. (1): Las "Investigaciones filosóficas" de Ludwig Wittgenstein. *Theoria* 2, 1954.

Workman, A. J. (1): L. Wittgenstein: Philosophical Investigations. *The Personalist* 36, 1955.

Wright, G. H. von (1): Ludwig Wittgenstein, a Biographical Sketch. *The Philosophical Review* 64, 1955. (Reprinted in: N. Malcolm: *Ludwig Wittgenstein*. Oxford 1958.)

Xenakis, J. (1): Meaning, *Methodos* 24, 1954.
(2) Function and Meaning of Names. *Theoria* 22, 1956.
(3): Using Expressions. *Philosophy and Phenomenological Research* 18, 1957.